SQL for Data Analysis
Advanced Techniques for Transforming Data into Insights

Cathy Tanimura

Beijing · Boston · Farnham · Sebastopol · Tokyo

SQL for Data Analysis

by Cathy Tanimura

Copyright © 2021 Cathy Tanimura. All rights reserved.

Published by O'Reilly Media, Inc., 1005 Gravenstein Highway North, Sebastopol, CA 95472.

O'Reilly books may be purchased for educational, business, or sales promotional use. Online editions are also available for most titles (*http://oreilly.com*). For more information, contact our corporate/institutional sales department: 800-998-9938 or *corporate@oreilly.com*.

Acquisitions Editor: Andy Kwan
Development Editors Amelia Blevins and Shira Evans
Production Editor: Kristen Brown
Copyeditor: Arthur Johnson
Proofreader: Paula L. Fleming

Indexer: Ellen Troutman-Zaig
Interior Designer: David Futato
Cover Designer: Karen Montgomery
Illustrator: Kate Dullea

September 2021:   First Edition

Revision History for the First Edition

2021-09-09:   First Release

See *http://oreilly.com/catalog/errata.csp?isbn=9781492088783* for release details.

978-1-492-08878-3

[LSI]

Table of Contents

Preface

Over the past 20 years, I've spent many of my working hours manipulating data with SQL. For most of those years, I've worked in technology companies spanning a wide range of consumer and business-to-business industries. In that time, volumes of data have increased dramatically, and the technology I get to use has improved by leaps and bounds. Databases are faster than ever, and the reporting and visualization tools used to communicate the meaning in the data are more powerful than ever. One thing that has remained remarkably constant, however, is SQL being a key part of my toolbox.

I remember when I first learned SQL. I started my career in finance, where spreadsheets rule, and I'd gotten pretty good at writing formulas and memorizing all those keyboard shortcuts. One day I totally geeked out and Ctrl- and Alt-clicked every key on my keyboard just to see what would happen (and then created a cheat sheet for my peers). That was part fun and part survival: the faster I was with my spreadsheets, the more likely I would be to finish my work before midnight so I could go home and get some sleep. Spreadsheet mastery got me in the door at my next role, a startup where I was first introduced to databases and SQL.

Part of my role involved crunching inventory data in spreadsheets, and thanks to early internet scale, the data sets were sometimes tens of thousands of rows. This was "big data" at the time, at least for me. I got in the habit of going for a cup of coffee or for lunch while my computer's CPU was occupied with running its vlookup magic. One day my manager went on vacation and asked me to tend to the data warehouse he'd built on his laptop using Access. Refreshing the data involved a series of steps: running SQL queries in a portal, loading the resulting csv files into the database, and then refreshing the spreadsheet reports. After the first successful load, I started tinkering, trying to understand how it worked, and pestering the engineers to show me how to modify the SQL queries.

I was hooked, and even when I thought I might change directions with my career, I've kept coming back to data. Manipulating data, answering questions, helping my colleagues work better and smarter, and learning about businesses and the world through sets of data have never stopped feeling fun and exciting.

When I started working with SQL, there weren't many learning resources. I got a book on basic syntax, read it in a night, and from there mostly learned through trial and error. Back in the days when I was learning, I queried production databases directly and brought the website down more than once with my overly ambitious (or more likely just poorly written) SQL. Fortunately my skills improved, and over the years I learned to work forward from the data in tables, and backward from the output needed, solving technical and logic challenges and puzzles to write queries that returned the right data. I ended up designing and building data warehouses to gather data from different sources and avoid bringing down critical production databases. I've learned a lot about when and how to aggregate data before writing the SQL query and when to leave data in a more raw form.

I've compared notes with others who got into data around the same time, and it's clear we mostly learned in the same ad hoc way. The lucky among us had peers with whom to share techniques. Most SQL texts are either introductory and basic (there's definitely a place for these!) or else aimed at database developers. There are few resources for advanced SQL users who are focused on analysis work. Knowledge tends to be locked up in individuals or small teams. A goal of this book is to change that, giving practitioners a reference for how to solve common analysis problems with SQL, and I hope inspiring new inquiries into data using techniques you might not have seen before.

Conventions Used in This Book

The following typographical conventions are used in this book:

Italic
> Indicates new terms, URLs, email addresses, filenames, file extensions, and keywords.

`Constant width`
> Used for program listings, as well as within paragraphs to refer to program elements such as variable or function names, databases, environment variables, and statements.

`Constant width bold`
> Shows commands or other text that should be typed literally by the user.

`Constant width italic`
> Shows text that should be replaced with user-supplied values or by values determined by context.

This element signifies a tip or suggestion.

This element signifies a general note.

This element indicates a warning or caution.

Using Code Examples

Supplemental material (code examples, exercises, etc.) is available for download at *https://github.com/cathytanimura/sql_book*.

If you have a technical question or a problem using the code examples, please send email to *bookquestions@oreilly.com*.

This book is here to help you get your job done. In general, if example code is offered with this book, you may use it in your programs and documentation. You do not need to contact us for permission unless you're reproducing a significant portion of the code. For example, writing a program that uses several chunks of code from this book does not require permission. Selling or distributing examples from O'Reilly books does require permission. Answering a question by citing this book and quoting example code does not require permission. Incorporating a significant amount of example code from this book into your product's documentation does require permission.

We appreciate, but generally do not require, attribution. An attribution usually includes the title, author, publisher, and ISBN. For example: "*SQL for Data Analysis* by Cathy Tanimura (O'Reilly). Copyright 2021 Cathy Tanimura, 978-1-492-08878-3."

If you feel your use of code examples falls outside fair use or the permission given above, feel free to contact us at *permissions@oreilly.com*.

O'Reilly Online Learning

 For more than 40 years, *O'Reilly Media* has provided technology and business training, knowledge, and insight to help companies succeed.

Our unique network of experts and innovators share their knowledge and expertise through books, articles, and our online learning platform. O'Reilly's online learning platform gives you on-demand access to live training courses, in-depth learning paths, interactive coding environments, and a vast collection of text and video from O'Reilly and 200+ other publishers. For more information, visit *http://oreilly.com*.

How to Contact Us

Please address comments and questions concerning this book to the publisher:

O'Reilly Media, Inc.
1005 Gravenstein Highway North
Sebastopol, CA 95472
800-998-9938 (in the United States or Canada)
707-829-0515 (international or local)
707-829-0104 (fax)

We have a web page for this book, where we list errata, examples, and any additional information. You can access this page at *https://oreil.ly/sql-data-analysis*.

Email *bookquestions@oreilly.com* to comment or ask technical questions about this book.

For news and information about our books and courses, visit *http://oreilly.com*.

Find us on Facebook: *http://facebook.com/oreilly*

Follow us on Twitter: *http://twitter.com/oreillymedia*

Watch us on YouTube: *http://www.youtube.com/oreillymedia*

Acknowledgments

This book wouldn't have been possible without the efforts of a number of people at O'Reilly. Andy Kwan recruited me to this project. Amelia Blevins and Shira Evans guided me through the process and gave helpful feedback along the way. Kristen Brown shepherded the book through the production process. Arthur Johnson improved the quality and clarity of the text and inadvertently made me think more deeply about SQL keywords.

Many colleagues over the years played an important role in my SQL journey, and I'm grateful for their tutorials, tips, and shared code, and the time spent brainstorming ways to solve analysis problems over the years. Sharon Lin opened my eyes to regular expressions. Elyse Gordon gave me lots of book-writing advice. Dave Hoch and our conversations about experiment analysis inspired Chapter 7. Dan, Jim, and Stu from the Star Chamber have long been my favorite guys to geek out with. I'm also grateful for all of the colleagues who asked hard questions over the years—and once those were answered, asked even harder ones.

I'd like to thank my husband Rick, son Shea, daughters Lily and Fiona, and mom Janet for their love, encouragement, and most of all the gift of time to work on this book. Amy, Halle, Jessi, and the Den of Slack kept me sane and laughing through months of writing and pandemic lockdown.

CHAPTER 1

Analysis with SQL

If you're reading this book, you're probably interested in data analysis and in using SQL to accomplish it. You may be experienced with data analysis but new to SQL, or perhaps you're experienced with SQL but new to data analysis. Or you may be new to both topics entirely. Whatever your starting point, this chapter lays the groundwork for the topics covered in the rest of the book and makes sure we have a common vocabulary. I'll start with a discussion of what data analysis is and then move on to a discussion of SQL: what it is, why it's so popular, how it compares to other tools, and how it fits into data analysis. Then, since modern data analysis is so intertwined with the technologies that have enabled it, I'll conclude with a discussion of different types of databases that you may encounter in your work, why they're used, and what all of that means for the SQL you write.

What Is Data Analysis?

Collecting and storing data for analysis is a very human activity. Systems to track stores of grain, taxes, and the population go back thousands of years, and the roots of statistics (*https://oreil.ly/1W6Jf*) date back hundreds of years. Related disciplines, including statistical process control, operations research, and cybernetics, exploded in the 20th century. Many different names are used to describe the discipline of data analysis, such as business intelligence (BI), analytics, data science, and decision science, and practitioners have a range of job titles. Data analysis is also done by marketers, product managers, business analysts, and a variety of other people. In this book, I'll use the terms *data analyst* and *data scientist* interchangeably to mean the person working with SQL to understand data. I will refer to the software used to build reports and dashboards as *BI tools*.

Data analysis in the contemporary sense was enabled by, and is intertwined with, the history of computing. Trends in both research and commercialization have shaped it, and the story includes a who's who of researchers and major companies, which we'll talk about in the section on SQL. Data analysis blends the power of computing with techniques from traditional statistics. Data analysis is part data discovery, part data interpretation, and part data communication. Very often the purpose of data analysis is to improve decision making, by humans and increasingly by machines through automation.

Sound methodology is critical, but analysis is about more than just producing the right number. It's about curiosity, asking questions, and the "why" behind the numbers. It's about patterns and anomalies, discovering and interpreting clues about how businesses and humans behave. Sometimes analysis is done on a data set gathered to answer a specific question, as in a scientific setting or an online experiment. Analysis is also done on data that is generated as a result of doing business, as in sales of a company's products, or that is generated for analytics purposes, such as user interaction tracking on websites and mobile apps. This data has a wide range of possible applications, from troubleshooting to planning user interface (UI) improvements, but it often arrives in a format and volume such that the data needs processing before yielding answers. Chapter 2 will cover preparing data for analysis, and Chapter 8 will discuss some of the ethical and privacy concerns with which all data practitioners should be familiar.

It's hard to think of an industry that hasn't been touched by data analysis: manufacturing, retail, finance, health care, education, and even government have all been changed by it. Sports teams have employed data analysis since the early years of Billy Beane's term as general manager of the Oakland Athletics, made famous by Michael Lewis's book *Moneyball* (Norton). Data analysis is used in marketing, sales, logistics, product development, user experience design, support centers, human resources, and more. The combination of techniques, applications, and computing power has led to the explosion of related fields such as data engineering and data science.

Data analysis is by definition done on historical data, and it's important to remember that the past doesn't necessarily predict the future. The world is dynamic, and organizations are dynamic as well—new products and processes are introduced, competitors rise and fall, sociopolitical climates change. Criticisms are leveled against data analysis for being backward looking. Though that characterization is true, I have seen organizations gain tremendous value from analyzing historical data. Mining historical data helps us understand the characteristics and behavior of customers, suppliers, and processes. Historical data can help us develop informed estimates and predicted ranges of outcomes, which will sometimes be wrong but quite often will be right. Past data can point out gaps, weaknesses, and opportunities. It allows organizations to optimize, save money, and reduce risk and fraud. It can also help organizations find opportunity, and it can become the building blocks of new products that delight customers.

Organizations that don't do some form of data analysis are few and far between these days, but there are still some holdouts. Why do some organizations not use data analysis? One argument is the cost-to-value ratio. Collecting, processing, and analyzing data takes work and some level of financial investment. Some organizations are too new, or they're too haphazard. If there isn't a consistent process, it's hard to generate data that's consistent enough to analyze. Finally, there are ethical considerations. Collecting or storing data about certain people in certain situations may be regulated or even banned. Data about children and health-care interventions is sensitive, for example, and there are extensive regulations around its collection. Even organizations that are otherwise data driven need to take care around customer privacy and to think hard about what data should be collected, why it is needed, and how long it should be stored. Regulations such as the European Union's General Data Protection Regulation, or GDPR, and the California Consumer Privacy Act, or CCPA, have changed the way businesses think about consumer data. We'll discuss these regulations in more depth in Chapter 8. As data practitioners, we should always be thinking about the ethical implications of our work.

When working with organizations, I like to tell people that data analysis is not a project that wraps up at a fixed date—it's a way of life. Developing a data-informed mindset is a process, and reaping the rewards is a journey. Unknowns become known, difficult questions are chipped away at until there are answers, and the most critical information is embedded in dashboards that power tactical and strategic decisions. With this information, new and harder questions are asked, and then the process repeats.

Data analysis is both accessible for those looking to get started and hard to master. The technology can be learned, particularly SQL. Many problems, such as optimizing marketing spend or detecting fraud, are familiar and translate across businesses. Every organization is different and every data set has quirks, so even familiar problems can pose new challenges. Communicating results is a skill. Learning to make good recommendations and becoming a trusted partner to an organization take time. In my experience, simple analysis presented persuasively has more impact than sophisticated analysis presented poorly. Successful data analysis also requires partnership. You can have great insights, but if there is no one to execute on them, you haven't really made an impact. Even with all the technology, it's still about people, and relationships matter.

Why SQL?

This section describes what SQL is, the benefits of using it, how it compares to other languages commonly used for analysis, and finally how SQL fits into the analysis workflow.

What Is SQL?

SQL is the language used to communicate with databases. The acronym stands for Structured Query Language and is pronounced either like "sequel" or by saying each letter, as in "ess cue el." This is only the first of many controversies and inconsistencies surrounding SQL that we'll see, but most people will know what you mean regardless of how you say it. There is some debate as to whether SQL is or isn't a programming language. It isn't a general purpose language in the way that C or Python are. SQL without a database and data in tables is just a text file. SQL can't build a website, but it is powerful for working with data in databases. On a practical level, what matters most is that SQL can help you get the job of data analysis done.

IBM was the first to develop SQL databases, from the relational model invented by Edgar Codd in the 1960s. The relational model was a theoretical description for managing data using relationships. By creating the first databases, IBM helped to advance the theory, but it also had commercial considerations, as did Oracle, Microsoft, and every other company that has commercialized a database since. From the beginning, there has been tension between computer theory and commercial reality. SQL became an International Organization for Standards (ISO) standard in 1987 and an American National Standards Institute (ANSI) standard in 1986. Although all major databases start from these standards in their implementation of SQL, many have variations and functions that make life easier for the users of those databases. These come at the cost of making SQL more difficult to move between databases without some modifications.

SQL is used to access, manipulate, and retrieve data from objects in a database. Databases can have one or more *schemas*, which provide the organization and structure and contain other objects. Within a schema, the objects most commonly used in data analysis are tables, views, and functions. Tables contain fields, which hold the data. Tables may have one or more *indexes*; an index is a special kind of data structure that allows data to be retrieved more efficiently. Indexes are usually defined by a database administrator. Views are essentially stored queries that can be referenced in the same way as a table. Functions allow commonly used sets of calculations or procedures to be stored and easily referenced in queries. They are usually created by a database administrator, or DBA. Figure 1-1 gives an overview of the organization of databases.

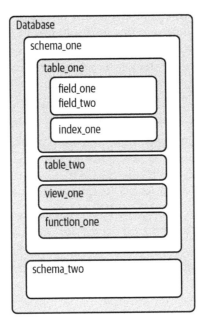

Figure 1-1. Overview of database organization and objects in a database

To communicate with databases, SQL has four sublanguages for tackling different jobs, and these are mostly standard across database types. Most people who work in data analysis don't need to recall the names of these sublanguages on a daily basis, but they might come up in conversation with database administrators or data engineers, so I'll briefly introduce them. The commands all work fluidly together, and some may coexist in the same SQL statement.

DQL, or *data query language*, is what this book is mainly about. It's used for *querying* data, which you can think of as using code to ask questions of a database. DQL commands include *SELECT*, which will be familiar to prior users of SQL, but the acronym DQL is not frequently used in my experience. SQL queries can be as short as a single line or span many tens of lines. SQL queries can access a single table (or view), can combine data from multiple tables through the use of joins, and can also query across multiple schemas in the same database. SQL queries generally cannot query across databases, but in some cases clever network settings or additional software can be used to retrieve data from multiple sources, even databases of different types. SQL queries are self-contained and, apart from tables, do not reference variables or outputs from previous steps not contained in the query, unlike scripting languages.

DDL, or *data definition language*, is used to create and modify tables, views, users, and other objects in the database. It affects the structure but not the contents. There are three common commands: *CREATE*, *ALTER*, and *DROP*. *CREATE* is used to make new objects. *ALTER* changes the structure of an object, such as by adding a column to a table. *DROP* deletes the entire object and its structure. You might hear DBAs and data engineers talk about working with DDLs—this is really just shorthand for the files or pieces of code that do the creates, alters, or drops. An example of how DDL is used in the context of analysis is the code to create temporary tables.

DCL, or *data control language*, is used for access control. Commands include *GRANT* and *REVOKE*, which give permission and remove permission, respectively. In an analysis context, *GRANT* might be needed to allow a colleague to query a table you created. You might also encounter such a command when someone has told you a table exists in the database but you can't see it—permissions might need to be *GRANT*ed to your user.

DML, or *data manipulation language*, is used to act on the data itself. The commands are *INSERT*, *UPDATE*, and *DELETE*. *INSERT* adds new records and is essentially the "load" step in extract, transform, load (ETL). *UPDATE* changes values in a field, and *DELETE* removes rows. You will encounter these commands if you have any kind of self-managed tables—temp tables, sandbox tables—or if you find yourself in the role of both owner and analyzer of the database.

These four sublanguages are present in all major databases. In this book, I'll focus mainly on DQL. We will touch on a few DDL and DML commands in Chapter 8, and you will also see some examples in the GitHub site for the book (*https://github.com/cathytanimura/sql_book*), where they are used to create and populate the data used in examples. Thanks to this common set of commands, SQL code written for any database will look familiar to anyone used to working with SQL. However, reading SQL from another database may feel a bit like listening to someone who speaks the same language as you but comes from another part of the country or the world. The basic structure of the language is the same, but the slang is different, and some words have different meanings altogether. Variations in SQL from database to database are often termed *dialects*, and database users will reference Oracle SQL, MSSQL, or other dialects.

Still, once you know SQL, you can work with different database types as long as you pay attention to details such as the handling of nulls, dates, and timestamps; the division of integers; and case sensitivity.

This book uses PostgreSQL, or Postgres, for the examples, though I will try to point out where the code would be meaningfully different in other types of databases. You can install Postgres (*https://www.postgresql.org/download*) on a personal computer in order to follow along with the examples.

Benefits of SQL

There are many good reasons to use SQL for data analysis, from computing power to its ubiquity in data analysis tools and its flexibility.

Perhaps the best reason to use SQL is that much of the world's data is already in databases. It's likely your own organization has one or more databases. Even if data is not already in a database, loading it into one can be worthwhile in order to take advantage of the storage and computing advantages, especially when compared to alternatives such as spreadsheets. Computing power has exploded in recent years, and data warehouses and data infrastructure have evolved to take advantage of it. Some newer cloud databases allow massive amounts of data to be queried in memory, speeding things up further. The days of waiting minutes or hours for query results to return may be over, though analysts may just write more complex queries in response.

SQL is the de facto standard for interacting with databases and retrieving data from them. A wide range of popular software connects to databases with SQL, from spreadsheets to BI and visualization tools and coding languages such as Python and R (discussed in the next section). Due to the computing resources available, performing as much data manipulation and aggregation as possible in the database often has advantages downstream. We'll discuss strategies for building complex data sets for downstream tools in depth in Chapter 8.

The basic SQL building blocks can be combined in an endless number of ways. Starting with a relatively small number of building blocks—the syntax—SQL can accomplish a wide array of tasks. SQL can be developed iteratively, and it's easy to review the results as you go. It may not be a full-fledged programming language, but it can do a lot, from transforming data to performing complex calculations and answering questions.

Last, SQL is relatively easy to learn, with a finite amount of syntax. You can learn the basic keywords and structure quickly and then hone your craft over time working with varied data sets. Applications of SQL are virtually infinite, when you take into account the range of data sets in the world and the possible questions that can be asked of data. SQL is taught in many universities, and many people pick up some skills on the job. Even employees who don't already have SQL skills can be trained, and the learning curve may be easier than that for other programming languages. This makes storing data for analysis in relational databases a logical choice for organizations.

SQL Versus R or Python

While SQL is a popular language for data analysis, it isn't the only choice. R and Python are among the most popular of the other languages used for data analysis. R is a statistical and graphing language, while Python is a general-purpose programming language that has strengths in working with data. Both are open source, can be installed on a laptop, and have active communities developing packages, or extensions, that tackle various data manipulation and analysis tasks. Choosing between R and Python is beyond the scope of this book, but there are many discussions online about the relative advantages of each. Here I will consider them together as coding-language alternatives to SQL.

One major difference between SQL and other coding languages is where the code runs and, therefore, how much computing power is available. SQL always runs on a database server, taking advantage of all its computing resources. For doing analysis, R and Python are usually run locally on your machine, so computing resources are capped by whatever is available locally. There are, of course, lots of exceptions: databases can run on laptops, and R and Python can be run on servers with more resources. When you are performing anything other than the simplest analysis on large data sets, pushing work onto a database server with more resources is a good option. Since databases are usually set up to continually receive new data, SQL is also a good choice when a report or dashboard needs to update periodically.

A second difference is in how data is stored and organized. Relational databases always organize data into rows and columns within tables, so SQL assumes this structure for every query. R and Python have a wider variety of ways to store data, including variables, lists, and dictionaries, among other options. These provide more flexibility, but at the cost of a steeper learning curve. To facilitate data analysis, R has data frames, which are similar to database tables and organize data into rows and columns. The pandas package makes DataFrames available in Python. Even when other options are available, the table structure remains valuable for analysis.

Looping is another major difference between SQL and most other computer programming languages. A *loop* is an instruction or a set of instructions that repeats until a specified condition is met. SQL aggregations implicitly loop over the set of data, without any additional code. We will see later how the lack of ability to loop over fields can result in lengthy SQL statements when pivoting or unpivoting data. While deeper discussion is beyond the scope of this book, some vendors have created extensions to SQL, such as PL/SQL in Oracle and T-SQL in Microsoft SQL Server, that allow functionality such as looping.

A drawback of SQL is that your data must be in a database,[1] whereas R and Python can import data from files stored locally or can access files stored on servers or websites. This is convenient for many one-off projects. A database can be installed on a laptop, but this does add an extra layer of overhead. In the other direction, packages such as dbplyr for R and SQLAlchemy for Python allow programs written in those languages to connect to databases, execute SQL queries, and use the results in further processing steps. In this sense, R or Python can be complementary to SQL.

R and Python both have sophisticated statistical functions that are either built in or available in packages. Although SQL has, for example, functions to calculate average and standard deviation, calculations of p-values and statistical significance that are needed in experiment analysis (discussed in Chapter 7) cannot be performed with SQL alone. In addition to sophisticated statistics, machine learning is another area that is better tackled with one of these other coding languages.

When deciding whether to use SQL, R, or Python for an analysis, consider:

- Where is the data located—in a database, a file, a website?
- What is the volume of data?
- Where is the data going—into a report, a visualization, a statistical analysis?
- Will it need to be updated or refreshed with new data? How often?
- What does your team or organization use, and how important is it to conform to existing standards?

There is no shortage of debate around which languages and tools are best for doing data analysis or data science. As with many things, there's often more than one way to accomplish an analysis. Programming languages evolve and change in popularity, and we're lucky to live and work in a time with so many good choices. SQL has been around for a long time and will likely remain popular for years to come. The ultimate goal is to use the best available tool for the job. This book will help you get the most out of SQL for data analysis, regardless of what else is in your toolkit.

SQL as Part of the Data Analysis Workflow

Now that I've explained what SQL is, discussed some of its benefits, and compared it to other languages, we'll turn to a discussion of where SQL fits in the data analysis process. Analysis work always starts with a question, which may be about how many new customers have been acquired, how sales are trending, or why some users stick around for a long time while others try a service and never return. Once the question is framed, we consider where the data originated, where the data is stored, the

---

[1] There are some newer technologies that allow SQL queries on data stored in nonrelational sources.

analysis plan, and how the results will be presented to the audience. Figure 1-2 shows the steps in the process. Queries and analysis are the focus of this book, though I will discuss the other steps briefly in order to put the queries and analysis stage into a broader context.

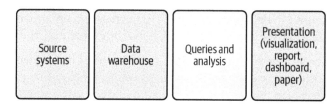

Figure 1-2. Steps in the data analysis process

First, data is generated by *source systems*, a term that includes any human or machine process that generates data of interest. Data can be generated by people by hand, such as when someone fills out a form or takes notes during a doctor's visit. Data can also be machine generated, such as when an application database records a purchase, an event-streaming system records a website click, or a marketing management tool records an email open. Source systems can generate many different types and formats of data, and Chapter 2 will discuss them, and how the type of source may impact the analysis, in more detail.

The second step is moving the data and storing it in a database for analysis. I will use the terms *data warehouse*, which is a database that consolidates data from across an organization into a central repository, and *data store*, which refers to any type of data storage system that can be queried. Other terms you might come across are *data mart*, which is typically a subset of a data warehouse, or a more narrowly focused data warehouse; and *data lake*, a term that can mean either that data resides in a file storage system or that it is stored in a database but without the degree of data transformation that is common in data warehouses. Data warehouses range from small and simple to huge and expensive. A database running on a laptop will be sufficient for you to follow along with the examples in this book. What matters is having the data you need to perform an analysis together in one place.

Usually a person or team is responsible for getting data into the data warehouse. This process is called *ETL*, or extract, transform, load. Extract pulls the data from the source system. Transform optionally changes the structure of the data, performs data quality cleaning, or aggregates the data. Load puts the data into the database. This process can also be called *ELT*, for extract, load, transform—the difference being that, rather than transformations being done before data is loaded, all the data is loaded and then transformations are performed, usually using SQL. You might also hear the terms *source* and *target* in the context of ETL. The source is where the data comes from, and the target is the destination, i.e., the database and the tables within it. Even when SQL is used to do the transforming, another language such as Python or Java is used to glue the steps together, coordinate scheduling, and raise alerts when something goes wrong. There are a number of commercial products as well as open source tools available, so teams don't have to create an ETL system entirely from scratch.

Once the data is in a database, the next step is performing queries and analysis. In this step, SQL is applied to explore, profile, clean, shape, and analyze the data. Figure 1-3 shows the general flow of the process. Exploring the data involves becoming familiar with the topic, where the data was generated, and the database tables in which it is stored. Profiling involves checking the unique values and distribution of records in the data set. Cleaning involves fixing incorrect or incomplete data, adding categorization and flags, and handling null values. Shaping is the process of arranging the data into the rows and columns needed in the result set. Finally, analyzing the data involves reviewing the output for trends, conclusions, and insights. Although this process is shown as linear, in practice it is often cyclical—for example, when shaping or analysis reveals data that should be cleaned.

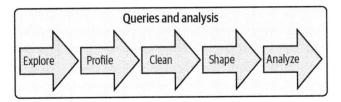

Figure 1-3. Stages within the queries and analysis step of the analysis workflow

Presentation of the data into a final output form is the last step in the overall workflow. Businesspeople won't appreciate receiving a file of SQL code; they expect you to present graphs, charts, and insights. Communication is key to having an impact with analysis, and for that we need a way to share the results with other people. At other times, you may need to apply more sophisticated statistical analysis than is possible in SQL, or you may want to feed the data into a machine learning (ML) algorithm. Fortunately, most reporting and visualization tools have SQL connectors that allow you to pull in data from entire tables or prewritten SQL queries. Statistical software and languages commonly used for ML also usually have SQL connectors.

Analysis workflows encompass a number of steps and often include multiple tools and technologies. SQL queries and analysis are at the heart of many analyses and are what we will focus on in the following chapters. Chapter 2 will discuss types of source systems and the types of data they generate. The rest of this chapter will take a look at the types of databases you are likely to encounter in your analysis journey.

Database Types and How to Work with Them

If you're working with SQL, you'll be working with databases. There is a range of database types—open source to proprietary, row-store to column-store. There are on-premises databases and cloud databases, as well as hybrid databases, where an organization runs the database software on a cloud vendor's infrastructure. There are also a number of data stores that aren't databases at all but can be queried with SQL.

Databases are not all created equal; each database type has its strengths and weaknesses when it comes to analysis work. Unlike tools used in other parts of the analysis workflow, you may not have much say in which database technology is used in your organization. Knowing the ins and outs of the database you have will help you work more efficiently and take advantage of any special SQL functions it offers. Familiarity with other types of databases will help you if you find yourself working on a project to build or migrate to a new data warehouse. You may want to install a database on your laptop for personal, small-scale projects, or get an instance of a cloud warehouse for similar reasons.

Databases and data stores have been a dynamic area of technology development since they were introduced. A few trends since the turn of the 21st century have driven the technology in ways that are really exciting for data practitioners today. First, data volumes have increased incredibly with the internet, mobile devices, and the Internet of Things (IoT). In 2020 IDC predicted (*https://oreil.ly/oEWDD*) that the amount of data stored globally will grow to 175 zettabytes by 2025. This scale of data is hard to even think about, and not all of it will be stored in databases for analysis. It's not uncommon for companies to have data in the scale of terabytes and petabytes these days, a scale that would have been impossible to process with the technology of the 1990s and earlier. Second, decreases in data storage and computing costs, along with the advent of the cloud, have made it cheaper and easier for organizations to collect and store these massive amounts of data. Computer memory has gotten cheaper, meaning that large amounts of data can be loaded into memory, calculations performed, and results returned, all without reading and writing to disk, greatly increasing the speed. Third, distributed computing has allowed the breaking up of workloads across many machines. This allows a large and tunable amount of computing to be pointed to complex data tasks.

Databases and data stores have combined these technological trends in a number of different ways in order to optimize for particular types of tasks. There are two broad categories of databases that are relevant for analysis work: row-store and column-store. In the next section I'll introduce them, discuss what makes them similar to and different from each other, and talk about what all of this means as far as doing analysis with data stored in them. Finally, I'll introduce some additional types of data infrastructure beyond databases that you may encounter.

Row-Store Databases

Row-store databases—also called *transactional* databases—are designed to be efficient at processing transactions: *INSERTs*, *UPDATEs*, and *DELETEs*. Popular open source row-store databases include MySQL and Postgres. On the commercial side, Microsoft SQL Server, Oracle, and Teradata are widely used. Although they're not really optimized for analysis, for a number of years row-store databases were the only option for companies building data warehouses. Through careful tuning and schema design, these databases can be used for analytics. They are also attractive due to the low cost of open source options and because they're familiar to the database administrators who maintain them. Many organizations replicate their production database in the same technology as a first step toward building out data infrastructure. For all of these reasons, data analysts and data scientists are likely to work with data in a row-store database at some point in their career.

We think of a table as rows and columns, but data has to be serialized for storage. A query searches a hard disk for the needed data. Hard disks are organized in a series of blocks of a fixed size. Scanning the hard disk takes both time and resources, so minimizing the amount of the disk that needs to be scanned to return query results is important. Row-store databases approach this problem by serializing data in a row. Figure 1-4 shows an example of row-wise data storage. When querying, the whole row is read into memory. This approach is fast when making row-wise updates, but it's slower when making calculations across many rows if only a few columns are needed.

id	sku	type	color	size	price
1	123	tshirt	black	S	19.99
2	124	shorts	green	M	24.99

Figure 1-4. Row-wise storage, in which each row is stored together on disk

To reduce the width of tables, row-store databases are usually modeled in *third normal form*, which is a database design approach that seeks to store each piece of information only once, to avoid duplication and inconsistencies. This is efficient for transaction processing but often leads to a large number of tables in the database, each with only a few columns. To analyze such data, many joins may be required, and it can be difficult for nondevelopers to understand how all of the tables relate to each other and where a particular piece of data is stored. When doing analysis, the goal is usually denormalization, or getting all the data together in one place.

Tables typically have a *primary key* that enforces uniqueness—in other words, it prevents the database from creating more than one record for the same thing. Tables will often have an id column that is an auto-incrementing integer, where each new record gets the next integer after the last one inserted, or an alphanumeric value that is created by a primary key generator. There should also be a set of columns that together make the row unique; this combination of fields is called a *composite key*, or sometimes a *business key*. For example, in a table of people, the columns first_name, last_name, and birthdate together might make the row unique. Social_security_id would also be a unique identifier, in addition to the table's person_id column.

Tables also optionally have indexes that make looking up specific records faster and make joins involving these columns faster. Indexes store the values in the field or fields indexed as single pieces of data along with a row pointer, and since the indexes are smaller than the whole table, they are faster to scan. Usually the primary key is indexed, but other fields or groups of fields can be indexed as well. When working with row-store databases, it's useful to get to know which fields in the tables you use have indexes. Common joins can be sped up by adding indexes, so it's worth investigating whether analysis queries take a long time to run. Indexes don't come for free: they take up storage space, and they slow down loading, as new values need to be added with each insert. DBAs may not index everything that might be useful for analysis. Beyond reporting, analysis work may not be routine enough to bother with optimizing indexes either. Exploratory and complex queries often use complex join patterns, and we may throw out one approach when we figure out a new way to solve a problem.

Star schema modeling (*https://oreil.ly/5WiSp*) was developed in part to make row-store databases more friendly to analytic workloads. The foundations are laid out in the book *The Data Warehouse Toolkit*,[2] which advocates modeling the data as a series of fact and dimension tables. Fact tables represent events, such as retail store transactions. Dimensions hold descriptors such as customer name and product type. Since data doesn't always fit neatly into fact and dimension categories, there's an extension called the snowflake schema (*https://oreil.ly/rpj4N*) in which some dimensions have dimensions of their own.

Column-Store Databases

Column-store databases took off in the early part of the 21st century, though their theoretical history goes back as far as that of row-store databases. Column-store databases store the values of a column together, rather than storing the values of a row together. This design is optimized for queries that read many records but not necessarily all the columns. Popular column-store databases include Amazon Redshift, Snowflake, and Vertica.

Column-store databases are efficient at storing large volumes of data thanks to compression. Missing values and repeating values can be represented by very small marker values instead of the full value. For example, rather than storing "United Kingdom" thousands or millions of times, a column-store database will store a surrogate value that takes up very little storage space, along with a lookup that stores the full "United Kingdom" value. Column-store databases also compress data by taking advantage of repetitions of values in sorted data. For example, the database can store the fact that the marker value for "United Kingdom" is repeated 100 times, and this takes up even less space than storing that marker 100 times.

Column-store databases do not enforce primary keys and do not have indexes. Repeated values are not problematic, thanks to compression. As a result, schemas can be tailored for analysis queries, with all the data together in one place as opposed to being in multiple tables that need to be joined. Duplicate data can easily sneak in without primary keys, however, so understanding the source of the data and quality checking are important.

Updates and deletes are expensive in most column-store databases, since data for a single row is distributed rather than stored together. For very large tables, a write-only policy may exist, so we also need to know something about how the data is generated in order to figure out which records to use. The data can also be slower to read, as it needs to be uncompressed before calculations are applied.

Column-store databases are generally the gold standard for fast analysis work. They use standard SQL (with some vendor-specific variations), and in many ways working with them is no different from working with a row-store database in terms of the

---

2 Ralph Kimball and Margy Ross, *The Data Warehouse Toolkit*, 3rd ed. (Indianapolis: Wiley, 2013).

queries you write. The size of the data matters, as do the computing and storage resources that have been allocated to the database. I have seen aggregations run across millions and billions of records in seconds. This does wonders for productivity.

 There are a few tricks to be aware of. Since certain types of compression rely on sorting, knowing the fields that the table is sorted on and using them to filter queries improves performance. Joining tables can be slow if both tables are large.

At the end of the day, some databases will be easier or faster to work with, but there is nothing inherent in the type of database that will prevent you from performing any of the analysis in this book. As with all things, using a tool that's properly powerful for the volume of data and complexity of the task will allow you to focus on creating meaningful analysis.

Other Types of Data Infrastructure

Databases aren't the only way data can be stored, and there is an increasing variety of options for storing data needed for analysis and powering applications. File storage systems, sometimes called *data lakes*, are probably the main alternative to database warehouses. NoSQL databases and search-based data stores are alternative data storage systems that offer low latency for application development and searching log files. Although not typically part of the analysis process, they are increasingly part of organizations' data infrastructure, so I will introduce them briefly in this section as well. One interesting trend to point out is that although these newer types of infrastructure at first aimed to break away from the confines of SQL databases, many have ended up implementing some kind of SQL interface to query the data.

Hadoop, also known as HDFS (for "Hadoop distributed filesystem"), is an open source file storage system that takes advantage of the ever-falling cost of data storage and computing power, as well as distributed systems. Files are split into blocks, and Hadoop distributes them across a filesystem that is stored on nodes, or computers, in a cluster. The code to run operations is sent to the nodes, and they process the data in parallel. Hadoop's big breakthrough was to allow huge amounts of data to be stored cheaply. Many large internet companies, with massive amounts of often unstructured data, found this to be an advantage over the cost and storage limitations of traditional databases. Hadoop's early versions had two major downsides: specialized coding skills were needed to retrieve and process data since it was not SQL compatible, and execution time for the programs was often quite long. Hadoop has since matured, and various tools have been developed that allow SQL or SQL-like access to the data and speed up query times.

Other commercial and open source products have been introduced in the last few years to take advantage of cheap data storage and fast, often in-memory data processing, while offering SQL querying ability. Some of them even permit the analyst to write a single query that returns data from multiple underlying sources. This is exciting for anyone who works with large amounts of data, and it is validation that SQL is here to stay.

NoSQL is a technology that allows for data modeling that is not strictly relational. It allows for very low latency storage and retrieval, critical in many online applications. The class includes key-value pair storage and graph databases, which store in a node-edge format, and document stores. Examples of these data stores that you might hear about in your organization are Cassandra, Couchbase, DynamoDB, Memcached, Giraph, and Neo4j. Early on, NoSQL was marketed as making SQL obsolete, but the acronym has more recently been marketed as "not only SQL." For analysis purposes, using data stored in a NoSQL key-value store for analysis typically requires moving it to a more traditional SQL data warehouse, since NoSQL is not optimized for querying many records at once. Graph databases have applications such as network analysis, and analysis work may be done directly in them with special query languages. The tool landscape is always evolving, however, and perhaps someday we'll be able to analyze this data with SQL as well.

Search-based data stores include Elasticsearch and Splunk. Elasticsearch and Splunk are often used to analyze machine-generated data, such as logs. These and similar technologies have non-SQL query languages, but if you know SQL, you can often understand them. Recognizing how common SQL skills are, some data stores, such as Elasticsearch, have added SQL querying interfaces. These tools are useful and powerful for the use cases they were designed for, but they're usually not well suited to the types of analysis tasks this book is covering. As I've explained to people over the years, they are great for finding needles in haystacks. They're not as great at measuring the haystack itself.

Regardless of the type of database or other data storage technology, the trend is clear: even as data volumes grow and use cases become more complex, SQL is still the standard tool for accessing data. Its large existing user base, approachable learning curve, and power for analytical tasks mean that even technologies that try to move away from SQL come back around and accommodate it.

Conclusion

Data analysis is an exciting discipline with a range of applications for businesses and other organizations. SQL has many benefits for working with data, particularly any data stored in a database. Querying and analyzing data is part of the larger analysis workflow, and there are several types of data stores that a data scientist might expect to work with. Now that we've set the groundwork for analysis, SQL, and data stores, the rest of the book will cover using SQL for analysis in depth. Chapter 2 focuses on data preparation, starting with an introduction to data types and then moving on to profiling, cleaning, and shaping data. Chapters 3 through 7 present applications of data analysis, focusing on time series analysis, cohort analysis, text analysis, anomaly detection, and experiment analysis. Chapter 8 covers techniques for developing complex data sets for further analysis in other tools. Finally, Chapter 9 concludes with thoughts on how types of analysis can be combined for new insights and lists some additional resources to support your analytics journey.

CHAPTER 2

Preparing Data for Analysis

Estimates of how long data scientists spend preparing their data vary, but it's safe to say that this step takes up a significant part of the time spent working with data. In 2014, the *New York Times* reported (*https://oreil.ly/HX1cO*) that data scientists spend from 50% to 80% of their time cleaning and wrangling their data. A 2016 survey by CrowdFlower (*https://oreil.ly/5h28Y*) found that data scientists spend 60% of their time cleaning and organizing data in order to prepare it for analysis or modeling work. Preparing data is such a common task that terms have sprung up to describe it, such as data munging, data wrangling, and data prep. ("Mung" is an acronym for Mash Until No Good, which I have certainly done on occasion.) Is all this data preparation work just mindless toil, or is it an important part of the process?

Data preparation is easier when a data set has a *data dictionary*, a document or repository that has clear descriptions of the fields, possible values, how the data was collected, and how it relates to other data. Unfortunately, this is frequently not the case. Documentation often isn't prioritized, even by people who see its value, or it becomes out-of-date as new fields and tables are added or the way data is populated changes. Data profiling creates many of the elements of a data dictionary, so if your organization already has a data dictionary, this is a good time to use it and contribute to it. If no data dictionary exists currently, consider starting one! This is one of the most valuable gifts you can give to your team and to your future self. An up-to-date data dictionary allows you to speed up the data-profiling process by building on profiling that's already been done rather than replicating it. It will also improve the quality of your analysis results, since you can verify that you have used fields correctly and applied appropriate filters.

Even when a data dictionary exists, you will still likely need to do data prep work as part of the analysis. In this chapter, I'll start with a review of data types you are likely to encounter. This is followed by a review of SQL query structure. Next, I will talk about profiling the data as a way to get to know its contents and check for data quality. Then I'll talk about some data-shaping techniques that will return the columns and rows needed for further analysis. Finally, I'll walk through some useful tools for cleaning data to deal with any quality issues.

Types of Data

Data is the foundation of analysis, and all data has a database data type and also belongs to one or more categories of data. Having a firm grasp of the many forms data can take will help you be a more effective data analyst. I'll start with the database data types most frequently encountered in analysis. Then I'll move on to some conceptual groupings that can help us understand the source, quality, and possible applications of the data.

Database Data Types

Fields in database tables all have defined data types. Most databases have good documentation on the types they support, and this is a good resource for any needed detail beyond what is presented here. You don't necessarily need to be an expert on the nuances of data types to be good at analysis, but later in the book we'll encounter situations in which considering the data type is important, so this section will cover the basics. The main types of data are strings, numeric, logical, and datetime, as summarized in Table 2-1. These are based on Postgres but are similar across most major database types.

Table 2-1. A summary of common database data types

Type	Name	Description
String	CHAR / VARCHAR	Holds strings. A CHAR is always of fixed length, whereas a VARCHAR is of variable length, up to some maximum size (256 characters, for example).
	TEXT / BLOB	Holds longer strings that don't fit in a VARCHAR. Descriptions or free text entered by survey respondents might be held in these fields.
Numeric	INT / SMALLINT / BIGINT	Holds integers (whole numbers). Some databases have SMALLINT and/or BIGINT. SMALLINT can be used when the field will only hold values with a small number of digits. SMALLINT takes less memory than a regular INT. BIGINT is capable of holding numbers with more digits than an INT, but it takes up more space than an INT.
	FLOAT / DOUBLE / DECIMAL	Holds decimal numbers, sometimes with the number of decimal places specified.
Logical	BOOLEAN	Holds values of TRUE or FALSE.
	DATETIME / TIMESTAMP	Holds dates with times. Typically in a YYYY-MM-DD hh:mi:ss format, where YYYY is the four-digit year, MM is the two-digit month number, DD is the two-digit day, hh is the two-digit hour (usually 24-hour time, or values of 0 to 23), mi is the two-digit minutes, and ss is the two-digit seconds. Some databases store only timestamps without time zone, while others have specific types for timestamps with and without time zones.
	TIME	Holds times.

String data types are the most versatile. These can hold letters, numbers, and special characters, including unprintable characters like tabs and newlines. String fields can be defined to hold a fixed or variable number of characters. A CHAR field could be defined to allow only two characters to hold US state abbreviations, for example, whereas a field storing the full names of states would need to be a VARCHAR to allow a variable number of characters. Fields can be defined as TEXT, CLOB (Character Large Object), or BLOB (Binary Large Object, which can include additional data types such as images), depending on the database to hold very long strings, though since they often take up a lot of space, these data types tend to be used sparingly. When data is loaded, if strings arrive that are too big for the defined data type, they may be truncated or rejected entirely. SQL has a number of string functions that we will make use of for various analysis purposes.

Numeric data types are all the ones that store numbers, both positive and negative. Mathematical functions and operators can be applied to numeric fields. Numeric data types include the INT types as well as FLOAT, DOUBLE, and DECIMAL types that allow decimal places. Integer data types are often implemented because they use less memory than their decimal counterparts. In some databases, such as Postgres, dividing integers results in an integer, rather than a value with decimal places as you might expect. We'll discuss converting numeric data types to obtain correct results later in this chapter.

The logical data type is called BOOLEAN. It has values of TRUE and FALSE and is an efficient way to store information where these options are appropriate. Operations that compare two fields return a BOOLEAN value as a result. This data type is often used to create *flags*, fields that summarize the presence or absence of a property in the data. For example, a table storing email data might have a BOOLEAN has_opened field.

The datetime types include DATE, TIMESTAMP, and TIME. Date and time data should be stored in a field of one of these database types whenever possible, since SQL has a number of useful functions that operate on them. Timestamps and dates are very common in databases and are critical to many types of analysis, particularly time series analysis (covered in Chapter 3) and cohort analysis (covered in Chapter 4). Chapter 3 will discuss date and time formatting, transformations, and calculations.

Other data types, such as JSON and geographical types, are supported by some but not all databases. I won't go into detail on all of them here since they are generally beyond the scope of this book. However, they are a sign that SQL continues to evolve to tackle emerging analysis tasks.

Beyond database data types, there are a number of conceptual ways that data is categorized. These can have an impact both on how data is stored and on how we think about analyzing it. I will discuss these categorical data types next.

Structured Versus Unstructured

Data is often described as structured or unstructured, or sometimes as semistructured. Most databases were designed to handle *structured data*, where each attribute is stored in a column, and instances of each entity are represented as rows. A data model is first created, and then data is inserted according to that data model. For example, an address table might have fields for street address, city, state, and postal code. Each row would hold a particular customer's address. Each field has a data type and allows only data of that type to be entered. When structured data is inserted into a table, each field is verified to ensure it conforms to the correct data type. Structured data is easy to query with SQL.

Unstructured data is the opposite of structured data. There is no predetermined structure, data model, or data types. Unstructured data is often the "everything else" that isn't database data. Documents, emails, and web pages are unstructured. Photos, images, videos, and audio files are also examples of unstructured data. They don't fit into the traditional data types, and thus they are more difficult for relational databases to store efficiently and for SQL to query. Unstructured data is often stored outside of relational databases as a result. This allows data to be loaded quickly, but lack of data validation can result in low data quality. As we saw in Chapter 1, the technology continues to evolve, and new tools are being developed to allow SQL querying of many types of unstructured data.

Semistructured data falls in between these two categories. Much "unstructured" data has some structure that we can make use of. For example, emails have from and to email addresses, subject lines, body text, and sent timestamps that can be stored separately in a data model with those fields. Metadata, or data about data, can be extracted from other file types and stored for analysis. For example, music audio files might be tagged with artist, song name, genre, and duration. Generally, the structured parts of semistructured data can be queried with SQL, and SQL can often be used to parse or otherwise extract structured data for further querying. We'll see some applications of this in the discussion of text analysis in Chapter 5.

Quantitative Versus Qualitative Data

Quantitative data is numeric. It measures people, things, and events. Quantitative data can include descriptors, such as customer information, product type, or device configurations, but it also comes with numeric information such as price, quantity, or visit duration. Counts, sums, average, or other numeric functions are applied to the data. Quantitative data is often machine generated these days, but it doesn't need to be. Height, weight, and blood pressure recorded on a paper patient intake form are quantitative, as are student quiz scores typed into a spreadsheet by a teacher.

Qualitative data is usually text based and includes opinions, feelings, and descriptions that aren't strictly quantitative. Temperature and humidity levels are quantitative, while descriptors like "hot and humid" are qualitative. The price a customer paid for a product is quantitative; whether they like or dislike it is qualitative. Survey feedback, customer support inquiries, and social media posts are qualitative. There are whole professions that deal with qualitative data. In a data analysis context, we usually try to quantify the qualitative. One technique for this is to extract keywords or phrases and count their occurrences. We'll look at this in more detail when we delve into text analysis in Chapter 5. Another technique is sentiment analysis, in which the structure of language is used to interpret the meaning of the words used, in addition to their frequency. Sentences or other bodies of text can be scored for their level of positivity or negativity, and then counts or averages are used to derive insights that would be hard to summarize otherwise. There have been exciting advances in the field of natural language processing, or NLP, though much of this work is done with tools such as Python.

First-, Second-, and Third-Party Data

First-party data is collected by the organization itself. This can be done through server logs, databases that keep track of transactions and customer information, or other systems that are built and controlled by the organization and generate data of interest for analysis. Since the systems were created in-house, finding the people who built them and learning about how the data is generated is usually possible. Data analysts may also be able to influence or have control over how certain pieces of data are created and stored, particularly when bugs are responsible for poor data quality.

Second-party data comes from vendors that provide a service or perform a business function on the organization's behalf. These are often software as a service (SaaS) products; common examples are CRM, email and marketing automation tools, ecommerce-enabling software, and web and mobile interaction trackers. The data is similar to first-party data since it is about the organization itself, created by its employees and customers. However, both the code that generates and stores the data and the data model are controlled externally, and the data analyst typically has little influence over these aspects. Second-party data is increasingly imported into an organization's data warehouse for analysis. This can be accomplished with custom code or ETL connectors, or with SaaS vendors that offer data integration.

Many SaaS vendors provide some reporting capabilities, so the question may arise of whether to bother copying the data to a data warehouse. The department that interacts with a tool may find that reporting sufficient, such as a customer service department that reports on time to resolve issues and agent productivity from within its helpdesk software. On the other hand, customer service interactions might be an important input to a customer retention model, which would require integrating that data into a data store with sales and cancellation data. Here's a good rule of thumb when deciding whether to import data from a particular data source: if the data will create value when combined with data from other systems, import it; if not, wait until there is a stronger case before doing the work.

Third-party data may be purchased or obtained from free sources such as those published by governments. Unless the data has been collected specifically on behalf of the organization, data teams usually have little control over the format, frequency, and data quality. This data often lacks the granularity of first- and second-party data. For example, most third-party sources do not have user-level data, and instead data might be joined with first-party data at the postal code or city level, or at a higher level. Third-party data can have unique and useful information, however, such as aggregate spending patterns, demographics, and market trends that would be very expensive or impossible to collect otherwise.

Sparse Data

Sparse data occurs when there is a small amount of information within a larger set of empty or unimportant information. Sparse data might show up as many nulls and only a few values in a particular column. Null, different from a value of 0, is the *absence* of data; that will be covered later in the section on data cleaning. Sparse data can occur when events are rare, such as software errors or purchases of products in the long tail of a product catalog. It can also occur in the early days of a feature or product launch, when only testers or beta customers have access. JSON is one approach that has been developed to deal with sparse data from a writing and storage perspective, as it stores only the data that is present and omits the rest. This is in contrast to a row-store database, which has to hold memory for a field even if there is no value in it.

Sparse data can be problematic for analysis. When events are rare, trends aren't necessarily meaningful, and correlations are hard to distinguish from chance fluctuations. It's worth profiling your data, as discussed later in this chapter, to understand if and where your data is sparse. Some options are to group infrequent events or items into categories that are more common, exclude the sparse data or time period from the analysis entirely, or show descriptive statistics along with cautionary explanations that the trends are not necessarily meaningful.

There are a number of different types of data and a variety of ways that data is described, many of which are overlapping or not mutually exclusive. Familiarity with these types is useful not only in writing good SQL but also for deciding how to analyze the data in appropriate ways. You may not always know the data types in advance, which is why data profiling is so critical. Before we get to that, and to our first code examples, I'll give a brief review of SQL query structure.

SQL Query Structure

SQL queries have common clauses and syntax, although these can be combined in a nearly infinite number of ways to achieve analysis goals. This book assumes you have some prior knowledge of SQL, but I'll review the basics here so that we have a common foundation for the code examples to come.

The *SELECT* clause determines the columns that will be returned by the query. One column will be returned for each expression within the *SELECT* clause, and expressions are separated by commas. An expression can be a field from the table, an aggregation such as a sum, or any number of calculations, such as CASE statements, type conversions, and various functions that will be discussed later in this chapter and throughout the book.

The *FROM* clause determines the tables from which the expressions in the *SELECT* clause are derived. A "table" can be a database table, a view (a type of saved query that otherwise functions like a table), or a subquery. A subquery is itself a query, wrapped in parentheses, and the result is treated like any other table by the query that references it. A query can reference multiple tables in the *FROM* clause, though they must use one of the *JOIN* types along with a condition that specifies how the tables relate. The *JOIN* condition usually specifies an equality between fields in each table, such as `orders.customer_id = customers.customer_id`. *JOIN* conditions can include multiple fields and can also specify inequalities or ranges of values, such as ranges of dates. We'll see a variety of *JOIN* conditions that achieve specific analysis goals throughout the book. An *INNER JOIN* returns all records that match in both tables. A *LEFT JOIN* returns all records from the first table, but only those records from the second table that match. A *RIGHT JOIN* returns all records from the second table, but only those records from the first table that match. A *FULL OUTER JOIN* returns all records from both tables. A Cartesian *JOIN* can result when each record in the first table matches more than one record in the second table. Cartesian *JOINs* should generally be avoided, though there are some specific use cases, such as generating data to fill in a time series, in which we will use them intentionally. Finally, tables in the *FROM* clause can be *aliased*, or given a shorter name of one or more letters that can be referenced in other clauses in the query. Aliases save query writers from having to type out long table names repeatedly, and they make queries easier to read.

 While both *LEFT JOIN* and *RIGHT JOIN* can be used in the same query, it's much easier to keep track of your logic when you stick with only one or the other. In practice, *LEFT JOIN* is much more commonly used than *RIGHT JOIN*.

The *WHERE* clause specifies restrictions or filters that are needed to exclude or remove rows from the result set. *WHERE* is optional.

The *GROUP BY* clause is required when the *SELECT* clause contains aggregations and at least one nonaggregated field. An easy way to remember what should go in the *GROUP BY* clause is that it should have every field that is not part of an aggregation. In most databases, there are two ways to list the *GROUP BY* fields: either by field name or by position, such as 1, 2, 3, and so on. Some people prefer to use the field name notation, and SQL Server requires this. I prefer the position notation, particularly when the *GROUP BY* fields contain complex expressions or when I'm doing a lot of iteration. This book will typically use the position notation.

How Not to Kill Your Database: LIMIT and Sampling

Database tables can be very large, containing millions or billions of records. Querying across all of these records can cause problems at the least and crash databases at the worst. To avoid receiving cranky calls from database administrators or getting locked out, it's a good idea to limit the results returned during profiling or while testing queries. *LIMIT* clauses and sampling are two techniques that should be part of your toolbox.

LIMIT is added as the last line of the query, or subquery, and can take any positive integer value:

```
SELECT column_a, column_b
FROM table
LIMIT 1000
;
```

When used in a subquery, the limit will be applied at that step, and only the restricted result set will be evaluated by the outer query:

```
SELECT...
FROM
(
        SELECT column_a, column_b, sum(sales) as total_sales
        FROM table
        GROUP BY 1,2
        LIMIT 1000
```

```
   ) a
   ;
```

SQL Server does not support the *LIMIT* clause, but a similar result can be obtained using `top`:

```
SELECT top 1000
column_a, column_b
FROM table
;
```

Sampling can be accomplished by using a function on an ID field that has a random distribution of digits at the beginning or end. The modulus or `mod` function returns the remainder when one integer is divided by another. If the ID field is an integer, `mod` can be used to find the last one, two, or more digits and filter on the result:

```
WHERE mod(integer_order_id,100) = 6
```

This will return every order whose last two digits are 06, which should be about 1% of the total. If the field is alphanumeric, you can use a `right()` function to find a certain number of digits at the end:

```
WHERE right(alphanum_order_id,1) = 'B'
```

This will return every order with a last digit of B, which will be about 3% of the total if all letters and numbers are equally common, an assumption worth validating.

Limiting the result set also makes your work faster, but be aware that subsets of data might not contain all of the variations in values and edge cases that exist in the full data set. Remember to remove the *LIMIT* or sampling before running your final analysis or report with your query, or you'll end up with funny results!

That covers the basics of SQL query structure. Chapter 8 will go into additional detail on each of these clauses, a few additional ones that are less commonly encountered but appear in this book, and the order in which each clause is evaluated. Now that we have this foundation, we can turn to one of the most important parts of the analysis process: data profiling.

Profiling: Distributions

Profiling is the first thing I do when I start working with any new data set. I look at how the data is arranged into schemas and tables. I look at the table names to get familiar with the topics covered, such as customers, orders, or visits. I check out the column names in a few tables and start to construct a mental model of how the tables relate to one another. For example, the tables might include an `order_detail` table with line-item breakouts that relate to the `order` table via an `order_id`, while the `order` table relates to the `customer` table via a `customer_id`. If there is a data dictionary, I review that and compare it to the data I see in a sample of rows.

The tables generally represent the operations of an organization, or some subset of the operations, so I think about what domain or domains are covered, such as ecommerce, marketing, or product interactions. Working with data is easier when we have knowledge of how the data was generated. Profiling can provide clues about this, or about what questions to ask of the source, or of people inside or outside the organization responsible for the collection or generation of the data. Even when you collect the data yourself, profiling is useful.

Another detail I check for is how history is represented, if at all. Data sets that are replicas of production databases may not contain previous values for customer addresses or order statuses, for example, whereas a well-constructed data warehouse may have daily snapshots of changing data fields.

Profiling data is related to the concept of *exploratory data analysis*, or EDA, named by John Tukey. In his book of that name,[1] Tukey describes how to analyze data sets by computing various summaries and visualizing the results. He includes techniques for looking at distributions of data, including stem-and-leaf plots, box plots, and histograms.

After checking a few samples of data, I start looking at distributions. Distributions allow me to understand the range of values that exist in the data and how often they occur, whether there are nulls, and whether negative values exist alongside positive ones. Distributions can be created with continuous or categorical data and are also called frequencies. In this section, we'll look at how to create histograms, how binning can help us understand the distribution of continuous values, and how to use n-tiles to get more precise about distributions.

Histograms and Frequencies

One of the best ways to get to know a data set, and to know particular fields within the data set, is to check the frequency of values in each field. Frequency checks are also useful whenever you have a question about whether certain values are possible or if you spot an unexpected value and want to know how commonly it occurs. Frequency checks can be done on any data type, including strings, numerics, dates, and booleans. Frequency queries are a great way to detect sparse data as well.

The query is straightforward. The number of rows can be found with count(*), and the profiled field is in the *GROUP BY*. For example, we can check the frequency of each type of fruit in a fictional fruit_inventory table:

---

1 John W. Tukey, *Exploratory Data Analysis* (Reading, MA: Addison-Wesley, 1977).

```
SELECT fruit, count(*) as quantity
FROM fruit_inventory
GROUP BY 1
;
```

 When using `count`, it's worth taking a minute to consider whether there might be any duplicate records in the data set. You can use `count(*)` when you want the number of records, but use `count distinct` to find out how many unique items there are.

A *frequency plot* is a way to visualize the number of times something occurs in the data set. The field being profiled is usually plotted on the x-axis, with the count of observations on the y-axis. Figure 2-1 shows an example of plotting the frequency of fruit from our query. Frequency graphs can also be drawn horizontally, which accommodates long value names well. Notice that this is categorical data without any inherent order.

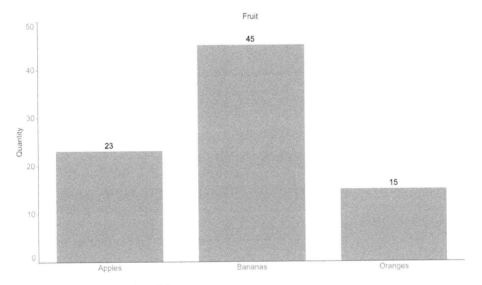

Figure 2-1. Frequency plot of fruit inventory

A *histogram* is a way to visualize the distribution of numerical values in a data set and will be familiar to those with a statistics background. A basic histogram might show the distribution of ages across a group of customers. Imagine that we have a `custom ers` table that contains names, registration date, age, and other attributes. To create a histogram by age, *GROUP BY* the numerical `age` field and `count customer_id`:

```
SELECT age, count(customer_id) as customers
FROM customers
GROUP BY 1
;
```

The results of our hypothetical age distribution are graphed in Figure 2-2.

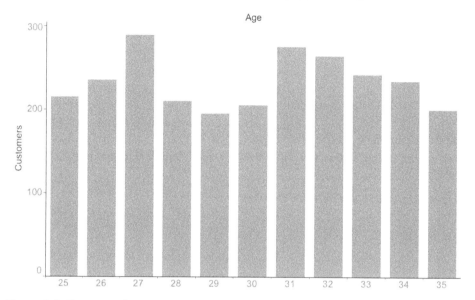

Figure 2-2. Customers by age

Another technique I've used repeatedly and that has become the basis for one of my favorite interview questions involves an aggregation followed by a frequency count. I give candidates a hypothetical table called orders, which has a date, customer identifier, order identifier, and an amount, and then ask them to write a SQL query that returns the distribution of orders per customer. This can't be solved with a simple query; it requires an intermediate aggregation step, which can be accomplished with a subquery. First, count the number of orders placed by each customer_id in the subquery. The outer query uses the number of orders as a category and counts the number of customers:

```
SELECT orders, count(*) as num_customers
FROM
(
    SELECT customer_id, count(order_id) as orders
    FROM orders
    GROUP BY 1
) a
GROUP BY 1
;
```

This type of profiling can be applied whenever you need to see how frequently certain entities or attributes appear in the data. In these examples, count has been used, but the other basic aggregations (sum, avg, min, and max) can be used to create histograms as well. For instance, we might want to profile customers by the sum of all their orders, their avg order size, their min order date, or their max (most recent) order date.

Binning

Binning is useful when working with continuous values. Rather than the number of observations or records for each value being counted, ranges of values are grouped together, and these groups are called *bins* or *buckets*. The number of records that fall into each interval is then counted. Bins can be variable in size or have a fixed size, depending on whether your goal is to group the data into bins that have particular meaning for the organization, are roughly equal width, or contain roughly equal numbers of records. Bins can be created with CASE statements, rounding, and logarithms.

A CASE statement allows for conditional logic to be evaluated. These statements are very flexible, and we will come back to them throughout the book, applying them to data profiling, cleaning, text analysis, and more. The basic structure of a CASE statement is:

```
case when condition1 then return_value_1
    when condition2 then return_value_2
    ...
    else return_value_default
    end
```

The WHEN condition can be an equality, inequality, or other logical condition. The THEN return value can be a constant, an expression, or a field in the table. Any number of conditions can be included, but the statement will stop executing and return the result the first time a condition evaluates to TRUE. ELSE tells the database what to use as a default value if no matches are found and can also be a constant or field. ELSE is optional, and if it is not included, any nonmatches will return null. CASE statements can also be nested so that the return value is another CASE statement.

> The return values following THEN must all be the same data type (strings, numeric, BOOLEAN, etc.), or else you'll get an error. Consider casting to a common data type such as string if you encounter this.

A CASE statement is a flexible way to control the number of bins, the range of values that fall into each bin, and how the bins are named. I find them particularly useful when there is a long tail of very small or very large values that I want to group together rather than have empty bins in part of the distribution. Certain ranges of values have a business meaning that needs to be re-created in the data. Many B2B companies separate their customers into "enterprise" and "SMB" (small- and medium-sized businesses) categories based on number of employees or revenue, because their buying patterns are different. As an example, imagine we are considering discounted shipping offers and we want to know how many customers will be affected. We can group order_amount into three buckets using a CASE statement:

```
SELECT
case when order_amount <= 100 then 'up to 100'
    when order_amount <= 500 then '100 - 500'
    else '500+' end as amount_bin
,case when order_amount <= 100 then 'small'
    when order_amount <= 500 then 'medium'
    else 'large' end as amount_category
,count(customer_id) as customers
FROM orders
GROUP BY 1,2
;
```

Arbitrary-sized bins can be useful, but at other times bins of fixed size are more appropriate for the analysis. Fixed-size bins can be accomplished in a few ways, including with rounding, logarithms, and n-tiles. To create equal-width bins, rounding is useful. Rounding reduces the precision of the values, and we usually think about rounding as reducing the number of decimal places or removing them altogether by rounding to the nearest integer. The round function takes the form:

```
round(value,number_of_decimal_places)
```

The number of decimal places can also be a negative number, allowing this function to round to the nearest tens, hundreds, thousands, and so on. Table 2-2 demonstrates the results of rounding with arguments ranging from –3 to 2.

Table 2-2. The number 123,456.789 rounded with various decimal places

Decimal places	Formula	Result
2	round(123456.789,2)	123456.79
1	round(123456.789,1)	123456.8
0	round(123456.789,0)	123457
-1	round(123456.789,-1)	123460
-2	round(123456.789,-2)	123500
-3	round(123456.789,-3)	123000

```
SELECT round(sales,-1) as bin
,count(customer_id) as customers
FROM table
GROUP BY 1
;
```

Logarithms are another way to create bins, particularly in data sets in which the largest values are orders of magnitude greater than the smallest values. The distribution of household wealth, the number of website visitors across different properties on the internet, and the shaking force of earthquakes are all examples of phenomena that have this property. While they don't create bins of equal width, logarithms create bins that increase in size with a useful pattern. To refresh your memory, a logarithm is the exponent to which 10 must be raised to produce that number:

$\log(number) = exponent$

In this case, 10 is called the base, and this is usually the default implementation in databases, but technically the base can be any number. Table 2-3 shows the logarithms for several powers of 10.

Table 2-3. Results of log function on powers of 10

Formula	Result
log(1)	0
log(10)	1
log(100)	2
log(1000)	3
log(10000)	4

In SQL, the `log` function returns the logarithm of its argument, which can be a constant or a field:

```
SELECT log(sales) as bin
,count(customer_id) as customers
FROM table
GROUP BY 1
;
```

The `log` function can be used on any positive value, not just multiples of 10. However, the logarithm function does not work when values can be less than or equal to 0; it will return null or an error, depending on the database.

n-Tiles

You're probably familiar with the *median*, or middle value, of a data set. This is the 50th percentile value. Half of the values are larger than the median, and the other half are smaller. With quartiles, we fill in the 25th and 75th percentile values. A quarter of the values are smaller and three quarters are larger for the 25th percentile; three quarters are smaller and one quarter are larger at the 75th percentile. Deciles break the data set into 10 equal parts. Making this concept generic, *n-tiles* allow us to calculate any percentile of the data set: 27th percentile, 50.5th percentile, and so on.

Window Functions

The n-tiles functions are part of a group of SQL functions called window or analytic functions. Unlike most SQL functions, which can operate only on the current row of data, window functions perform calculations that span multiple rows. Window functions have special syntax that includes the function name and an *OVER* clause that is used to determine the rows on which to operate and the ordering of those rows. The general format of a window function is:

```
function(field_name) over (partition by field_name order by field_name)
```

The function can be any of the normal aggregations (count, sum, avg, min, max) as well as a number of special functions, including rank, first_value, and ntile. The *PARTITION BY* clause can include zero or more fields. When no fields are specified, the function operates over the entire table, but when one or more fields are specified, the function will operate only on that section of rows. For example, we might *PARTITION BY* a customer_id to perform calculations about all of the records per customer, restarting the calculation for each customer. The *ORDER BY* clause determines the ordering of the rows for functions that rely on this; for example, to rank customers, we need to specify a field by which to order them, such as number of orders. All of the major database types have window functions, except for versions of MySQL prior to 8.0.2. We will see these useful functions throughout the book, along with additional explanations of how they work and how to set up the arguments correctly.

Many databases have a median function built in but rely on more generic n-tile functions for the rest. These functions are window functions, computing across a range of rows to return a value for a single row. They take an argument that specifies the number of bins to split the data into and, optionally, a *PARTITION BY* and/or an *ORDER BY* clause:

```
ntile(num_bins) over (partition by... order by...)
```

As an example, imagine we had 12 transactions with order_amounts of $19.99, $9.99, $59.99, $11.99, $23.49, $55.98, $12.99, $99.99, $14.99, $34.99, $4.99, and $89.99. Performing an ntile calculation with 10 bins sorts each order_amount and assigns a bin from 1 to 10:

```
order_amount   ntile
------------   -----
4.99            1
9.99            1
11.99           2
12.99           2
14.99           3
19.99           4
23.49           5
34.99           6
```

```
55.98       7
59.99       8
89.99       9
99.99      10
```

This can be used to bin records in practice by first calculating the `ntile` of each row in a subquery and then wrapping it in an outer query that uses `min` and `max` to find the upper and lower boundaries of the value range:

```
SELECT ntile
,min(order_amount) as lower_bound
,max(order_amount) as upper_bound
,count(order_id) as orders
FROM
(
    SELECT customer_id, order_id, order_amount
    ,ntile(10) over (order by order_amount) as ntile
    FROM orders
) a
GROUP BY 1
;
```

A related function is `percent_rank`. Instead of returning the bins that the data falls into, `percent_rank` returns the percentile. It takes no argument but requires parentheses and optionally takes a *PARTITION BY* and/or an *ORDER BY* clause:

```
percent_rank() over (partition by... order by...)
```

While not as useful as `ntile` for binning, `percent_rank` can be used to create a continuous distribution, or it can be used as an output itself for reporting or further analysis. Both `ntile` and `percent_rank` can be expensive to compute over large data sets, since they require sorting all the rows. Filtering the table to only the data set you need helps. Some databases have implemented approximate versions of the functions that are faster to compute and generally return high-quality results if absolute precision is not required. We will look at additional uses for n-tiles in the discussion of anomaly detection in Chapter 6.

In many contexts, there is no single correct or objectively best way to look at distributions of data. There is significant leeway for analysts to use the preceding techniques to understand data and present it to others. However, data scientists need to use judgment and must bring their ethical radar along whenever sharing distributions of sensitive data.

Profiling: Data Quality

Data quality is absolutely critical when it comes to creating good analysis. Although this may seem obvious, it has been one of the hardest lessons I've learned in my years of working with data. It's easy to get overly focused on the mechanics of processing the data, finding clever query techniques and just the right visualization, only to have stakeholders ignore all of that and point out the one data inconsistency. Ensuring data quality can be one of the hardest and most frustrating parts of analysis. The saying "garbage in, garbage out" captures only part of the problem. Good ingredients in plus incorrect assumptions can also lead to garbage out.

Comparing data against ground truth, or what is otherwise known to be true, is ideal though not always possible. For example, if you are working with a replica of a production database, you could compare the row counts in each system to verify that all rows arrived in the replica database. In other cases, you might know the dollar value and count of sales in a particular month and thus can query for this information in the database to make sure the sum of sales and count of records match. Often the difference between your query results and the expected value comes down to whether you applied the correct filters, such as excluding cancelled orders or test accounts; how you handled nulls and spelling anomalies; and whether you set up correct *JOIN* conditions between tables.

Profiling is a way to uncover data quality issues early on, before they negatively impact results and conclusions drawn from the data. Profiling reveals nulls, categorical codings that need to be deciphered, fields with multiple values that need to be parsed, and unusual datetime formats. Profiling can also uncover gaps and step changes in the data that have resulted from tracking changes or outages. Data is rarely perfect, and it's often only through its use in analysis that data quality issues are uncovered.

Detecting Duplicates

A *duplicate* is when you have two (or more) rows with the same information. Duplicates can exist for any number of reasons. A mistake might have been made during data entry, if there is some manual step. A tracking call might have fired twice. A processing step might have run multiple times. You might have created it accidentally with a hidden many-to-many *JOIN*. However they come to be, duplicates can really throw a wrench in your analysis. I can recall times early in my career when I thought I had a great finding, only to have a product manager point out that my sales figure was twice the actual sales. It's embarrassing, it erodes trust, and it requires rework and sometimes painstaking reviews of the code to find the problem. I've learned to check for duplicates as I go.

Fortunately, it's relatively easy to find duplicates in our data. One way is to inspect a sample, with all columns ordered:

```
SELECT column_a, column_b, column_c...
FROM table
ORDER BY 1,2,3...
;
```

This will reveal whether the data is full of duplicates, for example, when looking at a brand-new data set, when you suspect that a process is generating duplicates, or after a possible Cartesian *JOIN*. If there are only a few duplicates, they might not show up in the sample. And scrolling through data to try to spot duplicates is taxing on your eyes and brain. A more systematic way to find duplicates is to *SELECT* the columns and then count the rows (this might look familiar from the discussion of histograms!):

```
SELECT count(*)
FROM
(
    SELECT column_a, column_b, column_c...
    , count(*) as records
    FROM...
    GROUP BY 1,2,3...
) a
WHERE records > 1
;
```

This will tell you whether there are any cases of duplicates. If the query returns 0, you're good to go. For more detail, you can list out the number of records (2, 3, 4, etc.):

```
SELECT records, count(*)
FROM
(
    SELECT column_a, column_b, column_c..., count(*) as records
    FROM...
    GROUP BY 1,2,3...
) a
WHERE records > 1
GROUP BY 1
;
```

As an alternative to a subquery, you can use a *HAVING* clause and keep everything in a single main query. Since it is evaluated after the aggregation and *GROUP BY*, *HAVING* can be used to filter on the aggregation value:

```
SELECT column_a, column_b, column_c..., count(*) as records
FROM...
GROUP BY 1,2,3...
HAVING count(*) > 1
;
```

I prefer to use subqueries, because I find that they're a useful way to organize my logic. Chapter 8 will discuss order of evaluation and strategies for keeping your SQL queries organized.

For full detail on which records have duplicates, you can list out all the fields and then use this information to chase down which records are problematic:

```
SELECT *
FROM
(
    SELECT column_a, column_b, column_c..., count(*) as records
    FROM...
    GROUP BY 1,2,3...
) a
WHERE records = 2
;
```

Detecting duplicates is one thing; figuring out what to do about them is another. It's almost always useful to understand why duplicates are occurring and, if possible, fix the problem upstream. Can a data process be improved to reduce or remove duplication? Is there an error in an ETL process? Have you failed to account for a one-to-many relationship in a *JOIN*? Next, we'll turn to some options for handling and removing duplicates with SQL.

Deduplication with GROUP BY and DISTINCT

Duplicates happen, and they're not always a result of bad data. For example, imagine we want to find a list of all the customers who have successfully completed a transaction so we can send them a coupon for their next order. We might *JOIN* the custom ers table to the transactions table, which would restrict the records returned to only those customers that appear in the transactions table:

```
SELECT a.customer_id, a.customer_name, a.customer_email
FROM customers a
JOIN transactions b on a.customer_id = b.customer_id
;
```

This will return a row for each customer for each transaction, however, and there are hopefully at least a few customers who have transacted more than once. We have accidentally created duplicates, not because there is any underlying data quality problem but because we haven't taken care to avoid duplication in the results. Fortunately, there are several ways to avoid this with SQL. One way to remove duplicates is to use the keyword *DISTINCT*:

```
SELECT distinct a.customer_id, a.customer_name, a.customer_email
FROM customers a
JOIN transactions b on a.customer_id = b.customer_id
;
```

Another option is to use a *GROUP BY*, which, although typically seen in connection with an aggregation, will also deduplicate in the same way as *DISTINCT*. I remember the first time I saw a colleague use *GROUP BY* without an aggregation dedupe—I didn't even realize it was possible. I find it somewhat less intuitive than *DISTINCT*, but the result is the same:

```
SELECT a.customer_id, a.customer_name, a.customer_email
FROM customers a
JOIN transactions b on a.customer_id = b.customer_id
GROUP BY 1,2,3
;
```

Another useful technique is to perform an aggregation that returns one row per entity. Although technically not deduping, it has a similar effect. For example, if we have a number of transactions by the same customer and need to return one record per customer, we could find the min (first) and/or the max (most recent) transaction_date:

```
SELECT customer_id
,min(transaction_date) as first_transaction_date
,max(transaction_date) as last_transaction_date
,count(*) as total_orders
FROM table
GROUP BY customer_id
;
```

Duplicate data, or data that contains multiple records per entity even if they technically are not duplicates, is one of the most common reasons for incorrect query results. You can suspect duplicates as the cause if all of a sudden the number of customers or total sales returned by a query is many times greater than what you were expecting. Fortunately, there are several techniques that can be applied to prevent this from occurring.

Another common problem is missing data, which we'll turn to next.

Preparing: Data Cleaning

Profiling often reveals where changes can make the data more useful for analysis. Some of the steps are CASE transformations, adjusting for null, and changing data types.

Cleaning Data with CASE Transformations

CASE statements can be used to perform a variety of cleaning, enrichment, and summarization tasks. Sometimes the data exists and is accurate, but it would be more useful for analysis if values were standardized or grouped into categories. The structure of CASE statements was presented earlier in this chapter, in the section on binning.

Nonstandard values occur for a variety of reasons. Values might come from different systems with slightly different lists of choices, system code might have changed, options might have been presented to the customer in different languages, or the customer might have been able to fill out the value rather than pick from a list.

Imagine a field containing information about the gender of a person. Values indicating a female person exist as "F," "female," and "femme." We can standardize the values like this:

```
CASE when gender = 'F' then 'Female'
     when gender = 'female' then 'Female'
     when gender = 'femme' then 'Female'
     else gender
     end as gender_cleaned
```

CASE statements can also be used to add categorization or enrichment that does not exist in the original data. As an example, many organizations use a Net Promoter Score, or NPS, to monitor customer sentiment. NPS surveys ask respondents to rate, on a scale of 0 to 10, how likely they are to recommend a company or product to a friend or colleague. Scores of 0 to 6 are considered detractors, 7 and 8 are passive, and 9 and 10 are promoters. The final score is calculated by subtracting the percentage of detractors from the percentage of promoters. Survey result data sets usually include optional free text comments and are sometimes enriched with information the organization knows about the person surveyed. Given a data set of NPS survey responses, the first step is to group the responses into the categories of detractor, passive, and promoter:

```
SELECT response_id
,likelihood
,case when likelihood <= 6 then 'Detractor'
      when likelihood <= 8 then 'Passive'
      else 'Promoter'
      end as response_type
FROM nps_responses
;
```

Note that the data type can differ between the field being evaluated and the return data type. In this case, we are checking an integer and returning a string. Listing out all the values with an IN list is also an option. The IN operator allows you to specify a list of items rather than having to write an equality for each one separately. It is useful when the input isn't continuous or when values in order shouldn't be grouped together:

```
case when likelihood in (0,1,2,3,4,5,6) then 'Detractor'
     when likelihood in (7,8) then 'Passive'
     when likelihood in (9,10) then 'Promoter'
     end as response_type
```

CASE statements can consider multiple columns and can contain AND/OR logic. They can also be nested, though often this can be avoided with AND/OR logic:

```
case when likelihood <= 6
        and country = 'US'
        and high_value = true
        then 'US high value detractor'
    when likelihood >= 9
        and (country in ('CA','JP')
            or high_value = true
            )
        then 'some other label'
    ... end
```

Alternatives for Cleaning Data

Cleaning or enriching data with a CASE statement works well as long as there is a relatively short list of variations, you can find them all in the data, and the list of values isn't expected to change. For longer lists and ones that change frequently, a lookup table can be a better option. A lookup table exists in the database and is either static or populated with code that checks for new values periodically. The query will *JOIN* to the lookup table to get the cleaned data. In this way, the cleaned values can be maintained outside your code and used by many queries, without your having to worry about maintaining consistency between them. An example of this might be a lookup table that maps state abbreviations to full state names. In my own work, I often start with a CASE statement and create a lookup table only after the list becomes unruly, or once it's clear that my team or I will need to use this cleaning step repeatedly.

Of course, it's worth investigating whether the data can be cleaned upstream. I once started with a CASE statement of 5 or so lines that grew to 10 lines and then eventually to more than 100 lines, at which point the list was unruly and difficult to maintain. The insights were valuable enough that I was able to convince engineers to change the tracking code and send the meaningful categorizations in the data stream in the first place.

Another useful thing you can do with CASE statements is to create flags indicating whether a certain value is present, without returning the actual value. This can be useful during profiling for understanding how common the existence of a particular attribute is. Another use for flagging is during preparation of a data set for statistical analysis. In this case, a flag is also known as a dummy variable, taking a value of 0 or 1 and indicating the presence or absence of some qualitative variable. For example, we can create is_female and is_promoter flags with CASE statements on gender and likelihood (to recommend) fields:

```
SELECT customer_id
,case when gender = 'F' then 1 else 0 end as is_female
,case when likelihood in (9,10) then 1 else 0 end as is_promoter
```

```
FROM ...
;
```

If you are working with a data set that has multiple rows per entity, such as with line items in an order, you can flatten the data with a CASE statement wrapped in an aggregate and turn it into a flag at the same time by using 1 and 0 as the return value. We saw previously that a BOOLEAN data type is often used to create flags (fields that represent the presence or absence of some attribute). Here, 1 is substituted for TRUE and 0 is substituted for FALSE so that a max aggregation can be applied. The way this works is that for each customer, the CASE statement returns 1 for any row with a fruit type of "apple." Then max is evaluated and will return the largest value from any of the rows. As long as a customer bought an apple at least once, the flag will be 1; if not, it will be 0:

```
SELECT customer_id
,max(case when fruit = 'apple' then 1
        else 0
        end) as bought_apples
,max(case when fruit = 'orange' then 1
        else 0
        end) as bought_oranges
FROM ...
GROUP BY 1
;
```

You can also construct more complex conditions for flags, such as requiring a threshold or amount of something before labeling with a value of 1:

```
SELECT customer_id
,max(case when fruit = 'apple' and quantity > 5 then 1
        else 0
        end) as loves_apples
,max(case when fruit = 'orange' and quantity > 5 then 1
        else 0
        end) as loves_oranges
FROM ...
GROUP BY 1
;
```

CASE statements are powerful, and as we saw, they can be used to clean, enrich, and flag or add dummy variables to data sets. In the next section, we'll look at some special functions related to CASE statements that handle null values specifically.

Type Conversions and Casting

Every field in a database is defined with a data type, which we reviewed at the beginning of this chapter. When data is inserted into a table, values that aren't of the field's type are rejected by the database. Strings can't be inserted into integer fields, and booleans are not allowed in date fields. Most of the time, we can take the data types for granted and apply string functions to strings, date functions to dates, and so on. Occasionally, however, we need to override the data type of the field and force it to be something else. This is where type conversions and casting come in.

Type conversion functions allow pieces of data with the appropriate format to be changed from one data type to another. The syntax comes in a few forms that are basically equivalent. One way to change the data type is with the `cast` function, `cast` (*input* as *data_type*), or two colons, *input* :: *data_type*. Both of these are equivalent and convert the integer 1,234 to a string:

```
cast (1234 as varchar)

1234::varchar
```

Converting an integer to a string can be useful in CASE statements when categorizing numeric values with some unbounded upper or lower value. For example, in the following code, leaving the values that are less than or equal to 3 as integers while returning the string "4+" for higher values would result in an error:

```
case when order_items <= 3 then order_items
     else '4+'
     end
```

Casting the integers to the VARCHAR type solves the problem:

```
case when order_items <= 3 then order_items::varchar
     else '4+'
     end
```

Type conversions also come in handy when values that should be integers are parsed out of a string, and then we want to aggregate the values or use mathematical functions on them. Imagine we have a data set of prices, but the values include the dollar sign ($), and so the data type of the field is VARCHAR. We can remove the $ character with a function called `replace`, which will be discussed more during our look at text analysis in Chapter 5:

```
SELECT replace('$19.99','$','');
replace
-------
9.99
```

The result is still a VARCHAR, however, so trying to apply an aggregation will return an error. To fix this, we can `cast` the result as a FLOAT:

```
replace('$19.99','$','')::float
cast(replace('$19.99','$','')) as float
```

Dates and datetimes can come in a bewildering array of formats, and understanding how to *cast* them to the desired format is useful. I'll show a few examples on type conversion here, and Chapter 3 will go into more detail on date and datetime calculations. As a simple example, imagine that transaction or event data often arrives in the database as a TIMESTAMP, but we want to summarize some value such as transactions by day. Simply grouping by the timestamp will result in more rows than necessary. Casting the TIMESTAMP to a DATE reduces the size of the results and achieves our summarization goal:

```
SELECT tx_timestamp::date, count(transactions) as num_transactions
FROM ...
GROUP BY 1
;
```

Likewise, a DATE can be cast to a TIMESTAMP when a SQL function requires a TIMESTAMP argument. Sometimes the year, month, and day are stored in separate columns, or they end up as separate elements because they've been parsed out of a longer string. These then need to be assembled back into a date. To do this, we use the concatenation operator || (double pipe) or concat function and then cast the result to a DATE. Any of these syntaxes works and returns the same value:

```
(year || ',' || month|| '-' || day)::date
```

Or equivalently:

```
cast(concat(year, '-', month, '-', day) as date)
```

Yet another way to convert between string values and dates is by using the date function. For example, we can construct a string value as above and convert it into a date:

```
date(concat(year, '-', month, '-', day))
```

The *to_datatype* functions can take both a value and a format string and thus give you more control over how the data is converted. Table 2-4 summarizes the functions and their purposes. They are particularly useful when converting in and out of DATE or DATETIME formats, as they allow you to specify the order of the date and time elements.

Table 2-4. The to_datatype functions

Function	Purpose
to_char	Converts other types to string
to_number	Converts other types to numeric
to_date	Converts other types to date, with specified date parts
to_timestamp	Converts other types to date, with specified date and time parts

Sometimes the database automatically converts a data type. This is called *type coercion*. For example, INT and FLOAT numerics can usually be used together in mathematical functions or aggregations without explicitly changing the type. CHAR and VARCHAR values can usually be mixed. Some databases will coerce BOOLEAN fields to 0 and 1 values, where 0 is FALSE and 1 is TRUE, but some databases require you to convert the values explicitly. Some databases are pickier than others about mixing dates and datetimes in result sets and functions. You can read through the documentation, or you can do some simple query experiments to learn how the database you're working with handles data types implicitly and explicitly. There is usually a way to accomplish what you want, though sometimes you need to get creative in using functions in your queries.

Dealing with Nulls: coalesce, nullif, nvl Functions

Null was one of the stranger concepts I had to get used to when I started working with data. Null just isn't something we think about in daily life, where we're used to dealing in concrete quantities of things. *Null* has a special meaning in databases and was introduced by Edgar Codd, the inventor of the relational database, to ensure that databases have a way to represent missing information. If someone asks me how many parachutes I have, I can answer "zero." But if the question is never asked, I have null parachutes.

Nulls can represent fields for which no data was collected or that aren't applicable for that row. When new columns are added to a table, the values for previously created rows will be null unless explicitly filled with some other value. When two tables are joined via an *OUTER JOIN*, nulls will appear in any fields for which there is no matching record in the second table.

Nulls are problematic for certain aggregations and groupings, and different types of databases handle them in different ways. For example, imagine I have five records, with 5, 10, 15, 20, and null. The sum of these is 50, but the average is either 10 or 12.5 depending on whether the null value is counted in the denominator. The whole question may also be considered invalid since one of the values is null. For most database functions, a null input will return a null output. Equalities and inequalities involving null also return null. A variety of unexpected and frustrating results can be output from your queries if you are not on the lookout for nulls.

When tables are defined, they can either allow nulls, reject nulls, or populate a default value if the field would otherwise be left null. In practice, this means that you can't always rely on a field to show up as null if the data is missing, because it may have been filled with a default value such as 0. I once had a long debate with a data engineer when it turned out that null dates in the source system were defaulting to "1970-01-01" in our data warehouse. I insisted that the dates should be null instead, to reflect the fact that they were unknown or not applicable. The engineer pointed out that I could remember to filter those dates or change them back to null with a CASE statement. I finally prevailed by pointing out that one day another user who wasn't as aware of the nuances of default dates would come along, run a query, and get the puzzling cluster of customers about a year before the company was even founded.

Nulls are often inconvenient or inappropriate for the analysis you want to do. They can also make output confusing to the intended audience for your analysis. Businesspeople don't necessarily understand how to interpret a null value or may assume that null values represent a problem with data quality.

Empty Strings

A concept related to but slightly different from nulls is *empty string*, where there is no value but the field is not technically null. One reason an empty string might be used is to indicate that a field is known to be blank, as opposed to null, where the value might be missing or unknown. For example, the database might have a name_suffix field that can be used to hold a value such as "Jr." Many people do not have a name_suffix, so an empty string is appropriate. Empty string can also be used as a default value instead of null, or as a way to overcome a NOT NULL constraint by inserting a value, even if empty. An empty string can be specified in a query with two quote marks:

```
WHERE my_field = '' or my_field <> 'apple'
```

Profiling the frequencies of values should reveal whether your data includes nulls, empty strings, or both.

There are a few ways to replace nulls with alternate values: CASE statements, and the specialized coalesce and nullif functions. We saw previously that CASE statements can check a condition and return a value. They can also be used to check for a null and, if one is found, replace it with another value:

```
case when num_orders is null then 0 else num_orders end

case when address is null then 'Unknown' else address end

case when column_a is null then column_b else column_a end
```

The coalesce function is a more compact way to achieve this. It takes two or more arguments and returns the first one that is not null:

```
coalesce(num_orders,0)

coalesce(address,'Unknown')

coalesce(column_a,column_b)

coalesce(column_a,column_b,column_c)
```

 The function nvl exists in some databases and is similar to coalesce, but it allows only two arguments.

The `nullif` function compares two numbers, and if they are not equal, it returns the first number; if they *are* equal, the function returns null. Running this code:

```
nullif(6,7)
```

returns 6, whereas null is returned by:

```
nullif(6,6)
```

`nullif` is equivalent to the following, more wordy case statement:

```
case when 6 = 7 then 6
     when 6 = 6 then null
     end
```

This function can be useful for turning values back into nulls when you know a certain default value has been inserted into the database. For example, with my default time example, we could change it back to null by using:

```
nullif(date,'1970-01-01')
```

 Nulls can be problematic when filtering data in the *WHERE* clause. Returning values that are null is fairly straightforward:

```
WHERE my_field is null
```

However, imagine that `my_field` contains some nulls and also some names of fruits. I would like to return all rows that are not apples. It seems like this should work:

```
WHERE my_field <> 'apple'
```

However, some databases will exclude both the "apple" rows and all rows with null values in `my_field`. To correct this, the SQL should both filter out "apple" and explicitly include nulls by connecting the conditions with OR:

```
WHERE my_field <> 'apple' or my_field is null
```

Nulls are a fact of life when working with data. Regardless of why they occur, we often need to consider them in profiling and as targets for data cleaning. Fortunately, there are a number of ways to detect them with SQL, as well as several useful functions that allow us to replace nulls with alternate values. Next we'll look at missing data, a problem that can cause nulls but has even wider implications and thus deserves a section of its own.

Missing Data

Data can be missing for a variety of reasons, each with its own implications for how you decide to handle the data's absence. A field might not have been required by the system or process that collected it, as with an optional "how did you hear about us?" field in an ecommerce checkout flow. Requiring this field might create friction for the customer and decrease successful checkouts. Alternatively, data might normally be required but wasn't collected due to a code bug or human error, such as in a medical questionnaire where the interviewer missed the second page of questions. A change in the way the data was collected can result in records before or after the change having missing values. A tool tracking mobile app interactions might add an additional field recording whether the interaction was a tap or a scroll, for example, or remove another field due to functionality change. Data can be orphaned when a table references a value in another table, and that row or the entire table has been deleted or is not yet loaded into the data warehouse. Finally, data may be available but not at the level of detail, or granularity, needed for the analysis. An example of this comes from subscription businesses, where customers pay on an annual basis for a monthly product and we want to analyze monthly revenue.

In addition to profiling the data with histograms and frequency analysis, we can often detect missing data by comparing values in two tables. For example, we might expect that each customer in the transactions table also has a record in the customer table. To check this, query the tables using a *LEFT JOIN* and add a *WHERE* condition to find the customers that do not exist in the second table:

```
SELECT distinct a.customer_id
FROM transactions a
LEFT JOIN customers b on a.customer_id = b.customer_id
WHERE b.customer_id is null
;
```

Missing data can be an important signal in and of itself, so don't assume that it always needs to be fixed or filled. Missing data can reveal the underlying system design or biases in the data collection process.

Records with missing fields can be filtered out entirely, but often we want to keep them and instead make some adjustments based on what we know about expected or typical values. We have some options, called *imputation* techniques, for filling in missing data. These include filling with an average or median of the data set, or with the previous value. Documenting the missing data and how it was replaced is important, as this may impact the downstream interpretation and use of the data. Imputed values can be particularly problematic when the data is used in machine learning, for example.

A common option is to fill missing data with a constant value. Filling with a constant value can be useful when the value is known for some records even though they were not populated in the database. For example, imagine there was a software bug that prevented the population of the price for an item called "xyz," but we know the price is always $20. A CASE statement can be added to the query to handle this:

```
case when price is null and item_name = 'xyz' then 20
                                  else price
                                  end as price
```

Another option is to fill with a derived value, either a mathematical function on other columns or a CASE statement. For example, imagine we have a field for the net_sales amount for each transaction. Due to a bug, some rows don't have this field populated, but they do have the gross_sales and discount fields populated. We can calculate net_sales by subtracting discount from gross_sales:

```
SELECT gross_sales - discount as net_sales...
```

Missing values can also be filled with values from other rows in the data set. Carrying over a value from the previous row is called *fill forward*, while using a value from the next row is called *fill backward*. These can be accomplished with the lag and lead window functions, respectively. For example, imagine that our transaction table has a product_price field that stores the undiscounted price a customer pays for a prod uct. Occasionally this field is not populated, but we can make an assumption that the price is the same as the price paid by the last customer to buy that product. We can fill with the previous value using the lag function, *PARTITION BY* the product to ensure the price is pulled only from the same product, and *ORDER BY* the appropriate date to ensure the price is pulled from the most recent prior transaction:

```
lag(product_price) over (partition by product order by order_date)
```

The lead function could be used to fill with product_price for the following transaction. Alternatively, we could take the avg of prices for the product and use that to fill in the missing value. Filling with previous, next, or average values involves making some assumptions about typical values and what's reasonable to include in an analysis. It's always a good idea to check the results to make sure they are plausible and to note that you have interpolated the data when not available.

For data that is available but not at the granularity needed, we often have to create additional rows in the data set. For example, imagine we have a customer_subscrip tions table with the fields subscription_date and annual_amount. We can spread this annual subscription amount into 12 equal monthly revenue amounts by dividing by 12, effectively converting ARR (annual recurring revenue) into MRR (monthly recurring revenue):

```
SELECT customer_id
,subscription_date
,annual_amount
,annual_amount / 12 as month_1
,annual_amount / 12 as month_2
...
,annual_amount / 12 as month_12
FROM customer_subscriptions
;
```

This gets a bit tedious, particularly if subscription periods can be two, three, or five years as well as one year. It's also not helpful if what we want is the actual dates of the months. In theory we could write a query like this:

```
SELECT customer_id
,subscription_date
,annual_amount
,annual_amount / 12 as '2020-01'
,annual_amount / 12 as '2020-02'
...
,annual_amount / 12 as '2020-12'
FROM customer_subscriptions
;
```

However, if the data includes orders from customers across time, hardcoding the month names won't be accurate. We could use CASE statements in combination with hardcoded month names, but again this is tedious and is likely to be error-prone as you add more convoluted logic. Instead, creating new rows through a *JOIN* to a table such as a date dimension provides an elegant solution.

A *date dimension* is a static table that has one row per day, with optional extended date attributes, such as day of the week, month name, end of month, and fiscal year. The dates extend far enough into the past and far enough into the future to cover all anticipated uses. Because there are only 365 or 366 days per year, tables covering even 100 years don't take up a lot of space. Figure 2-3 shows a sample of the data in a date dimension table. Sample code to create a date dimension using SQL functions is on the book's GitHub site (*https://oreil.ly/kv3dZ*).

date	day_of_month	day_of_year	day_of_week	day_name	week	month_number	month_name	quarter_number	quarter_name	year	decade
2000-01-01	1	1	6	Saturday	1999-12-27	1	January	1	Q1	2000	2000
2000-01-02	2	2	0	Sunday	1999-12-27	1	January	1	Q1	2000	2000
2000-01-03	3	3	1	Monday	2000-01-03	1	January	1	Q1	2000	2000
2000-01-04	4	4	2	Tuesday	2000-01-03	1	January	1	Q1	2000	2000
2000-01-05	5	5	3	Wednesday	2000-01-03	1	January	1	Q1	2000	2000
2000-01-06	6	6	4	Thursday	2000-01-03	1	January	1	Q1	2000	2000
2000-01-07	7	7	5	Friday	2000-01-03	1	January	1	Q1	2000	2000
2000-01-08	8	8	6	Saturday	2000-01-03	1	January	1	Q1	2000	2000
2000-01-09	9	9	0	Sunday	2000-01-03	1	January	1	Q1	2000	2000
2000-01-10	10	10	1	Monday	2000-01-10	1	January	1	Q1	2000	2000
2000-01-11	11	11	2	Tuesday	2000-01-10	1	January	1	Q1	2000	2000
2000-01-12	12	12	3	Wednesday	2000-01-10	1	January	1	Q1	2000	2000
2000-01-13	13	13	4	Thursday	2000-01-10	1	January	1	Q1	2000	2000
2000-01-14	14	14	5	Friday	2000-01-10	1	January	1	Q1	2000	2000
2000-01-15	15	15	6	Saturday	2000-01-10	1	January	1	Q1	2000	2000
2000-01-16	16	16	0	Sunday	2000-01-10	1	January	1	Q1	2000	2000
2000-01-17	17	17	1	Monday	2000-01-17	1	January	1	Q1	2000	2000
2000-01-18	18	18	2	Tuesday	2000-01-17	1	January	1	Q1	2000	2000
2000-01-19	19	19	3	Wednesday	2000-01-17	1	January	1	Q1	2000	2000
2000-01-20	20	20	4	Thursday	2000-01-17	1	January	1	Q1	2000	2000
2000-01-21	21	21	5	Friday	2000-01-17	1	January	1	Q1	2000	2000
2000-01-22	22	22	6	Saturday	2000-01-17	1	January	1	Q1	2000	2000
2000-01-23	23	23	0	Sunday	2000-01-17	1	January	1	Q1	2000	2000
2000-01-24	24	24	1	Monday	2000-01-24	1	January	1	Q1	2000	2000
2000-01-25	25	25	2	Tuesday	2000-01-24	1	January	1	Q1	2000	2000
2000-01-26	26	26	3	Wednesday	2000-01-24	1	January	1	Q1	2000	2000

Figure 2-3. A date dimension table with date attributes

If you're using a Postgres database, the `generate_series` function can be used to create a date dimension either to populate the table initially or if creating a table is not an option. It takes the following form:

```
generate_series(start, stop, step interval)
```

In this function, *start* is the first date you want in the series, *stop* is the last date, and *step interval* is the time period between values. The *step interval* can take any value, but one day is appropriate for a date dimension:

```
SELECT *
FROM generate_series('2000-01-01'::timestamp,'2030-12-31', '1 day')
```

The generate_series function requires at least one of the arguments to be a TIME-STAMP, so "2000-01-01" is cast as a TIMESTAMP. We can then create a query that results in a row for every day, regardless of whether a customer ordered on a particular day. This is useful when we want to ensure that a customer is counted for each day, or when we specifically want to count or otherwise analyze days on which a customer did not make a purchase:

```
SELECT a.generate_series as order_date, b.customer_id, b.items
FROM
(
    SELECT *
    FROM generate_series('2020-01-01'::timestamp,'2020-12-31','1 day')
) a
LEFT JOIN
(
    SELECT customer_id, order_date, count(item_id) as items
    FROM orders
    GROUP BY 1,2
) b on a.generate_series = b.order_date
;
```

Returning to our subscription example, we can use the date dimension to create a record for each month by *JOIN*ing the date dimension on dates that are between the subscription_date and 11 months later (for 12 total months):

```
SELECT a.date
,b.customer_id
,b.subscription_date
,b.annual_amount / 12 as monthly_subscription
FROM date_dim a
JOIN customer_subscriptions b on a.date between b.subscription_date
and b.subscription_date + interval '11 months'
;
```

Data can be missing for various reasons, and understanding the root cause is important in deciding how to deal with it. There are a number of options for finding and replacing missing data. These include using CASE statements to set default values, deriving values by performing calculations on other fields in the same row, and interpolating from other values in the same column.

Data cleaning is an important part of the data preparation process. Data may need to be cleaned for many different reasons. Some data cleaning needs to be done to fix poor data quality, such as when there are inconsistent or missing values in the raw data, while other data cleaning is done to make further analysis easier or more meaningful. The flexibility of SQL allows us to perform cleaning tasks in a variety of ways.

After data is cleaned, a common next step in the preparation process is shaping the data set.

Preparing: Shaping Data

Shaping data refers to manipulating the way the data is represented in columns and rows. Each table in the database has a shape. The result set of each query has a shape. Shaping data may seem like a rather abstract concept, but if you work with enough data, you will come to see its value. It is a skill that can be learned, practiced, and mastered.

One of the most important concepts in shaping data is figuring out the *granularity* of data that you need. Just as rocks can range in size from giant boulders down to grains of sand, and even further down to microscopic dust, so too can data have varying levels of detail. For example, if the population of a country is a boulder, then the population of a city is a small rock, and that of a household is a grain of sand. Data at a smaller level of detail might include individual births and deaths, or moves from one city or country to another.

Flattening data is another important concept in shaping. This refers to reducing the number of rows that represent an entity, including down to a single row. Joining multiple tables together to create a single output data set is one way to flatten data. Another way is through aggregation.

In this section, we'll first cover some considerations for choosing data shapes. Then we'll look at some common use cases: pivoting and unpivoting. We'll see examples of shaping data for specific analyses throughout the remaining chapters. Chapter 8 will go into more detail on keeping complex SQL organized when creating data sets for further analysis.

For Which Output: BI, Visualization, Statistics, ML

Deciding how to shape your data with SQL depends a lot on what you are planning to do with the data afterward. It's generally a good idea to output a data set that has as few rows as possible while still meeting your need for granularity. This will leverage the computing power of the database, reduce the time it takes to move data from the database to somewhere else, and reduce the amount of processing you or someone else needs to do in other tools. Some of the other tools that your output might go to are a BI tool for reporting and dashboarding, a spreadsheet for business users to examine, a statistics tool such as R, or a machine learning model in Python—or you might output the data straight to a visualization created with a range of tools.

When outputting data to a business intelligence tool for reports and dashboards, it's important to understand the use case. Data sets may need to be very detailed to enable exploration and slicing by end users. They may need to be small and aggregated and include specific calculations to enable fast loading and response times in executive dashboards. Understanding how the tool works, and whether it performs better with smaller data sets or is architected to perform its own aggregations across larger data sets, is important. There is no "one size fits all" answer. The more you know about how the data will be used, the better prepared you will be to shape the data appropriately.

Smaller, aggregated, and highly specific data sets often work best for visualizations, whether they are created in commercial software or using a programming language like R, Python, or JavaScript. Think about the level of aggregation and slices, or various elements, the end users will need to filter on. Sometimes the data sets require a row for each slice, as well as an "everything" slice. You may need to *UNION* together two queries—one at the detail level and one at the "everything" level.

When creating output for statistics packages or machine learning models, it's important to understand the core entity being studied, the level of aggregation desired, and the attributes or features needed. For example, a model might need one record per customer with several attributes, or a record per transaction with its associated attributes as well as customer attributes. Generally, the output for modeling will follow the notion of "tidy data" proposed by Hadley Wickham.[2] Tidy data has these properties:

1. Each variable forms a column.
2. Each observation forms a row.
3. Each value is a cell.

We will next look at how to use SQL to transform data from the structure in which it exists in your database into any other pivoted or unpivoted structure that is needed for analysis.

Pivoting with CASE Statements

A *pivot table* is a way to summarize data sets by arranging the data into rows, according to the values of an attribute, and columns, according to the values of another attribute. At the intersection of each row and column, a summary statistic such as sum, count, or avg is calculated. Pivot tables are often a good way to summarize data for business audiences, since they reshape the data into a more compact and easily

---

2 Hadley Wickham, "Tidy Data," *Journal of Statistical Software* 59, no. 10 (2014): 1–23, *https://doi.org/10.18637/jss.v059.i10*.

understandable form. Pivot tables are widely known from their implementation in Microsoft Excel, which has a drag-and-drop interface to create the summaries of data.

Pivot tables, or pivoted output, can be created in SQL using a CASE statement along with one or more aggregation functions. We've seen CASE statements several times so far, and reshaping data is another major use case for them. For example, imagine we have an orders table with a row for each purchase made by customers. To flatten the data, *GROUP BY* the customer_id and sum the order_amount:

```
SELECT customer_id
,sum(order_amount) as total_amount
FROM orders
GROUP BY 1
;

customer_id  total_amount
-----------  ------------
123          59.99
234          120.55
345          87.99
...          ...
```

To create a pivot, we will additionally create columns for each of the values of an attribute. Imagine the orders table also has a product field that contains the type of item purchased and the order_date. To create pivoted output, *GROUP BY* the order_date, and sum the result of a CASE statement that returns the order_amount whenever the row meets the product name criteria:

```
SELECT order_date
,sum(case when product = 'shirt' then order_amount
          else 0
          end) as shirts_amount
,sum(case when product = 'shoes' then order_amount
          else 0
          end) as shoes_amount
,sum(case when product = 'hat' then order_amount
          else 0
          end) hats_amount
FROM orders
GROUP BY 1
;

order_date  shirts_amount  shoes_amount  hats_amount
----------  -------------  -------------  -----------
2020-05-01  5268.56        1211.65        562.25
2020-05-02  5533.84        522.25         325.62
2020-05-03  5986.85        1088.62        858.35
...         ...            ...            ...
```

Note that with the sum aggregation, you can optionally use "else 0" to avoid nulls in the result set. With count or count distinct, however, you should not include an

ELSE statement, as doing so would inflate the result set. This is because the database won't count a null, but it will count a substitute value such as zero.

Pivoting with CASE statements is quite handy, and having this ability opens up data warehouse table designs that are long and narrow rather than wide, which can be better for storing sparse data, because adding columns to a table can be an expensive operation. For example, rather than storing various customer attributes in many different columns, a table could contain multiple records per customer, with each attribute in a separate row, and with `attribute_name` and `attribute_value` fields specifying what the attribute is and its value. The data can then be pivoted as needed to assemble a customer record with the desired attributes. This design is efficient when there are many sparse attributes (only a subset of customers have values for many of the attributes).

Pivoting data with a combination of aggregation and CASE statements works well when there are a finite number of items to pivot. For people who have worked with other programming languages, it's essentially looping, but written out explicitly line by line. This gives you a lot of control, such as if you want to calculate different metrics in each column, but it can also be tedious. Pivoting with case statements doesn't work well when new values arrive constantly or are rapidly changing, since the SQL code would need to be constantly updated. In those cases, pushing the computing to another layer of your analysis stack, such as a BI tool or statistical language, may be more appropriate.

Unpivoting with UNION Statements

Sometimes we have the opposite problem and need to move data stored in columns into rows instead to create tidy data. This operation is called *unpivoting*. Data sets that may need unpivoting are those that are in a pivot table format. As an example, the populations of North American countries at 10-year intervals starting in 1980 are shown in Figure 2-4.

Country	year_1980	year_1990	year_2000	year_2010
Canada	24,593	27,791	31,100	34,207
Mexico	68,347	84,634	99,775	114,061
United States	227,225	249,623	282,162	309,326

Figure 2-4. Country population by year (in thousands)[3]

---

3 US Census Bureau, "International Data Base (IDB)," last updated December 2020, *https://www.census.gov/data-tools/demo/idb.*

To turn this into a result set with a row per country per year, we can use a *UNION* operator. *UNION* is a way to combine data sets from multiple queries into a single result set. There are two forms, *UNION* and *UNION ALL*. When using *UNION* or *UNION ALL*, the numbers of columns in each component query must match. The data types must match or be compatible (integers and floats can be mixed, but integers and strings cannot). The column names in the result set come from the first query. Aliasing the fields in the remaining queries is therefore optional but can make a query easier to read:

```
SELECT country
,'1980' as year
,year_1980 as population
FROM country_populations
    UNION ALL
SELECT country
,'1990' as year
,year_1990 as population
FROM country_populations
    UNION ALL
SELECT country
,'2000' as year
,year_2000 as population
FROM country_populations
    UNION ALL
SELECT country
,'2010' as year
,year_2010 as population
FROM country_populations
;

country        year  population
-------------  ----  ----------
Canada         1980  24593
Mexico         1980  68347
United States  1980  227225
...             ...   ...
```

In this example, we use a constant to hardcode the year, in order to keep track of the year that the population value corresponds to. The hardcoded values can be of any type, depending on your use case. You may need to explicitly cast certain hardcoded values, such as when entering a date:

```
'2020-01-01'::date as date_of_interest
```

What is the difference between *UNION* and *UNION ALL*? Both can be used to append or stack data together in this fashion, but they are slightly different. *UNION* removes duplicates from the result set, whereas *UNION ALL* retains all records, whether duplicates or not. *UNION ALL* is faster, since the database doesn't have to do a pass over the data to find duplicates. It also ensures that every record ends up in the result set. I tend to use *UNION ALL*, using *UNION* only when I have a reason to suspect duplicate data.

*UNION*ing data can also be useful for bringing together data from different sources. For example, imagine we have a `populations` table with yearly data per country, and another `gdp` table with yearly gross domestic product, or GDP. One option is to *JOIN* the tables and obtain a result set with one column for population and another for GDP:

```
SELECT a.country, a.population, b.gdp
FROM populations a
JOIN gdp b on a.country = b.country
;
```

Another option is to *UNION ALL* the data sets so that we end up with a stacked data set:

```
SELECT country, 'population' as metric, population as metric_value
FROM populations
    UNION ALL
SELECT country, 'gdp' as metric, gdp as metric_value
FROM gdp
;
```

Which approach you use largely depends on the output that you need for your analysis. The latter option can be useful when you have a number of different metrics in different tables and no single table has a full set of entities (in this case, countries). This is an alternative approach to a *FULL OUTER JOIN*.

pivot and unpivot Functions

Recognizing that the pivot and unpivot use cases are common, some database vendors have implemented functions to do this with fewer lines of code. Microsoft SQL Server and Snowflake have `pivot` functions that take the form of extra expressions in the *WHERE* clause. Here, aggregation is any aggregation function, such as `sum` or `avg`, the `value_column` is the field to be aggregated, and a column will be created for each value of the `label_column` listed as a label:

```
SELECT...
FROM...
    pivot(aggregation(value_column)
            for label_column in (label_1, label_2, ...)
;
```

We could rewrite the earlier pivoting example that used CASE statements as follows:

```
SELECT *
FROM orders
  pivot(sum(order_amount) for product in ('shirt','shoes'))
GROUP BY order_date
;
```

Although this syntax is more compact than the CASE construction we saw earlier, the desired columns still need to be specified. As a result, pivot doesn't solve the problem of newly arriving or rapidly changing sets of fields that need to be turned into columns. Postgres has a similar crosstab function, available in the tablefunc module.

Microsoft SQL Server and Snowflake also have unpivot functions that work in a similar fashion to expressions in the *WHERE* clause and transform rows into columns:

```
SELECT...
FROM...
    unpivot( value_column for label_column in (label_1, label_2, ...))
;
```

For example, the country_populations data from the previous example could be reshaped in the following manner:

```
SELECT *
FROM country_populations
    unpivot(population for year in (year_1980, year_1990, year_2000, year_2010))
;
```

Here again the syntax is more compact than the *UNION* or *UNION ALL* approach we looked at earlier, but the list of columns must be specified in the query.

Postgres has an unnest array function that can be used to unpivot data, thanks to its array data type. An array is a collection of elements, and in Postgres you can list the elements of an array in square brackets. The function can be used in the *SELECT* clause and takes this form:

```
unnest(array[element_1, element_2, ...])
```

Returning to our earlier example with countries and populations, this query returns the same result as the query with the repeated *UNION ALL* clauses:

```
SELECT
country
,unnest(array['1980', '1990', '2000', '2010']) as year
,unnest(array[year_1980, year_1990, year_2000, year_2010]) as pop
FROM country_populations
;
```

```
country  year  pop
-------  ----  -----
Canada   1980  24593
Canada   1990  27791
Canada   2000  31100
...      ...   ...
```

Data sets arrive in many different formats and shapes, and they aren't always in the format needed in our output. There are several options for reshaping data through pivoting or unpivoting it, either with CASE statements or *UNIONs*, or with database-specific functions. Understanding how to manipulate your data in order to shape it in the way you want will give you greater flexibility in your analysis and in the way you present your results.

Conclusion

Preparing data for analysis can feel like the work you do before you get to the real work of analysis, but it is so fundamental to understanding the data that I always find it is time well spent. Understanding the different types of data you're likely to encounter is critical, and you should take the time to understand the data types in each table you work with. Profiling data helps us learn more about what is in the data set and examine it for quality. I often return to profiling throughout my analysis projects, as I learn more about the data and need to check my query results along the way as I build in complexity. Data quality will likely never stop being a problem, so we've looked at some ways to handle the cleaning and enhancement of data sets. Finally, knowing how to shape the data to create the right output format is essential. We'll see these topics recur in the context of various analyses throughout the book. The next chapter, on time series analysis, starts our journey into specific analysis techniques.

CHAPTER 3

Time Series Analysis

Now that I've covered SQL and databases and the key steps in preparing data for analysis, it's time to turn to specific types of analysis that can be done with SQL. There are a seemingly unending number of data sets in the world, and correspondingly infinite ways in which they could be analyzed. In this and the following chapters, I have organized types of analysis into themes that I hope will be helpful as you build your analysis and SQL skills. Many of the techniques to be discussed build on those shown in Chapter 2 and then on the preceding chapters as the book progresses. Time series of data are so prevalent and so important that I'll start the series of analysis themes here.

Time series analysis is one of the most common types of analysis done with SQL. A *time series* is a sequence of measurements or data points recorded in time order, often at regularly spaced intervals. There are many examples of time series data in daily life, such as the daily high temperature, the closing value of the S&P 500 stock index, or the number of daily steps recorded by your fitness tracker. Time series analysis is used in a wide variety of industries and disciplines, from statistics and engineering to weather forecasting and business planning. Time series analysis is a way to understand and quantify how things change over time.

Forecasting is a common goal of time series analysis. Since time only marches forward, future values can be expressed as a function of past values, while the reverse is not true. However, it's important to note that the past doesn't perfectly predict the future. Any number of changes to wider market conditions, popular trends, product introductions, or other large changes make forecasting difficult. Still, looking at historical data can lead to insights, and developing a range of plausible outcomes is useful for planning. As I'm writing this, the world is in the midst of a global COVID-19 pandemic, the likes of which haven't been seen in 100 years—predating all but the most long-lived organizations' histories. Thus many current organizations haven't seen this specific event before, but they have existed through other economic crises, such as those following the dot-com burst and the 9/11 attacks in 2001, as well as the global financial crisis of 2007–2008. With careful analysis and understanding of context, we can often extract useful insights.

In this chapter, we'll first cover the SQL building blocks of time series analysis: syntax and functions for working with dates, timestamps, and time. Next, I'll introduce the retail sales data set used for examples throughout the rest of the chapter. A discussion of methods for trending analysis follows, and then I'll cover calculating rolling time windows. Next are period-over-period calculations to analyze data with seasonality components. Finally, we'll wrap up with some additional techniques that are useful for time series analysis.

Date, Datetime, and Time Manipulations

Dates and times come in a wide variety of formats, depending on the data source. We often need or want to transform the raw data format for our output, or to perform calculations to arrive at new dates or parts of dates. For example, the data set might contain transaction timestamps, but the goal of the analysis is to trend monthly sales. At other times, we might want to know how many days or months have elapsed since a particular event. Fortunately, SQL has powerful functions and formatting capabilities that can transform just about any raw input to almost any output we might need for analysis.

In this section, I'll show you how to convert between time zones, and then I'll go into depth on formatting dates and datetimes. Next, I'll explore date math and time manipulations, including those that make use of intervals. An interval is a data type that holds a span of time, such as a number of months, days, or hours. Although data can be stored in a database table as an interval type, in practice I rarely see this done, so I will talk about intervals alongside the date and time functions that you can use them with. Last, I'll discuss some special considerations when joining or otherwise combining data from different sources.

Time Zone Conversions

Understanding the standard time zone used in a data set can prevent misunderstandings and mistakes further into the analysis process. Time zones split the world into north-south regions that observe the same time. Time zones allow different parts of the world to have similar clock times for daytime and nighttime—so, for example, the sun is overhead at 12 p.m. wherever you are in the world. The zones follow irregular boundaries that are as much political as geographic ones. Most are one hour apart, but some are offset only 30 or 45 minutes, and so there are more than 30 time zones spanning the globe. Many countries that are distant from the equator observe daylight savings time for parts of the year as well, but there are exceptions, such as in the

United States and Australia, where some states observe daylight savings time and others do not. Each time zone has a standard abbreviation, such as PST for Pacific Standard Time and PDT for Pacific Daylight Time.

Many databases are set to *Coordinated Universal Time* (UTC), the global standard used to regulate clocks, and record events in this time zone. It replaced *Greenwich Mean Time* (GMT), which you might still see if your data comes from an older database. UTC does not have daylight savings time, so it stays consistent all year long. This turns out to be quite useful for analysis. I remember one time a panicked product manager asked me to figure out why sales on a particular Sunday dropped so much compared to the prior Sunday. I spent hours writing queries and investigating possible causes before eventually figuring out that our data was recorded in Pacific Time (PT). Daylight savings started early Sunday morning, the database clock moved ahead 1 hour, and the day had only 23 hours instead of 24, and thus sales appeared to drop. Half a year later we had a corresponding 25-hour day, when sales appeared unusually high.

Often timestamps in the database are not encoded with the time zone, and you will need to consult with the source or developer to figure out how your data was stored. UTC has become most common in the data sets I see, but that is certainly not universal.

One drawback to UTC, or really to any logging of machine time, is that we lose information about the local time for the human doing the actions that generated the event recorded in the database. I might want to know whether people tend to use my mobile app more during the workday or during nights and weekends. If my audience is clustered in one time zone, it's not hard to figure this out. But if the audience spans multiple time zones or is international, then it becomes a calculation task of converting each recorded time to its local time zone.

All local time zones have a UTC offset. For example, the offset for PDT is UTC – 7 hours, while the offset for PST is UTC – 8 hours. Timestamps in databases are stored in the format YYYY-MM-DD hh:mi:ss (for years-months-days hours:minutes:seconds). Timestamps with the time zone have an additional piece of information for the UTC offset, expressed as a positive or negative number. Converting from one time zone to another can be accomplished with `at time zone` followed by the destination time zone's abbreviation. For example, we can convert a timestamp in UTC (offset – 0) to PST:

```
SELECT '2020-09-01 00:00:00 -0' at time zone 'pst';

timezone
-------------------
2020-08-31 16:00:00
```

The destination time zone name can be a constant, or a database field, allowing this conversion to be dynamic to the data set. Some databases have a `convert_timezone` or `convert_tz` function that works similarly. One argument is the time zone of the result, and the other argument is the time zone from which to convert:

```
SELECT convert_timezone('pst','2020-09-01 00:00:00 -0');

timezone
------------------
2020-08-31 16:00:00
```

Check your database's documentation for the exact name and ordering of the target time zone and the source timestamp arguments. Many databases contain a list of time zones and their abbreviations in a system table. Some common ones are seen in Table 3-1. These can be queried with *SELECT * FROM* the table name. Wikipedia also has a useful list of standard time zone abbreviations and their UTC offsets (*https:// oreil.ly/im0wi*).

Table 3-1. Time zone information system tables in common databases

Postgres	`pg_timezone_names`
MySQL	`mysql.time_zone_names`
SQL Server	`sys.time_zone_info`
Redshift	`pg_timezone_names`

Time zones are an innate part of working with timestamps. With time zone conversion functions, moving between the time zone in which the data was recorded and any other world time zone is possible. Next, I'll show you a variety of techniques for manipulating dates and timestamps with SQL.

Date and Timestamp Format Conversions

Dates and timestamps are key to time series analysis. Due to the wide variety of ways in which dates and times can be represented in source data, it is almost inevitable that you will need to convert date formats at some point. In this section, I'll cover several of the most common conversions and how to accomplish them with SQL: changing the data type, extracting parts of a date or timestamp, and creating a date or timestamp from parts. I'll begin by introducing some handy functions that return the current date and/or time.

Returning the current date or time is a common analysis task—for example, to include a timestamp for the result set or to use in date math, covered in the next section. The current date and time are referred to as *system time*, and while returning them is easy to do with SQL, there are some syntax differences between databases.

To return the current date, some databases have a `current_date` function, with no parentheses:

```
SELECT current_date;
```

There is a wider variety of functions to return the current date and time. Check your database's documentation or just experiment by typing into a SQL window to see whether a function returns a value or an error. The functions with parentheses do not take arguments, but it is important to include the parentheses:

```
current_timestamp
localtimestamp
get_date()
now()
```

Finally, there are functions to return only the timestamp portion of the current system time. Again, consult documentation or experiment to figure out which function(s) to use with your database:

```
current_time
localtime
timeofday()
```

SQL has a number of functions for changing the format of dates and times. To reduce the granularity of a timestamp, use the `date_trunc` function. The first argument is a text value indicating the time period level to which to truncate the timestamp in the second argument. The result is a timestamp value:

```
date_trunc (text, timestamp)

SELECT date_trunc('month','2020-10-04 12:33:35'::timestamp);

date_trunc
------------------
2020-10-01 00:00:00
```

Standard arguments that can be used are listed in Table 3-2. They range all the way from microseconds to millennia, providing plenty of flexibility. Databases that don't support `date_trunc`, such as MySQL, have an alternate function called `date_format` that can be used in a similar way:

```
SELECT date_format('2020-10-04 12:33:35','%Y-%m-01') as date_trunc;

date_trunc
------------------
2020-10-01 00:00:00
```

Table 3-2. Standard time period arguments

Time period arguments
microsecond
millisecond
second
minute
hour
day
week
month
quarter
year
decade
century
millennium

Rather than returning dates or timestamps, sometimes our analysis calls for parts of dates or times. For example, we might want to group sales by month, day of the week, or hour of the day.

SQL provides a few functions for returning just the part of the date or timestamp required. Dates and timestamps are usually interchangeable, except when the request is to return a time part. In those cases, time is of course required.

The `date_part` function takes a text value for the part to be returned and a date or timestamp value. The returned value is a FLOAT, which is a numeric value with a decimal part; depending on your needs, you may want to cast the value to an integer data type:

```
SELECT date_part('day',current_timestamp);
SELECT date_part('month',current_timestamp);
SELECT date_part('hour',current_timestamp);
```

Another function that works similarly is `extract`, which takes a part name and a date or timestamp value and returns a FLOAT value:

```
SELECT extract('day' from current_timestamp);

date_part
---------
27.0

SELECT extract('month' from current_timestamp);
```

```
date_part
---------
5.0

SELECT extract('hour' from current_timestamp);

date_part
---------
14.0
```

The functions `date_part` and `extract` can be used with intervals, but note that the requested part must match the units of the interval. So, for example, requesting days from an interval stated in days returns the expected value of 30:

```
SELECT date_part('day',interval '30 days');

SELECT extract('day' from interval '30 days');

date_part
---------
30.0
```

However, requesting days from an interval stated in months returns a value of 0.0:

```
SELECT extract('day' from interval '3 months');

date_part
---------
0.0
```

 A full list of date parts can be found in your database's documentation or by searching online, but some of the most common are "day," "month," and "year" for dates, and "second," "minute," and "hour" for timestamps.

To return text values of the date parts, use the `to_char` function, which takes the input value and the output format as arguments:

```
SELECT to_char(current_timestamp,'Day');
SELECT to_char(current_timestamp,'Month');
```

 If you ever encounter timestamps stored as Unix epochs (the number of seconds that have elapsed since January 1, 1970, at 00:00:00 UTC), you can convert them to timestamps using the `to_time stamp` function.

Sometimes analysis calls for creating a date from parts from different sources. This can occur when the year, month, and day values are stored in different columns in the database. It can also be necessary when the parts have been parsed out of text, a topic I'll cover in more depth in Chapter 5.

A simple way to create a timestamp from separate date and time components is to concatenate them together with a plus sign (+):

```
SELECT date '2020-09-01' + time '03:00:00' as timestamp;

timestamp
-------------------
2020-09-01 03:00:00
```

A date can be assembled using the make_date, makedate, date_from_parts, or date fromparts function. These are equivalent, but different databases name the functions differently. The function takes arguments for the year, month, and day parts and returns a value with a date format:

```
SELECT make_date(2020,09,01);

make_date
----------
2020-09-01
```

The arguments can be constants or reference field names and must be integers. Yet another way to assemble a date or timestamp is to concatenate the values together and then cast the result to a date format using one of the casting syntaxes or the to_date function:

```
SELECT to_date(concat(2020,'-',09,'-',01), 'yyyy-mm-dd');

to_date
----------
2020-09-01

SELECT cast(concat(2020,'-',09,'-',01) as date);

to_date
----------
2020-09-01
```

SQL has a number of ways to format and convert dates and timestamps and retrieve system dates and times. In the next section, I will start putting them to use in date math.

Date Math

SQL allows us to do various mathematical operations on dates. This might be surprising since, strictly speaking, dates are not numeric data types, but the concept should be familiar if you've ever tried to figure out what day it will be four weeks from now. Date math is useful for a variety of analytics tasks. For example, we can use it to find the age or tenure of a customer, how much time elapsed between two events, and how many things occurred within a window of time.

Date math involves two types of data: the dates themselves and intervals. We need the concept of intervals because date and time components don't behave like integers. One-tenth of 100 is 10; one-tenth of a year is 36.5 days. Half of 100 is 50; half of a day is 12 hours. Intervals allow us to move smoothly between units of time. Intervals come in two types: year-month intervals and day-time ones. We'll start with a few operations that return integer values and then move on to functions that work with or return intervals.

First, let's find the days elapsed between two dates. There are several ways to do this in SQL. The first way is by using a mathematical operator, the minus sign (–):

```
SELECT date('2020-06-30') - date('2020-05-31') as days;

days
----
30
```

This returns the number of days between these two dates. Note that the answer is 30 days and not 31. The number of days is inclusive of only one of the endpoints. Subtracting the dates in the reverse also works and returns an interval of –30 days:

```
SELECT date('2020-05-31') - date('2020-06-30') as days;

days
----
-30
```

Finding the difference between two dates can also be accomplished with the datediff function. Postgres does not support it, but many other popular databases do, including SQL Server, Redshift, and Snowflake, and it's quite handy, particularly when the goal is to return an interval other than the number of days. The function takes three arguments—the time period units you want to return, a starting timestamp or date, and an ending timestamp or date:

```
datediff(interval_name, start_timestamp, end_timestamp)
```

So our previous example would look like this:

```
SELECT datediff('day',date('2020-05-31'), date('2020-06-30')) as days;

days
----
30
```

We can also find the number of months between two dates, and the database will do the correct math even though month lengths differ throughout the year:

```
SELECT datediff('month'
                ,date('2020-01-01')
                ,date('2020-06-30')
                ) as months;

months
------
5
```

In Postgres, this can be accomplished using the age function, which calculates the interval between two dates:

```
SELECT age(date('2020-06-30'),date('2020-01-01'));

age
--------------
5 mons 29 days
```

We can then find the number of months component of the interval with the date_part() function:

```
SELECT date_part('month',age('2020-06-30','2020-01-01')) as months;

months
------
5.0
```

Subtracting dates to find the time elapsed between them is quite powerful. Adding dates does not work in the same way. To do addition with dates, we need to leverage intervals or special functions.

For example, we can add seven days to a date by adding the interval '7 days':

```
SELECT date('2020-06-01') + interval '7 days' as new_date;

new_date
-------------------
2020-06-08 00:00:00
```

Some databases don't require the interval syntax and instead automatically convert the provided number to days, although it's generally good practice to use the interval notation, both for cross-database compatibility and to make your code easier to read:

```
SELECT date('2020-06-01') + 7 as new_date;

new_date
-------------------
2020-06-08 00:00:00
```

If you want to add a different unit of time, use the interval notation with months, years, hours, or another date or time period. Note that this can also be used to subtract intervals from dates by using a "-" instead of a "+." Many but not all databases have a `date_add` or `dateadd` function that takes the desired interval, a value, and the starting date and does the math:

```
SELECT date_add('month',1,'2020-06-01') as new_date;

new_date
----------
2020-07-01
```

 Consult your database's documentation, or just experiment with queries, to figure out the syntax and functions that are available and appropriate for your project.

Any of these formulations can be used in the *WHERE* clause in addition to the *SELECT* clause. For example, we can filter to records that occurred at least three months ago:

```
WHERE event_date < current_date - interval '3 months'
```

They can also be used in *JOIN* conditions, but note that database performance will usually be slower when the *JOIN* condition contains a calculation rather than an equality or inequality between dates.

Using date math is common in analysis with SQL, both to find the time elapsed between dates or timestamps and to calculate new dates based on an interval from a known date. There are several ways to find the elapsed time between two dates, add intervals to dates, and subtract intervals from dates. Next, we'll turn to time manipulations, which are similar.

Time Math

Time math is less common in many areas of analysis, but it can be useful in some situations. For example, we might want to know how long it takes for a support representative to answer a phone call in a call center or respond to an email requesting assistance. Whenever the elapsed time between two events is less than a day, or when rounding the result to a number of days doesn't provide enough information, time manipulation comes into play. Time math works similarly to date math, by leveraging intervals. We can add time intervals to times:

```
SELECT time '05:00' + interval '3 hours' as new_time;

new_time
--------
08:00:00
```

We can subtract intervals from times:

```
SELECT time '05:00' - interval '3 hours' as new_time;

new_time
--------
02:00:00
```

We can also subtract times, resulting in an interval:

```
SELECT time '05:00' - time '03:00' as time_diff;

time_diff
---------
02:00:00
```

Times, unlike dates, can be multiplied:

```
SELECT time '05:00' * 2 as time_multiplied;

time_multiplied
---------------
10:00:00
```

Intervals can also be multiplied, resulting in a time value:

```
SELECT interval '1 second' * 2000 as interval_multiplied;

interval_multiplied
------------------
00:33:20


SELECT interval '1 day' * 45 as interval_multiplied;

interval_multiplied
------------------
45 days
```

These examples use constant values, but you can include database field names or calculations in the SQL query as well to make the calculations dynamic. Next, I'll discuss special date considerations to keep in mind when combining data sets from different source systems.

Joining Data from Different Sources

Combining data from different sources is one of the most compelling use cases for a data warehouse. However, different source systems can record dates and times in different formats or different time zones or even just be off slightly due to issues with the internal clock time of the server. Even tables from the same data source can have differences, though this is less common. Reconciling and standardizing dates and timestamps is an important step before moving further in the analysis.

Dates and timestamps that are in different formats can be standardized with SQL. *JOIN*ing on dates or including date fields in *UNION*s generally requires that the dates or timestamps be in the same format. Earlier in the chapter, I showed techniques for formatting dates and timestamps that will serve well with these problems. Take care with time zones when combining data from different sources. For example, an internal database may use UTC time, but data from a third party could be in a local time zone. I have seen data sourced from software as a service (SaaS) that was recorded in a variety of local times. Note that the timestamp values themselves won't necessarily have the time zone embedded. You may need to consult the vendor's documentation and convert the data to UTC if the rest of your data is stored that way. Another option is to store the time zone in a field so that the timestamp value can be converted as needed.

Another thing to look out for when working with data from different sources is timestamps that are slightly out of sync. This can happen when timestamps are recorded from client devices—for example, from a laptop or mobile phone in one data source and a server in the other data source. I once saw a series of experiment results be miscalculated because the client mobile device that recorded a user's action was offset by a few minutes from the server that recorded the treatment group to which the user was assigned. Data from the mobile clients appeared to arrive before the treatment group timestamp, so some events were inadvertently excluded. A fix for something like this is relatively straightforward: rather than filter for action timestamps greater than the treatment group timestamp, allow events within a short interval or window of time prior to the treatment timestamp to be included in the results. This can be accomplished with a *BETWEEN* clause and date math, as seen in the last section.

When working with data from mobile apps, pay particular attention to whether the timestamps represent when the action happened on the device *or* when the event arrived in the database. The difference can range from negligible all the way up to days, depending on whether the mobile app allows offline usage and on how it handles sending data during periods of low signal strength. Data from mobile apps can be late-arriving or may make its way into the database days after it occurred on the device. Dates and timestamps can also become corrupted en route, and you may see ones that are impossibly distant in the past or future as a result.

Now that I've shown how to manipulate dates, datetimes, and time by changing the formats, converting time zones, performing date math, and working across data sets from different sources, we're ready to get into some time series examples. First, I'll introduce the data set for examples in the rest of the chapter.

The Retail Sales Data Set

The examples in the rest of this chapter use a data set of monthly US retail sales from the Monthly Retail Trade Report: Retail and Food Services Sales: Excel (1992–present) (*https://www.census.gov/retail/index.html#mrts*), available on the Census.gov website (*http://Census.gov*). The data in this report is used as an economic indicator to understand trends in US consumer spending patterns. While gross domestic product (GDP) figures are published quarterly, this retail sales data is published monthly, so it is also used to help predict GDP. For both of these reasons, the latest figures are usually covered in the business press when they are released.

The data spans from 1992 to 2020 and includes both total sales as well as details for subcategories of retail sales. It contains both unadjusted and seasonally adjusted numbers. This chapter will use the unadjusted numbers, since one of the goals is analyzing seasonality. Sales figures are in millions of US dollars. The original file format is an Excel file, with a tab for each year and with months as columns. The GitHub site for this book (*https://oreil.ly/LMiHw*) has the data in a format that's easier to import into a database, along with code specifically for importing into Postgres. Figure 3-1 shows a sample of the `retail_sales` table.

*	sales_month	naics_code	kind_of_business	reason_for_null	sales
1	2020-01-01	441	Motor vehicle and parts dealers	(null)	93268
2	2020-01-01	4411	Automobile dealers	(null)	80728
3	2020-01-01	4411, 4412	Automobile and other motor vehicle dealers	(null)	85823
4	2020-01-01	44111	New car dealers	(null)	71757
5	2020-01-01	44112	Used car dealers	(null)	8971
6	2020-01-01	4413	Automotive parts, acc., and tire stores	(null)	7445
7	2020-01-01	442	Furniture and home furnishings stores	(null)	9257
8	2020-01-01	442, 443	Furniture, home furn, electronics, and appliance stores	(null)	16993
9	2020-01-01	4421	Furniture stores	(null)	4904
10	2020-01-01	4422	Home furnishings stores	(null)	4353
11	2020-01-01	44221	Floor covering stores	Supressed	(null)
12	2020-01-01	442299	All other home furnishings stores	(null)	2408
13	2020-01-01	443	Electronics and appliance stores	(null)	7736
14	2020-01-01	443141	Household appliance stores	(null)	1197
15	2020-01-01	443142	Electronics stores	(null)	6539
16	2020-01-01	444	Building mat. and garden equip. and supplies dealers	(null)	27887
17	2020-01-01	4441	Building mat. and supplies dealers	(null)	24555
18	2020-01-01	44412	Paint and wallpaper stores	(null)	903
19	2020-01-01	44413	Hardware stores	(null)	1902
20	2020-01-01	445	Food and beverage stores	(null)	63590
21	2020-01-01	4451	Grocery stores	(null)	57667
22	2020-01-01	44511	Supermarkets and other grocery (except convenience) stores	(null)	55178
23	2020-01-01	4453	Beer, wine, and liquor stores	(null)	4388
24	2020-01-01	446	Health and personal care stores	(null)	30047
25	2020-01-01	44611	Pharmacies and drug stores	(null)	25209

Figure 3-1. Preview of the US retail sales data set

Trending the Data

With time series data, we often want to look for trends in the data. A trend is simply the direction in which the data is moving. It may be moving up or increasing over time, or it may be moving down or decreasing over time. It can remain more or less flat, or there could be so much noise, or movement up and down, that it's hard to determine a trend at all. This section will cover several techniques for trending time series data, from simple trends for graphing to comparing components of a trend, using percent of total calculations to compare parts to the whole, and finally indexing to see the percent change from a reference time period.

Simple Trends

Creating a trend may be a step in profiling and understanding data, or it may be the final output. The result set is a series of dates or timestamps and a numerical value. When graphing a time series, the dates or timestamps will become the x-axis, and the numerical value will be the y-axis. For example, we can check the trend of total retail and food services sales in the US:

```
SELECT sales_month
,sales
FROM retail_sales
WHERE kind_of_business = 'Retail and food services sales, total'
;

sales_month  sales
-----------  ------
1992-01-01   146376
1992-02-01   147079
1992-03-01   159336
...          ...
```

The results are graphed in Figure 3-2.

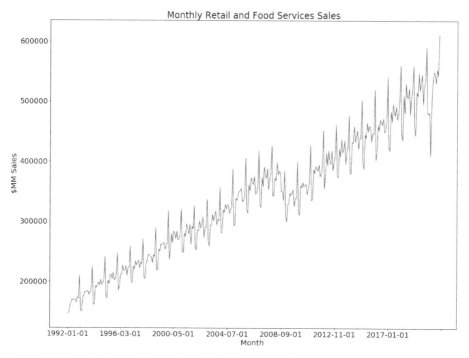

Figure 3-2. Trend of monthly retail and food services sales

This data clearly has some patterns, but it also has some noise. Transforming the data and aggregating at the yearly level can help us gain a better understanding. First, we'll use the `date_part` function to return just the year from the `sales_month` field and then `sum` the `sales`. The results are filtered to the "Retail and food services sales, total" `kind_of_business` in the *WHERE* clause:

```
SELECT date_part('year',sales_month) as sales_year
,sum(sales) as sales
FROM retail_sales
WHERE kind_of_business = 'Retail and food services sales, total'
GROUP BY 1
;

sales_year  sales
----------  -------
1992.0      2014102
1993.0      2153095
1994.0      2330235
...         ...
```

After graphing this data, as in Figure 3-3, we now have a smoother time series that is generally increasing over time, as might be expected, since the sales values are not adjusted for inflation. Sales for all retail and food services fell in 2009, during the global financial crisis. After growing every year throughout the 2010s, sales were flat in 2020 compared to 2019, due to the impact of the COVID-19 pandemic.

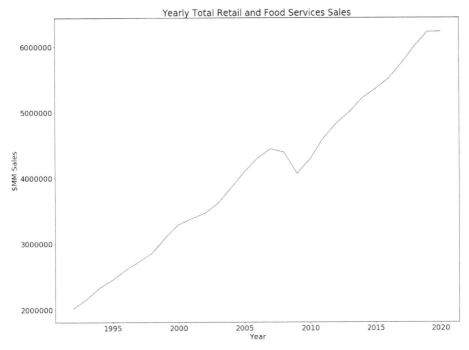

Figure 3-3. Trend of yearly total retail and food services sales

Graphing time series data at different levels of aggregation, such as weekly, monthly, or yearly, is a good way to understand trends. This step can be used to simply profile the data, but it can also be the final output, depending on the goals of the analysis. Next, we'll turn to using SQL to compare components of a time series.

Comparing Components

Often data sets contain not just a single time series but multiple slices or components of a total across the same time range. Comparing these slices often reveals interesting patterns. In the retail sales data set, there are values for total sales but also a number of subcategories. Let's compare the yearly sales trend for a few categories that are associated with leisure activities: book stores, sporting goods stores, and hobby stores. This query adds kind_of_business in the *SELECT* clause and, since it is another attribute rather than an aggregation, adds it to the *GROUP BY* clause as well:

```
SELECT date_part('year',sales_month) as sales_year
,kind_of_business
,sum(sales) as sales
FROM retail_sales
```

```
WHERE kind_of_business in ('Book stores'
  ,'Sporting goods stores','Hobby, toy, and game stores')
GROUP BY 1,2
;

sales_year  kind_of_business            sales
----------  --------------------------  -----
1992.0      Book stores                 8327
1992.0      Hobby, toy, and game stores 11251
1992.0      Sporting goods stores       15583
...         ...                         ...
```

The results are graphed in Figure 3-4. Sales at sporting goods retailers started the highest among the three categories and grew much faster during the time period, and by the end of the time series, those sales were substantially higher. Sales at sporting goods stores started declining in 2017 but had a big rebound in 2020. Sales at hobby, toy, and game stores were relatively flat over this time span, with a slight dip in the mid-2000s and another slight decline prior to a rebound in 2020. Sales at book stores grew until the mid-2000s and have been on the decline since then. All of these categories have been impacted by the growth of online retailers, but the timing and magnitude seem to differ.

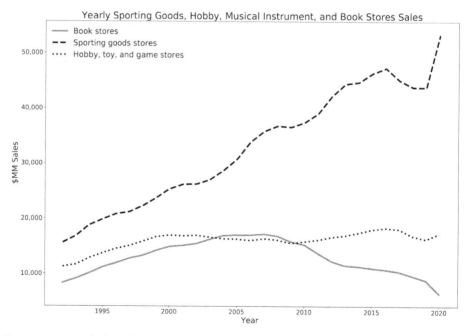

Figure 3-4. Trend of yearly retail sales for sporting goods stores; hobby, toy, and game stores; and book stores

In addition to looking at simple trends, we might want to perform more complex comparisons between parts of the time series. For the next few examples, we'll look at sales at women's clothing stores and at men's clothing stores. Note that since the names contain apostrophes, the character otherwise used to indicate the beginning and end of strings, we need to escape them with an extra apostrophe. This lets the database know that the apostrophe is part of the string rather than the end. Although we might consider adding a step in a data-loading pipeline that removes extra apostrophes in names, I've left them in here as a demonstration of the types of code adjustments that are often needed in the real world. First, we'll trend the data for each type of store by month:

```
SELECT sales_month
,kind_of_business
,sales
FROM retail_sales
WHERE kind_of_business in ('Men''s clothing stores'
  ,'Women''s clothing stores')
;

sales_month  kind_of_business         sales
-----------  ----------------------   -----
1992-01-01   Men's clothing stores    701
1992-01-01   Women's clothing stores  1873
1992-02-01   Women's clothing stores  1991
...          ...                      ...
```

The results are graphed in Figure 3-5. Sales at women's clothing retailers are much higher than those at men's clothing retailers. Both types of stores exhibit seasonality, a topic I'll cover in depth in "Analyzing with Seasonality" on page 107. Both experienced significant drops in 2020 due to store closures and a reduction in shopping because of the COVID-19 pandemic.

Figure 3-5. Monthly trend of sales at women's and men's clothing stores

The monthly data has intriguing patterns but is noisy, so we'll use yearly aggregates for the next few examples. We've seen this query format previously when rolling up total sales and sales for leisure categories:

```
SELECT date_part('year',sales_month) as sales_year
,kind_of_business
,sum(sales) as sales
FROM retail_sales
WHERE kind_of_business in ('Men''s clothing stores'
  ,'Women''s clothing stores')
GROUP BY 1,2
;
```

Are sales at women's clothing stores uniformly higher than those at men's clothing stores? In the yearly trend shown in Figure 3-6, the gap between men's and women's sales does not appear constant but rather was increasing during the early to mid-2000s. Women's clothing sales in particular dipped during the global financial crisis of 2008–2009, and sales in both categories dropped a lot during the pandemic in 2020.

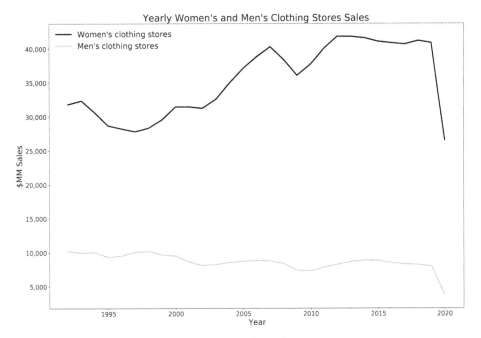

Figure 3-6. Yearly trend of sales at women's and men's clothing stores

We don't need to rely on visual estimation, however. For more precision on this gap, we can calculate the gap between the two categories, the ratio, and the percent difference between them. To do this, the first step is to arrange the data so that there is a single row for each month, with a column for each category. Pivoting the data with aggregate functions combined with CASE statements accomplishes this:

```
SELECT date_part('year',sales_month) as sales_year
,sum(case when kind_of_business = 'Women''s clothing stores'
        then sales
        end) as womens_sales
,sum(case when kind_of_business = 'Men''s clothing stores'
        then sales
        end) as mens_sales
FROM retail_sales
WHERE kind_of_business in ('Men''s clothing stores'
 ,'Women''s clothing stores')
GROUP BY 1
;

sales_year  womens_sales  mens_sales
----------  ------------  ----------
1992.0      31815         10179
1993.0      32350         9962
1994.0      30585         10032
...         ...           ...
```

With this building block calculation, we can find the difference, ratio, and percent difference between time series in the data set. The difference can be calculated by subtracting one value from the other using the mathematical "−" operator. Depending on the goals of the analysis, either finding the difference from men's sales or finding the difference from women's sales might be appropriate. Both are shown here and are equivalent except for the sign:

```
SELECT sales_year
,womens_sales - mens_sales as womens_minus_mens
,mens_sales - womens_sales as mens_minus_womens
FROM
(
    SELECT date_part('year',sales_month) as sales_year
    ,sum(case when kind_of_business = 'Women''s clothing stores'
            then sales
            end) as womens_sales
    ,sum(case when kind_of_business = 'Men''s clothing stores'
            then sales
            end) as mens_sales
    FROM retail_sales
    WHERE kind_of_business in ('Men''s clothing stores'
     ,'Women''s clothing stores')
    and sales_month <= '2019-12-01'
    GROUP BY 1
) a
;
```

sales_year	womens_minus_mens	mens_minus_womens
1992.0	21636	-21636
1993.0	22388	-22388
1994.0	20553	-20553
...	...	...

The subquery is not required from a query execution standpoint, since aggregations can be added to or subtracted from each other. A subquery is often more legible but does add more lines to the code. Depending on how long or complex the rest of your SQL query is, you might prefer to place the intermediate calculation in a subquery, or just calculate it in the main query. Here is an example without the subquery, subtracting men's sales from women's sales, with an added *WHERE* clause filter to remove 2020, since a few months have null values:[1]

```
SELECT date_part('year',sales_month) as sales_year
,sum(case when kind_of_business = 'Women''s clothing stores'
        then sales end)
```

---

[1] October and November 2020 data points were suppressed by the publisher of the data, due to concerns about the data quality. Collecting the data likely became more difficult due to store closures during the 2020 pandemic.

```
  -
  sum(case when kind_of_business = 'Men''s clothing stores'
          then sales end)
  as womens_minus_mens
FROM retail_sales
WHERE kind_of_business in ('Men''s clothing stores'
  ,'Women''s clothing stores')
and sales_month <= '2019-12-01'
GROUP BY 1
;

sales_year   womens_minus_mens
----------   -----------------
1992.0       21636
1993.0       22388
1994.0       20553
...          ...
```

Figure 3-7 shows that the gap decreased between 1992 and about 1997, began a long increase through about 2011 (with a brief dip in 2007), and then was more or less flat through 2019.

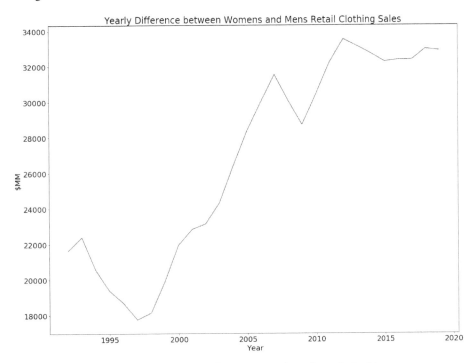

Figure 3-7. Yearly difference between sales at women's and men's clothing stores

Let's continue our investigation and look at the ratio of these categories. We'll use men's sales as the baseline or denominator, but note that we could just as easily use women's store sales instead:

```
SELECT sales_year
,womens_sales / mens_sales as womens_times_of_mens
FROM
(
    SELECT date_part('year',sales_month) as sales_year
    ,sum(case when kind_of_business = 'Women''s clothing stores'
                then sales
                end) as womens_sales
    ,sum(case when kind_of_business = 'Men''s clothing stores'
                then sales
                end) as mens_sales
    FROM retail_sales
    WHERE kind_of_business in ('Men''s clothing stores'
     ,'Women''s clothing stores')
    and sales_month <= '2019-12-01'
    GROUP BY 1
) a
;

sales_year  womens_times_of_mens
----------  --------------------
1992.0      3.1255526083112290
1993.0      3.2473398915880345
1994.0      3.0487440191387560
...         ...
```

 SQL returns a lot of decimal digits when performing division. You should generally consider rounding the result before presenting the analysis. Use the level of precision (number of decimal places) that tells the story.

Plotting the result, shown in Figure 3-8, reveals that the trend is similar to the difference trend, but while there was a drop in the difference in 2009, the ratio actually increased.

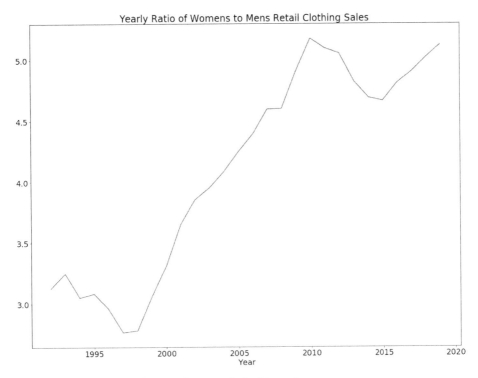

Figure 3-8. Yearly ratio of women's to men's clothing sales

Next, we can calculate the percent difference between sales at women's and men's clothing stores:

```
SELECT sales_year
,(womens_sales / mens_sales - 1) * 100 as womens_pct_of_mens
FROM
(
    SELECT date_part('year',sales_month) as sales_year
    ,sum(case when kind_of_business = 'Women''s clothing stores'
            then sales
            end) as womens_sales
    ,sum(case when kind_of_business = 'Men''s clothing stores'
            then sales
            end) as mens_sales
    FROM retail_sales
    WHERE kind_of_business in ('Men''s clothing stores'
      ,'Women''s clothing stores')
    and sales_month <= '2019-12-01'
    GROUP BY 1
) a
;
```

```
sales_year  womens_pct_of_mens
----------  --------------------
1992.0      212.5552608311229000
1993.0      224.7339891588034500
1994.0      204.8744019138756000
...         ...
```

Although the units for this output are different from those in the previous example, the shape of this graph is the same as that of the ratio graph. The choice of which to use depends on your audience and the norms in your domain. All of these statements are accurate: in 2009, sales at women's clothing stores were $28.7 billion higher than sales at men's stores; in 2009, sales at women's clothing stores were 4.9 times the sales at men's stores; in 2009, sales at women's stores were 390% higher than sales at men's stores. Which version to select depends on the story you want to tell with the analysis.

The transformations we've seen in this section allow us to analyze time series by comparing related parts. The next section will continue the theme of comparing time series by showing ways to analyze series that represent parts of a whole.

Percent of Total Calculations

When working with time series data that has multiple parts or attributes that constitute a whole, it's often useful to analyze each part's contribution to the whole and whether that has changed over time. Unless the data already contains a time series of the total values, we'll need to calculate the overall total in order to calculate the percent of total for each row. This can be accomplished with a self-*JOIN*, or a window function, which as we saw in Chapter 2 is a special kind of SQL function that can reference any row within a specified partition of the table.

First I'll show the self-*JOIN* method. A self-*JOIN* is any time a table is joined to itself. As long as each instance of the table in the query is given a different alias, the database will treat them all as distinct tables. For example, to find the percent of combined men's and women's clothing sales that each series represents, we can *JOIN* retail_sales, aliased as a, to retail_sales, aliased as b, on the sales_month field. We then *SELECT* the individual series name (kind_of_business) and sales values from alias a. Then, from alias b we sum the sales for both categories and call the result total_sales. Note that the *JOIN* between the tables on the sales_month field creates a partial Cartesian *JOIN*, which results in two rows from alias b for each row in alias a. Grouping by a.sales_month, a.kind_of_business, and a.sales and aggregating b.sales returns exactly the results needed, however. In the outer query, the percent of total for each row is calculated by dividing sales by total_sales:

```
SELECT sales_month
,kind_of_business
,sales * 100 / total_sales as pct_total_sales
```

```
FROM
(
    SELECT a.sales_month, a.kind_of_business, a.sales
    ,sum(b.sales) as total_sales
    FROM retail_sales a
    JOIN retail_sales b on a.sales_month = b.sales_month
    and b.kind_of_business in ('Men''s clothing stores'
      ,'Women''s clothing stores')
    WHERE a.kind_of_business in ('Men''s clothing stores'
      ,'Women''s clothing stores')
    GROUP BY 1,2,3
) aa
;
```

```
sales_month  kind_of_business        pct_total_sales
-----------  ----------------------  -------------------
1992-01-01   Men's clothing stores   27.2338772338772339
1992-01-01   Women's clothing stores 72.7661227661227661
1992-02-01   Men's clothing stores   24.8395620989052473
...          ...                     ...
```

The subquery isn't required here, as the same result could be obtained without it, but it makes the code a little easier to follow. A second way to calculate the percent of total sales for each category is to use the sum window function and *PARTITION BY* the sales_month. Recall that the *PARTITION BY* clause indicates the section of the table within which the function should calculate. The *ORDER BY* clause is not required in this sum window function, because the order of calculation doesn't matter. Additionally, the query does not need a *GROUP BY* clause, because window functions look across multiple rows, but they do not reduce the number of rows in the result set:

```
SELECT sales_month, kind_of_business, sales
,sum(sales) over (partition by sales_month) as total_sales
,sales * 100 / sum(sales) over (partition by sales_month) as pct_total
FROM retail_sales
WHERE kind_of_business in ('Men''s clothing stores'
  ,'Women''s clothing stores')
;
```

```
sales_month  kind_of_business        sales  total_sales  pct_total
-----------  ----------------------  -----  -----------  ---------
1992-01-01   Men's clothing stores   701    2574         27.233877
1992-01-01   Women's clothing stores 1873   2574         72.766122
1992-02-01   Women's clothing stores 1991   2649         75.160437
...          ...                     ...    ...          ...
```

Graphing this data, as in Figure 3-9, reveals some interesting trends. First, starting in the late 1990s, women's clothing store sales became an increasing percentage of the total. Second, early in the series a seasonal pattern is evident, where men's sales spike as a percent of total sales in December and January. In the first decade of the 21st century, two seasonal peaks appear, in the summer and the winter, but by the late 2010s, the seasonal patterns are dampened almost to the point of randomness. We'll take a look at analyzing seasonality in greater depth later in this chapter.

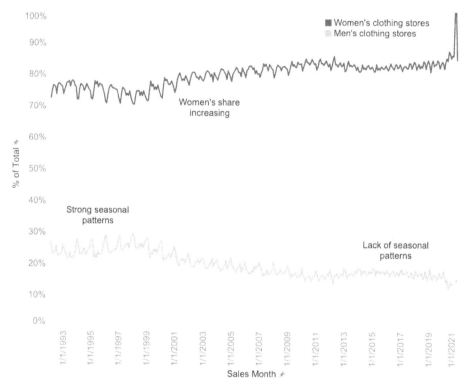

Figure 3-9. Men's and women's clothing store sales as percent of monthly total

Another percent of total we might want to find is the percent of sales within a longer time period, such as the percent of yearly sales each month represents. Again, either a self-*JOIN* or a window function will do the job. In this example, we'll use a self-*JOIN* in the subquery:

```
SELECT sales_month
,kind_of_business
,sales * 100 / yearly_sales as pct_yearly
FROM
(
    SELECT a.sales_month, a.kind_of_business, a.sales
    ,sum(b.sales) as yearly_sales
    FROM retail_sales a
    JOIN retail_sales b on
     date_part('year',a.sales_month) = date_part('year',b.sales_month)
     and a.kind_of_business = b.kind_of_business
     and b.kind_of_business in ('Men''s clothing stores'
```

```
      ,'Women''s clothing stores')
   WHERE a.kind_of_business in ('Men''s clothing stores'
      ,'Women''s clothing stores')
   GROUP BY 1,2,3
) aa
;
```

```
sales_month  kind_of_business      pct_yearly
-----------  --------------------  ------------------
1992-01-01   Men's clothing stores  6.8867275763827488
1992-02-01   Men's clothing stores  6.4642892229099126
1992-03-01   Men's clothing stores  7.1814520090382159
...          ...                    ...
```

Alternatively, the window function method can be used:

```
SELECT sales_month, kind_of_business, sales
,sum(sales) over (partition by date_part('year',sales_month)
                              ,kind_of_business
                  ) as yearly_sales
,sales * 100 /
 sum(sales) over (partition by date_part('year',sales_month)
                              ,kind_of_business
                  ) as pct_yearly
FROM retail_sales
WHERE kind_of_business in ('Men''s clothing stores'
  ,'Women''s clothing stores')
;
```

```
sales_month  kind_of_business      pct_yearly
-----------  --------------------  ------------------
1992-01-01   Men's clothing stores  6.8867275763827488
1992-02-01   Men's clothing stores  6.4642892229099126
1992-03-01   Men's clothing stores  7.1814520090382159
...          ...                    ...
```

The results, zoomed in to 2019, are shown in Figure 3-10. The two time series track fairly closely, but men's stores had a greater percentage of their sales in January than did women's stores. Men's stores had a summer dip in July, while the corresponding dip in women's store sales wasn't until September.

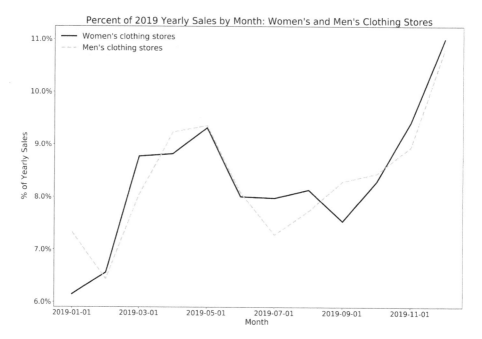

Figure 3-10. Percent of yearly sales for 2019 for women's and men's clothing sales

Now that I've shown how to use SQL for percent of total calculations and the types of analysis that can be accomplished, I'll turn to indexing and calculating percent change over time.

Indexing to See Percent Change over Time

The values in time series usually fluctuate over time. Sales increase with growing popularity and availability of a product, while web page response time decreases with engineers' efforts to optimize code. Indexing data is a way to understand the changes in a time series relative to a base period (starting point). Indices are widely used in economics as well as business settings. One of the most famous indices is the Consumer Price Index (CPI), which tracks the change in the prices of items that a typical consumer purchases and is used to track inflation, to decide salary increases, and for many other applications. The CPI is a complex statistical measure using various weights and data inputs, but the basic premise is straightforward. Pick a base period and compute the percent change in value from that base period for each subsequent period.

Indexing time series data with SQL can be done with a combination of aggregations and window functions, or self-*JOINs*. As an example, we index women's clothing store sales to the first year in the series, 1992. The first step is to aggregate the `sales` by `sales_year` in a subquery, as we've done previously. In the outer query, the `first_value` window function finds the value associated with the first row in the *PARTITION BY* clause, according to the sort in the *ORDER BY* clause. In this example, we can omit the *PARTITION BY* clause, because we want to return the `sales` value for the first row in the entire data set returned by the subquery:

```
SELECT sales_year, sales
,first_value(sales) over (order by sales_year) as index_sales
FROM
(
    SELECT date_part('year',sales_month) as sales_year
    ,sum(sales) as sales
    FROM retail_sales
    WHERE kind_of_business = 'Women''s clothing stores'
    GROUP BY 1
) a
;

sales_year  sales  index_sales
----------  -----  -----------
1992.0      31815  31815
1993.0      32350  31815
1994.0      30585  31815
...         ...    ...
```

With this sample of data, we can visually verify that the index value is correctly set at the value for 1992. Next, find the percent change from this base year for each row:

```
SELECT sales_year, sales
,(sales / first_value(sales) over (order by sales_year) - 1) * 100
 as pct_from_index
FROM
(
    SELECT date_part('year',sales_month) as sales_year
    ,sum(sales) as sales
    FROM retail_sales
    WHERE kind_of_business = 'Women''s clothing stores'
    GROUP BY 1
) a
;

sales_year  sales  pct_from_index
----------  -----  --------------
1992.0      31815  0
1993.0      32350  1.681596731101
1994.0      30585  -3.86610089580
...         ...    ...
```

The percent change can be either positive or negative, and we'll see that does in fact occur in this time series. The `last_value` window function could be substituted for `first_value` in this query. Indexing from the last value in a series is much less common, however, since analysis questions more often relate to change from a starting point rather than looking back from an arbitrary ending point; still, the option is there. Additionally, the sort order can be used to achieve indexing from the first or last value by switching between *ASC* and *DESC*:

```
first_value(sales) over (order by sales_year desc)
```

Window functions provide a lot of flexibility. Indexing can be accomplished without them through a series of self-*JOINs*, though more lines of code are required:

```
SELECT sales_year, sales
,(sales / index_sales - 1) * 100 as pct_from_index
FROM
(
    SELECT date_part('year',aa.sales_month) as sales_year
    ,bb.index_sales
    ,sum(aa.sales) as sales
    FROM retail_sales aa
    JOIN
    (
        SELECT first_year, sum(a.sales) as index_sales
        FROM retail_sales a
        JOIN
        (
            SELECT min(date_part('year',sales_month)) as first_year
            FROM retail_sales
            WHERE kind_of_business = 'Women''s clothing stores'
        ) b on date_part('year',a.sales_month) = b.first_year
        WHERE a.kind_of_business = 'Women''s clothing stores'
        GROUP BY 1
    ) bb on 1 = 1
    WHERE aa.kind_of_business = 'Women''s clothing stores'
    GROUP BY 1,2
) aaa
;

sales_year   sales   pct_from_index
----------   -----   --------------
1992.0       31815   0
1993.0       32350   1.681596731101
1994.0       30585   -3.86610089580
...          ...     ...
```

Notice the unusual *JOIN* clause on `1 = 1` between alias `aa` and subquery `bb`. Since we want the `index_sales` value to populate for every row in the result set, we can't *JOIN* on the year or any other value, which would restrict the results. However, the database will return an error if no *JOIN* clause is specified. We can fool the database by using any expression that evaluates to TRUE in order to create the desired Cartesian *JOIN*. Any other TRUE statement, such as `on 2 = 2` or `on 'apples' = 'apples'`, could be used instead.

 Beware of zeros in the denominator of division operations such as `sales / index_sales` in the last example. Databases return an error when they encounter division by zero, which can be frustrating. Even when you think a zero in the denominator field is unlikely, it's good practice to prevent this by telling the database to return an alternate default value when it encounters a zero. This can be done with a CASE statement. The examples in this section do not have zeros in the denominator, so I will omit this extra code for the sake of legibility.

To wrap up this section, let's look at a graph of the indexed time series for men's and women's clothing stores, shown in Figure 3-11. The SQL code looks like:

```
SELECT sales_year, kind_of_business, sales
,(sales / first_value(sales) over (partition by kind_of_business
                                   order by sales_year)
 - 1) * 100 as pct_from_index
FROM
(
    SELECT date_part('year',sales_month) as sales_year
    ,kind_of_business
    ,sum(sales) as sales
    FROM retail_sales
    WHERE kind_of_business in ('Men''s clothing stores'
      ,'Women''s clothing stores')
    and sales_month <= '2019-12-31'
    GROUP BY 1,2
) a
;
```

Figure 3-11. Men's and women's clothing store sales, indexed to 1992 sales

It's apparent from this graph that 1992 was something of a high-water mark for sales at men's clothing stores. After 1992 sales dropped, then returned briefly to the same level in 1998, and have been declining ever since. This is striking since the data set is not adjusted for inflation, the tendency for prices to rise over time. Sales at women's clothing stores decreased from 1992 levels initially, but they returned to the 1992 level by 2003. They have increased since, with the exception of the drop during the financial crisis that decreased sales in 2009 and 2010. One explanation for these trends is that men simply decreased spending on clothes over time, perhaps becoming less fashion conscious relative to women. Perhaps men's clothing simply became less expensive as global supply chains decreased costs. Yet another explanation might be that men shifted their clothing purchases from retailers categorized as "men's clothing stores" to other types of retailers, such as sporting goods stores or online retailers.

Indexing time series data is a powerful analysis technique, allowing us to find a range of insights in the data. SQL is well suited to this task, and I've shown how to construct indexed time series with and without window functions. Next, I'll show you how to analyze data by using rolling time windows to find patterns in noisy time series.

Rolling Time Windows

Time series data is often noisy, a challenge for one of our primary goals of finding patterns. We've seen how aggregating data, such as from monthly to yearly, can smooth out the results and make them easier to interpret. Another technique for smoothing data is *rolling time windows*, also known as moving calculations, that take into account multiple periods. Moving averages are probably the most common, but with the power of SQL, any aggregate function is available for analysis. Rolling time windows are used in a wide variety of analysis areas, including stock markets, macroeconomic trends, and audience measurement. Some calculations are so commonly used that they have their own acronyms: last twelve months (LTM), trailing twelve months (TTM), and year-to-date (YTD).

Figure 3-12 shows an example of a rolling time window and a cumulative calculation, relative to the month of October in the time series.

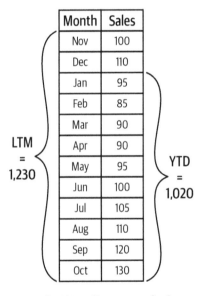

Month	Sales
Nov	100
Dec	110
Jan	95
Feb	85
Mar	90
Apr	90
May	95
Jun	100
Jul	105
Aug	110
Sep	120
Oct	130

LTM = 1,230

YTD = 1,020

Figure 3-12. Example of LTM and YTD rolling sum of sales

There are several important pieces of any rolling time series calculation. First is the size of the window, which is the number of periods to include in the calculation. Larger windows with more time periods have a greater smoothing effect, but at the risk of losing sensitivity to important short-term changes in the data. Shorter windows with fewer time periods do less smoothing and thus are more sensitive to short-term changes, but at the risk of too little noise reduction.

The second piece of time series calculations is the aggregate function used. As noted previously, moving averages are probably the most common. Moving sums, counts, minimums, and maximums can also be calculated with SQL. Moving counts are useful in user population metrics (see the following sidebar). Moving minimums and maximums can help in understanding the extremes of the data, useful for planning analyses.

The third piece of time series calculations is choosing the partitioning, or grouping, of the data that is included in the window. The analysis might call for resetting the window every year. Or the analysis might need a different moving series for each component or user group. Chapter 4 will go into more detail on cohort analysis of user groups, where we will consider how retention and cumulative values such as spend differ between populations over time. Partitioning will be controlled through grouping as well as the *PARTITION BY* statement of window functions.

With these three pieces in mind, we'll move into the SQL code and calculations for moving time periods, continuing with the US retail sales data set for examples.

Measuring "Active Users": DAU, WAU, and MAU

Many consumer and some B2B SaaS applications use active user calculations such as daily active users (DAU), weekly active users (WAU), and monthly active users (MAU) to estimate their audience size. Since each of these are rolling windows, they can be calculated on a daily basis. I've often been asked what is the right or best metric to use, and my answer is always "it depends."

DAU helps companies with capacity planning, such as estimating how much load to expect on servers. Depending on the service, however, even more detailed data might be needed, such as peak hourly or even minute-by-minute concurrent user information.

MAU is commonly used to estimate relative sizes of applications or services. It is useful for measuring fairly stable or growing user populations that have regular usage patterns that aren't necessarily daily, such as higher use on the weekend for leisure products, or higher weekday use for work- or school-related products. MAU is not as well suited to detecting changes in underlying churn from users who stop using an application. Since it takes a user 30 days, the most common window, to pass through MAU, a user can have been absent from the product for 29 days before they trigger a drop in MAU.

WAU, calculated over 7 days, can be a happy medium between DAU and MAU. WAU is more sensitive to short-term fluctuations, alerting teams to changes in churn more quickly than MAU while smoothing over day of week fluctuations that are tracked by DAU. A drawback to WAU is that it is still sensitive to short-term fluctuations driven by events such as holidays.

Calculating Rolling Time Windows

Now that we know what rolling time windows are, how they're useful, and their key components, let's get into calculating them using the US retail sales data set. We'll start with the simpler case, when the data set contains a record for each period that should be in the window, and then in the next section we'll look at what to do when this is not the case.

There are two main methods for calculating a rolling time window: a self-*JOIN*, which can be used in any database, and a window function, which as we've seen isn't available in some databases. In both cases we need the same result: a date and a number of data points that corresponds to the size of the window to which we will apply an average or another aggregate function.

For this example, we'll use a window of 12 months to get rolling annual sales, since the data is at a monthly level of granularity. We'll then apply an average to get a 12-month moving average of retail sales. First, let's develop the intuition for what will go into the calculation. In this query, alias a of the table is our "anchor" table, the one from which we gather the dates. To start, we'll look at a single month, December 2019. From alias b, the query gathers the 12 individual months of sales that will go into the moving average. This is accomplished with the *JOIN* clause b.sales_month between a.sales_month - interval '11 months' and a.sales_month, which creates an intentional Cartesian *JOIN*:

```
SELECT a.sales_month
,a.sales
,b.sales_month as rolling_sales_month
,b.sales as rolling_sales
FROM retail_sales a
JOIN retail_sales b on a.kind_of_business = b.kind_of_business
 and b.sales_month between a.sales_month - interval '11 months'
 and a.sales_month
 and b.kind_of_business = 'Women''s clothing stores'
WHERE a.kind_of_business = 'Women''s clothing stores'
and a.sales_month = '2019-12-01'
;

sales_month  sales  rolling_sales_month  rolling_sales
-----------  -----  -------------------  -------------
2019-12-01   4496   2019-01-01           2511
2019-12-01   4496   2019-02-01           2680
2019-12-01   4496   2019-03-01           3585
2019-12-01   4496   2019-04-01           3604
2019-12-01   4496   2019-05-01           3807
2019-12-01   4496   2019-06-01           3272
2019-12-01   4496   2019-07-01           3261
2019-12-01   4496   2019-08-01           3325
2019-12-01   4496   2019-09-01           3080
2019-12-01   4496   2019-10-01           3390
```

```
2019-12-01    4496    2019-11-01              3850
2019-12-01    4496    2019-12-01              4496
```

Notice that the `sales_month` and `sales` figures from alias `a` are repeated for each row of the 12 months in the window.

 Remember that the dates in a *BETWEEN* clause are inclusive (both will be returned in the result set). It's a common mistake to use 12 instead of 11 in the preceding query. When in doubt, check the intermediate query results as I've done here to make sure the intended number of periods ends up in the window calculation.

The next step is to apply the aggregation—in this case, `avg`, since we want a rolling average. The `count` of records returned from alias `b` is included to confirm that each row averages 12 data points, a useful data quality check. Alias `a` also has a filter on `sales_month`. Since this data set starts in 1992, months in that year, except for December, have fewer than 12 historical records:

```
SELECT a.sales_month
,a.sales
,avg(b.sales) as moving_avg
,count(b.sales) as records_count
FROM retail_sales a
JOIN retail_sales b on a.kind_of_business = b.kind_of_business
 and b.sales_month between a.sales_month - interval '11 months'
 and a.sales_month
 and b.kind_of_business = 'Women''s clothing stores'
WHERE a.kind_of_business = 'Women''s clothing stores'
and a.sales_month >= '1993-01-01'
GROUP BY 1,2
;
```

```
sales_month  sales  moving_avg  records_count
-----------  -----  ----------  -------------
1993-01-01   2123   2672.08     12
1993-02-01   2005   2673.25     12
1993-03-01   2442   2676.50     12
...          ...    ...         ...
```

The results are graphed in Figure 3-13. While the monthly trend is noisy, the smoothed moving average trend makes detecting changes such as the increase from 2003 to 2007 and the subsequent dip through 2011 easier to spot. Notice that the extreme drop in early 2020 pulls the moving average down even after sales start to rebound later in the year.

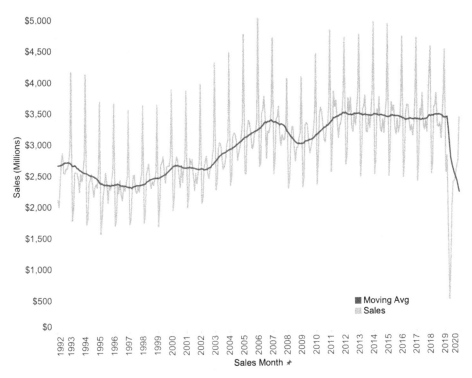

Figure 3-13. Monthly sales and 12-month moving average sales for women's clothing stores

Adding the filter `kind_of_business = 'Women''s clothing stores'` to each alias isn't strictly necessary. Since the query uses an *INNER JOIN*, filtering on one table will automatically filter on the other. However, filtering on both tables often makes queries run faster, particularly when the tables are large.

Window functions are another way to calculate rolling time windows. To make a rolling window, we need to use another optional part of a window calculation: the *frame clause*. The frame clause allows you to specify which records to include in the window. By default, all records in the partition are included, and for many cases this works just fine. However, controlling the included records at a more fine-grained level is useful for cases like moving window calculations. The syntax is simple and yet can be confusing when encountering it for the first time. The frame clause can be specified as:

```
{ RANGE | ROWS | GROUPS } BETWEEN frame_start AND frame_end
```

Within the curly braces are three options for the frame type: range, rows, and groups. These are the ways you can specify which records to include in the result, relative to the current row. Records are always chosen from the current partition and follow the *ORDER BY* specified. The default sorting is ascending (*ASC*), but it can be changed to descending (*DESC*). *Rows* is the most straightforward and will allow you to specify the exact number of rows that should be returned. *Range* includes records that are within some boundary of values relative to the current row. *Groups* can be used when there are multiple records with the same *ORDER BY* value, such as when a data set includes multiple lines per sales month, one for each customer.

The *frame_start* and *frame_end* can be any of the following:

```
UNBOUNDED PRECEDING
offset PRECEDING
CURRENT ROW
offset FOLLOWING
UNBOUNDED FOLLOWING
```

Preceding means to include rows before the current row, according to the *ORDER BY* sorting. *Current row* is just that, and *following* means to include rows that occur after the current row according to the *ORDER BY* sorting. The *UNBOUNDED* keyword means to include all records in the partition before or after the current row. The *offset* is the number of records, often just an integer constant, though a field or an expression that returns an integer could also be used. Frame clauses also have an optional *frame_exclusion* option, which is beyond the scope of the discussion here. Figure 3-14 shows an example of the rows that each of the window frame options will pick up.

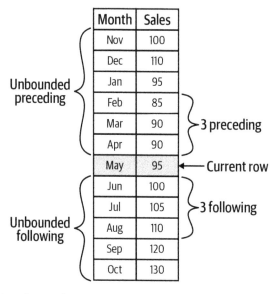

Figure 3-14. Window frame clauses and the rows they include

From partition to ordering to window frames, window functions have a variety of options that control the calculations, making them incredibly powerful and well suited to tackling complex calculations with relatively simple syntax. Returning to our retail sales example, the moving average that we calculated using a self-*JOIN* can be accomplished with window functions in fewer lines of code:

```
SELECT sales_month
,avg(sales) over (order by sales_month
                  rows between 11 preceding and current row
                  ) as moving_avg
,count(sales) over (order by sales_month
                  rows between 11 preceding and current row
                  ) as records_count
FROM retail_sales
WHERE kind_of_business = 'Women''s clothing stores'
;

sales_month  moving_avg  records_count
-----------  ----------  -------------
1992-01-01   1873.00     1
1992-02-01   1932.00     2
1992-03-01   2089.00     3
...          ...         ...
1993-01-01   2672.08     12
1993-02-01   2673.25     12
1993-03-01   2676.50     12
...          ...         ...
```

In this query, the window orders the sales by month (ascending) to ensure that the window records are in chronological order. The frame clause is rows between 11 preceding and current row, since I know that I have one record for each month and I want the 11 prior months and the month from the current row included in the average and count calculations. The query returns all months, including those that don't have 11 prior months, and we might want to filter these out by placing this query in a subquery and filtering by month or number of records in the outer query.

 While calculating moving averages from prior time periods is common in many business contexts, SQL window functions are flexible enough to include future time periods as well. They can also be used in any scenario in which the data has some ordering, not just in time series analysis.

Calculating rolling averages or other moving aggregations can be accomplished with self-*JOIN*s or window functions when records exist in the data set for each time period in the window. There may be performance differences between the two methods, depending on the type of database and the size of the data set. Unfortunately, it's difficult to predict which one will be performant or to give general advice on which to use. It's worth trying both methods and paying attention to how long it takes to return your query results; then make whichever one seems to run faster your default choice. Now that we've seen how to calculate rolling time windows, I'll show how to calculate rolling windows with sparse data sets.

Rolling Time Windows with Sparse Data

Data sets in the real world may not contain a record for every time period that falls within the window. The measurement of interest might be seasonal or intermittent by nature. For example, customers might return to purchase from a website at irregular intervals, or a particular product might go in and out of stock. This results in sparse data.

In the last section, I showed how to calculate a rolling window with a self-*JOIN* and a date interval in the *JOIN* clause. You might be thinking that this will pick up any records within the 12-month time window, whether all were in the data set or not, and you'd be correct. The problem with this approach comes when there is no record for the month (or day or year) itself. For example, imagine I want to calculate the rolling 12-month sales for each model of shoe my store stocks as of December 2019. Some of the shoes went out of stock prior to December, however, and so don't have sales records in that month. Using a self-*JOIN* or window function will return a data set of rolling sales for all the shoes that sold in December, but the data will be missing the shoes that went out of stock. Fortunately, we have a way to solve this problem: by using a date dimension.

The *date dimension*, a static table that contains a row for each calendar date, was introduced in Chapter 2. With such a table we can ensure that a query returns a result for every date of interest, whether or not there was a data point for that date in the underlying data set. Since the `retail_sales` data does include rows for all months, I've simulated a sparse data set by adding a subquery to filter the table to only `sales_months` from January and July (1 and 7). Let's look at the results when *JOIN*ed to the `date_dim`, but before aggregation, to develop intuition about the data before applying calculations:

```
SELECT a.date, b.sales_month, b.sales
FROM date_dim a
JOIN
(
    SELECT sales_month, sales
    FROM retail_sales
    WHERE kind_of_business = 'Women''s clothing stores'
      and date_part('month',sales_month) in (1,7)
) b on b.sales_month between a.date - interval '11 months' and a.date
WHERE a.date = a.first_day_of_month
  and a.date between '1993-01-01' and '2020-12-01'
;
```

```
date        sales_month   sales
----------  -----------   -----
1993-01-01  1992-07-01    2373
1993-01-01  1993-01-01    2123
1993-02-01  1992-07-01    2373
1993-02-01  1993-01-01    2123
1993-03-01  1992-07-01    2373
...         ...           ...
```

Notice that the query returns results for February and March dates in addition to
January, even though there are no sales for these months in the subquery results. This
is possible because the date dimension contains records for all months. The filter
a.date = a.first_day_of_month restricts the result set to one value per month,
instead of the 28 to 31 rows per month that would result from joining to every date.
The construction of this query is otherwise very similar to the self-*JOIN* query in the
last section, with the *JOIN* clause on b.sales_month between a.date - interval
'11 months' and a.date of the same form as the *JOIN* clause in the self-*JOIN*. Now
that we have developed an understanding of what the query will return, we can go
ahead and apply the avg aggregation to get the moving average:

```
SELECT a.date
,avg(b.sales) as moving_avg
,count(b.sales) as records
FROM date_dim a
JOIN
(
    SELECT sales_month, sales
    FROM retail_sales
    WHERE kind_of_business = 'Women''s clothing stores'
      and date_part('month',sales_month) in (1,7)
) b on b.sales_month between a.date - interval '11 months' and a.date
WHERE a.date = a.first_day_of_month
 and a.date between '1993-01-01' and '2020-12-01'
GROUP BY 1
;

date        moving_avg  records
----------  ----------  -------
1993-01-01  2248.00     2
1993-02-01  2248.00     2
1993-03-01  2248.00     2
...         ...         ...
```

As we saw above, the result set includes a row for every month; however, the moving
average stays constant until a new data point (in this case, a January or July) is added.
Each moving average consists of two underlying data points. In a real use case, the
number of underlying data points is likely to vary. To return the current month's
value when using a data dimension, an aggregation with a CASE statement can be
used—for example:

```
    ,max(case when a.date = b.sales_month then b.sales end)
    as sales_in_month
```

The conditions inside the CASE statement can be changed to return any of the underlying records that the analysis requires through use of equality, inequality, or offsets with date math. If a date dimension is not available in your database, then another technique can be used to simulate one. In a subquery, *SELECT* the *DISTINCT* dates needed and *JOIN* them to your table in the same way as in the preceding examples:

```
SELECT a.sales_month, avg(b.sales) as moving_avg
FROM
(
    SELECT distinct sales_month
    FROM retail_sales
    WHERE sales_month between '1993-01-01' and '2020-12-01'
) a
JOIN retail_sales b on b.sales_month between
 a.sales_month - interval '11 months' and a.sales_month
 and b.kind_of_business = 'Women''s clothing stores'
GROUP BY 1
;

sales_month  moving_avg
-----------  ----------
1993-01-01   2672.08
1993-02-01   2673.25
1993-03-01   2676.50
...          ...
```

In this example, I used the same underlying table because I know it contains all the months. However, in practice any database table that contains the needed dates can be used, whether or not it is related to the table from which you want to calculate the rolling aggregation.

Calculating rolling time windows with sparse or missing data can be done in SQL with controlled application of Cartesian *JOIN*s. Next, we'll look at how to calculate cumulative values that are often used in analysis.

Calculating Cumulative Values

Rolling window calculations, such as moving averages, typically use fixed-size windows, such as 12 months, as we saw in the last section. Another commonly used type of calculation is the *cumulative value*, such as YTD, quarter-to-date (QTD), and month-to-date (MTD). Rather than a fixed-length window, these rely on a common starting point, with the window size growing with each row.

The simplest way to calculate cumulative values is with a window function. In this example, sum is used to find total sales YTD as of each month. Other analyses might call for a monthly average YTD or a monthly maximum YTD, which can be accomplished by swapping sum for avg or max. The window resets according to the *PARTITION BY* clause, in this case the year of the sales month. The *ORDER BY* clause typically includes a date field in time series analysis. Omitting the *ORDER BY* can lead to incorrect results due to the way the data is sorted in the underlying table, so it's a good idea to include it even if you think the data is already sorted by date:

```
SELECT sales_month, sales
,sum(sales) over (partition by date_part('year',sales_month)
                  order by sales_month
                  ) as sales_ytd
FROM retail_sales
WHERE kind_of_business = 'Women''s clothing stores'
;

sales_month   sales   sales_ytd
-----------   -----   ---------
1992-01-01    1873    1873
1992-02-01    1991    3864
1992-03-01    2403    6267
...           ...     ...
1992-12-01    4416    31815
1993-01-01    2123    2123
1993-02-01    2005    4128
...           ...     ...
```

The query returns a record for each sales_month, the sales for that month, and the running total sales_ytd. The series starts in 1992 and then resets in January 1993, as it will for every year in the data set. The results for years 2016 through 2020 are graphed in Figure 3-15. The first four years show similar patterns through the year, but of course 2020 looks very different.

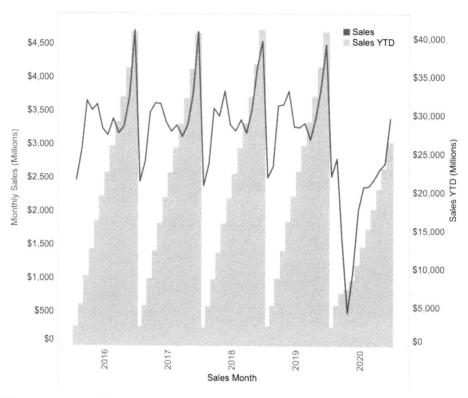

Figure 3-15. Monthly sales and cumulative annual sales for women's clothing stores

The same results can be achieved without window functions, by using a self-*JOIN* that leverages a Cartesian *JOIN*. In this example, the two table aliases are *JOIN*ed on the year of the `sales_month` to ensure that the aggregated values are for the same year, resetting each year. The *JOIN* clause also specifies that the results should include `sales_months` from alias b that are less than or equal to the `sales_month` in alias a. In January 1992, only the January 1992 row from alias b meets this criterion; in February 1992, both January and February 1992 do; and so on:

```
SELECT a.sales_month, a.sales
,sum(b.sales) as sales_ytd
FROM retail_sales a
JOIN retail_sales b on
 date_part('year',a.sales_month) = date_part('year',b.sales_month)
 and b.sales_month <= a.sales_month
 and b.kind_of_business = 'Women''s clothing stores'
WHERE a.kind_of_business = 'Women''s clothing stores'
GROUP BY 1,2
;
```

```
sales_month   sales   sales_ytd
-----------   -----   ---------
1992-01-01    1873    1873
1992-02-01    1991    3864
1992-03-01    2403    6267
...             ...     ...
1992-12-01    4416    31815
1993-01-01    2123    2123
1993-02-01    2005    4128
...             ...     ...
```

Window functions require fewer characters of code, and it's usually easier to keep track of exactly what they are calculating once you are familiar with the syntax. There's often more than one way to approach a problem in SQL, and rolling time windows are a good example of that. I find it useful to know multiple approaches, because every once in a while I run into a tricky problem that is actually better solved with an approach that seems less efficient in other contexts. Now that we've covered rolling time windows, we'll move on to our final topic in time series analysis with SQL: seasonality.

Analyzing with Seasonality

Seasonality is any pattern that repeats over regular intervals. Unlike other noise in the data, seasonality can be predicted. The word *seasonality* brings to mind the four seasons of the year—spring, summer, fall, winter—and some data sets include these patterns. Shopping patterns change with the seasons, from the clothes and food people buy to the money spent on leisure and travel. The winter holiday shopping season can be make-or-break for many retailers. Seasonality can also exist at other time scales, from years down to minutes. Presidential elections in the United States happen every four years, leading to distinct patterns in media coverage. Day of week cyclicality is common, as work and school dominate Monday to Friday, while chores and leisure activities dominate the weekend. Time of day is another type of seasonality that restaurants experience, with rushes around lunch and dinner time and slower sales in between.

To understand whether seasonality exists in a time series, and at what scale, it's useful to graph it and then visually inspect for patterns. Try aggregating at different levels, from hourly to daily, weekly, and monthly. You should also incorporate knowledge about the data set. Are there patterns that you can guess based on what you know about the entity or process it represents? Consult subject matter experts, if available.

Let's take a look at some seasonal patterns in the retail sales data set, shown in Figure 3-16. Jewelry stores have a highly seasonal pattern, with annual peaks in December related to holiday gift giving. Book stores have two peaks each year: one peak is in August, corresponding with back-to-school time in the United States; the other peak starts in December and lasts through January, including both the holiday gift period and back-to-school time for the spring semester. A third example is grocery stores, which have much less monthly seasonality than the other two time series (although they likely have seasonality at the day of week and time of day level). This isn't surprising: people need to eat year-round. Grocery store sales increase a bit in December for the holidays, and they decline in February, since that month simply has fewer days.

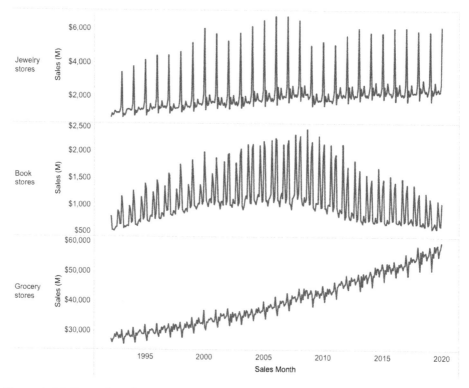

Figure 3-16. Examples of seasonality patterns in book store, grocery store, and jewelry store sales

Seasonality can take many forms, though there are some common approaches to analyzing it regardless. One way to deal with seasonality is to smooth it out, either by aggregating the data to a less granular time period or by using rolling windows, as we saw previously. Another way to work with seasonal data is to benchmark against similar time periods and analyze the difference. I'll show several ways to accomplish this next.

Period-over-Period Comparisons: YoY and MoM

Period-over-period comparisons can take multiple forms. The first one is to compare a time period to the previous value in the series, a practice so common in analysis that there are acronyms for the most often-used comparisons. Depending on the level of aggregation the comparison might be year-over-year (YoY), month-over-month (MoM), day-over-day (DoD), and so on.

For these calculations we'll use the lag function, another one of the window functions. The lag function returns a previous or lagging value from a series. The lag function has the following form:

```
lag(return_value [,offset [,default]])
```

The *return_value* is any field from the data set and thus can be any data type. The optional *OFFSET* indicates how many rows back in the partition to take the *return_value* from. The default is 1, but any integer value can be used. You can also optionally specify a *default* value to use if there is no lagging record to retrieve a value from. Like other window functions, lag is also calculated over a partition, with sorting determined by the *ORDER BY* clause. If no *PARTITION BY* clause is specified, lag looks back over the whole data set, and likewise if no *ORDER BY* clause is specified, the database order is used. It's usually a good idea to at least include an *ORDER BY* clause in a lag window function to control the output.

 The lead window function works in the same way as the lag function, except that it returns a subsequent value as determined by the offset. Changing the *ORDER BY* from ascending (*ASC*) to descending (*DESC*) in a time series has the effect of turning a lag statement into the equivalent of a lead statement. Alternatively, a negative integer can be used as the *OFFSET* value to return a value from a subsequent row.

Let's apply this to our retail sales data set to calculate MoM and YoY growth. In this section, we'll focus on book store sales, since I'm a real book store nerd. First, we'll develop our intuition about what is returned by the lag function by returning both the lagging month and the lagging sales values:

```
SELECT kind_of_business, sales_month, sales
,lag(sales_month) over (partition by kind_of_business
                        order by sales_month
                        ) as prev_month
,lag(sales) over (partition by kind_of_business
                  order by sales_month
                  ) as prev_month_sales
FROM retail_sales
WHERE kind_of_business = 'Book stores'
```

```
;
```

kind_of_business	sales_month	sales	prev_month	prev_month_sales
Book stores	1992-01-01	790	(null)	(null)
Book stores	1992-02-01	539	1992-01-01	790
Book stores	1992-03-01	535	1992-02-01	539
...	...	...	...	...

For each row, the previous `sales_month` is returned, as well as the `sales` for that month, and we can confirm this by inspecting the first few lines of the result set. The first row has null for `prev_month` and `prev_month_sales` since there is no earlier record in this data set. With an understanding of the values returned by the `lag` function, we can calculate the percent change from the previous value:

```
SELECT kind_of_business, sales_month, sales
,(sales / lag(sales) over (partition by kind_of_business
                           order by sales_month)
 - 1) * 100 as pct_growth_from_previous
FROM retail_sales
WHERE kind_of_business = 'Book stores'
;
```

kind_of_business	sales_month	sales	pct_growth_from_previous
Book stores	1992-01-01	790	(null)
Book stores	1992-02-01	539	-31.77
Book stores	1992-03-01	535	-0.74
...	...	...	...

Sales dropped 31.8% from January to February, due at least in part to the seasonal decline after the holidays and the return to school for the spring semester. Sales were down only 0.7% from February to March.

The calculation for the YoY comparison is similar, but first we need to aggregate sales to the yearly level. Since we're looking at only one `kind_of_business`, I'll drop that field from the rest of the examples to simplify the code:

```
SELECT sales_year, yearly_sales
,lag(yearly_sales) over (order by sales_year) as prev_year_sales
,(yearly_sales / lag(yearly_sales) over (order by sales_year)
 -1) * 100 as pct_growth_from_previous
FROM
(
    SELECT date_part('year',sales_month) as sales_year
    ,sum(sales) as yearly_sales
    FROM retail_sales
    WHERE kind_of_business = 'Book stores'
    GROUP BY 1
) a
;
```

sales_year	yearly_sales	prev_year_sales	pct_growth_from_previous
1992.0	8327	(null)	(null)
1993.0	9108	8327	9.37
1994.0	10107	9108	10.96
...	...	...	...

Sales grew more than 9.3% from 1992 to 1993, and almost 11% from 1993 to 1994. These period-over-period calculations are useful, but they don't quite allow us to analyze the seasonality in the data set. For example, in Figure 3-17 the MoM percent growth values are plotted, and they contain just as much seasonality as the original time series.

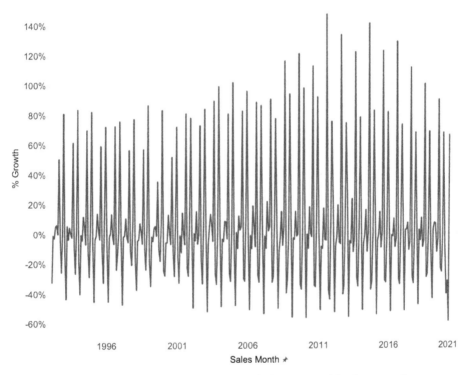

Figure 3-17. Percent growth from previous month for US retail book store sales

To tackle this, the next section will demonstrate how to use SQL to compare current values to the values for the same month in the previous year.

Period-over-Period Comparisons: Same Month Versus Last Year

Comparing data for one time period to data for a similar previous time period can be a useful way to control for seasonality. The previous time period may be the same day of the week in the previous week, the same month in the previous year, or another variation that makes sense for the data set.

To accomplish this comparison, we can use the lag function along with some clever partitioning: the unit of time with which we want to compare the current value. In this case, we will compare monthly sales to the sales for the same month in the previous year. For example, January sales will be compared to prior year January sales, February sales will be compared to prior year February sales, and so on.

First, recall that the date_part function returns a numeric value when used with the "month" argument:

```
SELECT sales_month
,date_part('month',sales_month)
FROM retail_sales
WHERE kind_of_business = 'Book stores'
;

sales_month  date_part
-----------  ---------
1992-01-01   1.0
1992-02-01   2.0
1992-03-01   3.0
...          ...
```

Next, we include the date_part in the *PARTITION BY* clause so that the window function looks up the value for the matching month number from the prior year.

This is an example of how window function clauses can include calculations in addition to database fields, giving them even more versatility. I find it useful to check intermediate results to build intuition about what the final query will return, so first we'll confirm that the lag function with partition by date_part('month', sales_month) returns the intended values:

```
SELECT sales_month, sales
,lag(sales_month) over (partition by date_part('month',sales_month)
                        order by sales_month
                        ) as prev_year_month
,lag(sales) over (partition by date_part('month',sales_month)
                  order by sales_month
                  ) as prev_year_sales
FROM retail_sales
WHERE kind_of_business = 'Book stores'
;
```

```
sales_month   sales   prev_year_month   prev_year_sales
-----------   -----   ---------------   ---------------
1992-01-01    790     (null)            (null)
1993-01-01    998     1992-01-01        790
1994-01-01    1053    1993-01-01        998
...           ...     ...               ...
1992-02-01    539     (null)            (null)
1993-02-01    568     1992-02-01        539
1994-02-01    635     1993-02-01        568
...           ...     ...               ...
```

The first lag function returns the same month for the prior year, which we can verify by looking at the prev_year_month value. The row for the 1993-01-01 sales_month returns 1992-01-01 for the prev_year_month as intended, and the prev_year_sales of 790 match the sales we can see in the 1992-01-01 row. Notice that the prev_year_month and prev_year_sales are null for 1992 since there are no prior records in the data set.

Now that we're confident the lag function as written returns the correct values, we can calculate comparison metrics such as absolute difference and percent change from previous:

```
SELECT sales_month, sales
,sales - lag(sales) over (partition by date_part('month',sales_month)
                          order by sales_month
                          ) as absolute_diff
,(sales / lag(sales) over (partition by date_part('month',sales_month)
                          order by sales_month)
 - 1) * 100 as pct_diff
FROM retail_sales
WHERE kind_of_business = 'Book stores'
;

sales_month   sales   absolute_diff   pct_diff
-----------   -----   -------------   --------
1992-01-01    790     (null)          (null)
1993-01-01    998     208             26.32
1994-01-01    1053    55              5.51
...           ...     ...             ...
```

We can now graph the results in Figure 3-18 and more easily see the months where growth was unusually high, such as January 2002, or unusually low, such as December 2001.

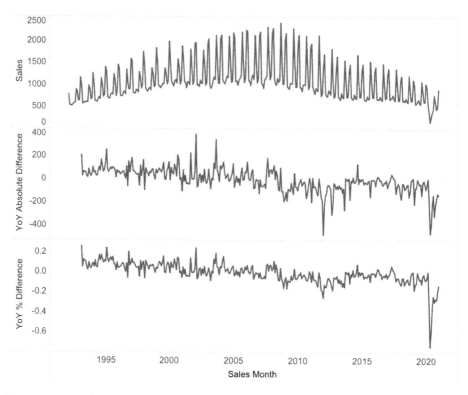

Figure 3-18. Book store sales, YoY absolute difference in sales, and YoY percent growth

Another useful analysis tool is to create a graph that lines up the same time period—in this case, months—with a line for each time series—in this case, years. To do this, we'll create a result set that has a row for each month number or name, and a column for each of the years we want to consider. To get the month, we can use either the date_part or the to_char function, depending on whether we want numeric or text values for the months. Then we'll pivot the data using an aggregate function.

This example uses the max aggregate, but depending on the analysis, a sum, count, or other aggregation might be appropriate. We'll zoom in on 1992 through 1994 for this example:

```
SELECT date_part('month',sales_month) as month_number
,to_char(sales_month,'Month') as month_name
,max(case when date_part('year',sales_month) = 1992 then sales end)
 as sales_1992
,max(case when date_part('year',sales_month) = 1993 then sales end)
 as sales_1993
,max(case when date_part('year',sales_month) = 1994 then sales end)
 as sales_1994
FROM retail_sales
```

```
WHERE kind_of_business = 'Book stores'
 and sales_month between '1992-01-01' and '1994-12-01'
GROUP BY 1,2
;

month_number  month_name  sales_1992  sales_1993  sales_1994
------------  ----------  ----------  ----------  ----------
1.0           January     790         998         1053
2.0           February    539         568         635
3.0           March       535         602         634
4.0           April       523         583         610
5.0           May         552         612         684
6.0           June        589         618         724
7.0           July        592         607         678
8.0           August      894         983         1154
9.0           September   861         903         1022
10.0          October     645         669         732
11.0          November    642         692         772
12.0          December    1165        1273        1409
```

By lining the data up in this way, we can see some trends immediately. December sales are the highest monthly sales of the year. Sales in 1994 were higher every month than sales in 1992 and 1993. The August-to-September sales bump is visible, and particularly easy to spot in 1994.

With a graph of the data, as in Figure 3-19, the trends are much easier to identify. Sales increased year to year in every month, though the increases were larger in some months than others. With this data and graph in hand, we can start to construct a story about book store sales that might help with inventory planning or scheduling of marketing promotions or might serve as a piece of evidence in a wider story about US retail sales.

With SQL there are a number of techniques for cutting through the noise of seasonality to compare data in time series. In this section, we've seen how to compare current values to prior comparable periods using lag functions and how to pivot the data with date_part, to_char, and aggregate functions. Next, I'll show some techniques for comparing multiple prior periods in order to further control for noisy time series data.

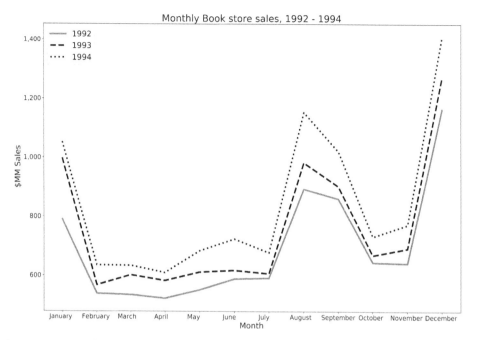

Figure 3-19. Book store sales for 1992–1994, aligned by month

Comparing to Multiple Prior Periods

Comparing data to prior comparable periods is a useful way to reduce the noise that arises from seasonality. Sometimes comparing to a single prior period is insufficient, particularly if that prior period was impacted by unusual events. Comparing a Monday to the previous Monday is difficult if one of them was a holiday. The month in the prior year might be unusual due to economic events, severe weather, or a site outage that changed typical behavior. Comparing current values to an aggregate of multiple prior periods can help smooth out these fluctuations. These techniques also combine what we've learned about using SQL to calculate rolling time periods and comparable prior period results.

The first technique uses the `lag` function, as in the last section, but here we'll take advantage of the optional offset value. Recall that when no offset is provided to `lag`, the function returns the immediate prior value according to the *PARTITION BY* and *ORDER BY* clauses. An offset value of 2 skips over the immediate prior value and returns the value prior to that, an offset value of 3 returns the value from 3 rows back, and so on.

For this example, we'll compare the current month's sales to the same month's sales over three prior years. As usual, first we'll inspect the returned values to confirm the SQL is working as expected:

```
SELECT sales_month, sales
,lag(sales,1) over (partition by date_part('month',sales_month)
                    order by sales_month
                    ) as prev_sales_1
,lag(sales,2) over (partition by date_part('month',sales_month)
                    order by sales_month
                    ) as prev_sales_2
,lag(sales,3) over (partition by date_part('month',sales_month)
                    order by sales_month
                    ) as prev_sales_3
FROM retail_sales
WHERE kind_of_business = 'Book stores'
;

sales_month  sales  prev_sales_1  prev_sales_2  prev_sales_3
-----------  -----  ------------  ------------  ------------
1992-01-01   790    (null)        (null)        (null)
1993-01-01   998    790           (null)        (null)
1994-01-01   1053   998           790           (null)
1995-01-01   1308   1053          998           790
1996-01-01   1373   1308          1053          998
...          ...    ...           ...           ...
```

Null is returned where no prior record exists, and we can confirm that the correct same month, prior year value appears. From here we can calculate whatever comparison metric the analysis calls for—in this case, the percent of the rolling average of three prior periods:

```
SELECT sales_month, sales
,sales / ((prev_sales_1 + prev_sales_2 + prev_sales_3) / 3)
 as pct_of_3_prev
FROM
(
    SELECT sales_month, sales
    ,lag(sales,1) over (partition by date_part('month',sales_month)
                        order by sales_month
                        ) as prev_sales_1
    ,lag(sales,2) over (partition by date_part('month',sales_month)
                        order by sales_month
                        ) as prev_sales_2
    ,lag(sales,3) over (partition by date_part('month',sales_month)
                        order by sales_month
                        ) as prev_sales_3
    FROM retail_sales
    WHERE kind_of_business = 'Book stores'
) a
;

sales_month  sales  pct_of_3_prev
-----------  -----  -------------
1995-01-01   1308   138.12
1996-01-01   1373   122.69
```

```
1997-01-01    1558    125.24
...           ...     ...
2017-01-01    1386    94.67
2018-01-01    1217    84.98
2019-01-01    1004    74.75
...           ...     ...
```

We can see from the result that book sales grew from the prior three-year rolling average in the mid-1990s, but the picture was different in the late 2010s, when sales were a shrinking percentage of that three-year rolling average each year.

You might have noticed that this problem resembles one we saw earlier when calculating rolling time windows. As an alternative to the last example, we can use an `avg` window function with a frame clause. To accomplish this, the *PARTITION BY* will use the same `date_part` function, and the *ORDER BY* is the same. A frame clause is added to include `rows between 3 preceding and 1 preceding`. This includes the values in the 1, 2, and 3 rows prior but excludes the value in the current row:

```
SELECT sales_month, sales
,sales / avg(sales) over (partition by date_part('month',sales_month)
                          order by sales_month
                          rows between 3 preceding and 1 preceding
                          ) as pct_of_prev_3
FROM retail_sales
WHERE kind_of_business = 'Book stores'
;

sales_month   sales   pct_of_prev_3
-----------   -----   -------------
1995-01-01    1308    138.12
1996-01-01    1373    122.62
1997-01-01    1558    125.17
...           ...     ...
2017-01-01    1386    94.62
2018-01-01    1217    84.94
2019-01-01    1004    74.73
...           ...     ...
```

The results match those of the previous example, confirming that the alternative code is equivalent.

> If you look closely, you'll notice that the decimal place values are slightly different in the result using the three `lag` windows and the result using the `avg` window function. This is due to how the database handles decimal rounding in intermediate calculations. For many analyses, the difference won't matter, but pay careful attention if you're working with financial or other highly regulated data.

Analyzing data with seasonality often involves trying to reduce noise in order to make clear conclusions about the underlying trends in the data. Comparing data points against multiple prior time periods can give us an even smoother trend to compare to and determine what is actually happening in the current time period. This does require that the data include enough history to make these comparisons, but when we have a long enough time series, it can be insightful.

Conclusion

Time series analysis is a powerful way to analyze data sets. We've seen how to set up our data for analysis with date and time manipulations. We talked about date dimensions and saw how to apply them to calculating rolling time windows. We looked at period-over-period calculations and how to analyze data with seasonality patterns. In the next chapter, we'll delve deep into a related topic that extends on time series analysis: cohort analysis.

CHAPTER 4

Cohort Analysis

In Chapter 3 we covered time series analysis. With those techniques in hand, we will now turn to a related type of analysis with many business and other applications: cohort analysis.

I remember the first time I encountered a cohort analysis. I was working at my first data analyst job, at a small startup. I was reviewing a purchase analysis I'd worked on with the CEO, and he suggested that I break up the customer base by cohorts to see whether behavior was changing over time. I assumed it was some fancy business school thing and probably useless, but he was the CEO, so of course I humored him. Turns out it wasn't just a lark. Breaking populations into cohorts and following them over time is a powerful way to analyze your data and avoid various biases. Cohorts can provide clues to how subpopulations differ from each other and how they change over time.

In this chapter, we'll first take a look at what cohorts are and at the building blocks of certain types of cohort analysis. After an introduction to the legislators data set used for the examples, we'll learn how to construct a retention analysis and deal with various challenges such as defining the cohort and handling sparse data. Next, we'll cover survivorship, returnship, and cumulative calculations, all of which are similar to retention analysis in the way the SQL code is structured. Finally, we'll look at how to combine cohort analysis with cross-sectional analysis to understand the makeup of populations over time.

Cohorts: A Useful Analysis Framework

Before we get into the code, I will define what cohorts are, consider the types of questions we can answer with this type of analysis, and describe the components of any cohort analysis.

A *cohort* is a group of individuals who share some characteristic of interest, described below, at the time we start observing them. Cohort members are often people but can be any type of entity we want to study: companies, products, or physical world phenomena. Individuals in a cohort may be aware of their membership, just as children in a first-grade class are aware they are part of a peer group of first graders, or participants in a drug trial are aware they are part of a group receiving a treatment. At other times, entities are grouped into cohorts virtually, as when a software company groups all customers acquired in a certain year to study how long they remain customers. It's always important to consider the ethical implications of cohorting entities without their awareness, if any different treatment is to be applied to them.

Cohort analysis is a useful way to compare groups of entities over time. Many important behaviors take weeks, months, or years to occur or evolve, and cohort analysis is a way to understand these changes. Cohort analysis provides a framework for detecting correlations between cohort characteristics and these long-term trends, which can lead to hypotheses about the causal drivers. For example, customers acquired through a marketing campaign may have different long-term purchase patterns than those who were persuaded by a friend to try a company's products. Cohort analysis can be used to monitor new cohorts of users or customers and assess how they compare to previous cohorts. Such monitoring can provide an early alert signal that something has gone wrong (or right) for new customers. Cohort analysis is also used to mine historical data. A/B tests, discussed in Chapter 7, are the gold standard for determining causality, but we can't go back in time and run every test for every question about the past in which we are interested. We should of course be cautious about attaching causal meaning to cohort analysis and instead use cohort analysis as a way to understand customers and generate hypotheses that can be tested rigorously in the future.

Cohort analyses have three components: the cohort grouping, a time series of data over which the cohort is observed, and an aggregate metric that measures an action done by cohort members.

Cohort grouping is often based on a start date: the customer's first purchase or subscription date, the date a student started school, and so on. However, cohorts can also be formed around other characteristics that are either innate or changing over time. Innate qualities include birth year and country of origin, or the year a company was founded. Characteristics that can change over time include city of residence and marital status. When these are used, we need to be careful to cohort only on the value on the starting date, or else entities can jump between cohort groups.

Cohort or Segment?

These two terms are often used in similar ways, or even interchangeably, but it's worth drawing a distinction between them for the sake of clarity. A *cohort* is a group of users (or other entities) who have a common starting date and are followed over time. A *segment* is a grouping of users who share a common characteristic or set of characteristics at a point in time, regardless of their starting date. Similar to cohorts, segments can be based on innate factors such as age or on behavioral characteristics. A segment of users that signs up in the same month can be put into a cohort and followed over time. Or different groupings of users can be explored with cohort analysis so that you can see which ones have the most valuable characteristics. The analyses we'll cover in this chapter, such as retention, can help put concrete data behind marketing segments.

The second component of any cohort analysis is the *time series*. This is a series of purchases, logins, interactions, or other actions that are taken by the customers or entities to be cohorted. It's important that the time series covers the entire life span of the entities, or there will be *survivorship bias* in early cohorts. Survivorship bias occurs when only customers who have stayed are in the data set; churned customers are excluded because they are no longer around, so the rest of the customers appear to be of higher quality or fit in comparison to newer cohorts (see "Survivorship Bias" on page 167). It's also important to have a time series that is long enough for the entities to complete the action of interest. For example, if customers tend to purchase once a month, a time series of several months is needed. If, on the other hand, purchases happen only once a year, a time series of several years would be preferable. Inevitably, more recently acquired customers will not have had as long to complete actions as those customers who were acquired further in the past. In order to normalize, cohort analysis usually measures the number of periods that have elapsed from a starting date, rather than calendar months. In this way, cohorts can be compared in period 1, period 2, and so on to see how they evolve over time, regardless of which month the action actually occurred. The intervals may be days, weeks, months, or years.

The *aggregate metric* should be related to the actions that matter to the health of the organization, such as customers continuing to use or purchase the product. Metric values are aggregated across the cohort, usually with `sum`, `count`, or `average`, though any relevant aggregation works. The result is a time series that can then be used to understand changes in behavior over time.

In this chapter, I'll cover four types of cohort analysis: retention, survivorship, returnship or repeat purchase behavior, and cumulative behavior.

Retention

Retention is concerned with whether the cohort member has a record in the time series on a particular date, expressed as a number of periods from the starting date. This is useful in any kind of organization in which repeated actions are expected, from playing an online game to using a product or renewing a subscription, and it helps to answer questions about how sticky or engaging a product is and how many entities can be expected to appear on future dates.

Survivorship

Survivorship is concerned with how many entities remained in the data set for a certain length of time or longer, regardless of the number or frequency of actions up to that time. Survivorship is useful for answering questions about the proportion of the population that can be expected to remain—either in a positive sense by not churning or passing away, or in a negative sense by not graduating or fulfilling some requirement.

Returnship

Returnship or repeat purchase behavior is concerned with whether an action has happened more than some minimum threshold of times—often simply more than once—during a fixed window of time. This type of analysis is useful in situations in which the behavior is intermittent and unpredictable, such as in retail, where it characterizes the share of repeat purchasers in each cohort within a fixed time window.

Cumulative

Cumulative calculations are concerned with the total number or amounts measured at one or more fixed time windows, regardless of when they happened during that window. Cumulative calculations are often used in calculations of customer lifetime value (LTV or CLTV).

The four types of cohort analysis allow us to compare subgroups and understand how they differ over time in order to make better product, marketing, and financial decisions. The calculations for the different types are similar, so we will set the stage with retention, and then I'll show how to modify retention code to calculate the other types. Before we dive into constructing our cohort analysis, let's take a look at the data set we'll be using for the examples in this chapter.

The Legislators Data Set

The SQL examples in this chapter will use a data set of past and present members of the United States Congress maintained in a GitHub repository (*https://github.com/ unitedstates/congress-legislators*). In the US, Congress is responsible for writing laws or legislation, so its members are also known as legislators. Since the data set is a JSON file, I have applied some transformations to produce a more suitable data model for analysis, and I have posted data in a format suitable for following along with the examples in the book's GitHub legislators folder (*https://oreil.ly/H2tYP*).

The source repository has an excellent data dictionary, so I won't repeat all the details here. I will provide a few details, however, that should help those who aren't familiar with the US government to follow along with the analyses in this chapter.

Congress has two chambers, the Senate ("sen" in the data set) and the House of Representatives ("rep"). Each state has two senators, and they are elected for six-year terms. Representatives are allocated to states based on population; each representative has a district that they alone represent. Representatives are elected for two-year terms. Actual terms in either chamber can be shorter in the event that the legislator dies or is elected or appointed to a higher office. Legislators accumulate power and influence via leadership positions the longer they are in office, and thus standing for re-election is common. Finally, a legislator may belong to a political party, or they may be an "independent." In the modern era, the vast majority of legislators are Democrats or Republicans, and the rivalry between the two parties is well known. Legislators occasionally change parties while in office.

For the analyses, we'll make use of two tables: legislators and legislators_terms. The legislators table contains a list of all the people included in the data set, with birthday, gender, and a set of ID fields that can be used to look up the person in other data sets. The legislators_terms table contains a record for each term in office for each legislator, with start and end date, and other attributes such as chamber and party. The id_bioguide field is used as the unique identifier of a legislator and appears in each table. Figure 4-1 shows a sample of the legislators data. Figure 4-2 shows a sample of the legislators_terms data.

*	full_name	first_name	last_name	birthday	gender	id_bioguide	id_govtrack
1	Sherrod Brown	Sherrod	Brown	1952-11-09	M	B000944	400050
2	Maria Cantwell	Maria	Cantwell	1958-10-13	F	C000127	300018
3	Benjamin L. Cardin	Benjamin	Cardin	1943-10-05	M	C000141	400064
4	Thomas R. Carper	Thomas	Carper	1947-01-23	M	C000174	300019
5	Robert P. Casey, Jr.	Robert	Casey	1960-04-13	M	C001070	412246
6	Dianne Feinstein	Dianne	Feinstein	1933-06-22	F	F000062	300043
7	Russ Fulcher	Russ	Fulcher	1973-07-19	M	F000469	412773
8	Amy Klobuchar	Amy	Klobuchar	1960-05-25	F	K000367	412242
9	Robert Menendez	Robert	Menendez	1954-01-01	M	M000639	400272
10	Bernard Sanders	Bernard	Sanders	1941-09-08	M	S000033	400357
11	Debbie Stabenow	Debbie	Stabenow	1950-04-29	F	S000770	300093
12	Jon Tester	Jon	Tester	1956-08-21	M	T000464	412244
13	Sheldon Whitehouse	Sheldon	Whitehouse	1955-10-20	M	W000802	412247
14	Nanette Diaz Barragán	Nanette	Barragán	1976-09-15	F	B001300	412687
15	John Barrasso	John	Barrasso	1952-07-21	M	B001261	412251
16	Roger F. Wicker	Roger	Wicker	1951-07-05	M	W000437	400432
17	Lamar Alexander	Lamar	Alexander	1940-07-03	M	A000360	300002
18	Susan M. Collins	Susan	Collins	1952-12-07	F	C001035	300025
19	John Cornyn	John	Cornyn	1952-02-02	M	C001056	300027

Figure 4-1. Sample of the legislators table

*	id_bioguide	term_id	term_type	term_start	term_end	state	district	party
1	B000944	B000944-0	rep	1993-01-05	1995-01-03	OH	13	Democrat
2	C000127	C000127-0	rep	1993-01-05	1995-01-03	WA	1	Democrat
3	C000141	C000141-0	rep	1987-01-06	1989-01-03	MD	3	Democrat
4	C000174	C000174-0	rep	1983-01-03	1985-01-03	DE	0	Democrat
5	C001070	C001070-0	sen	2007-01-04	2013-01-03	PA	(null)	Democrat
6	F000062	F000062-0	sen	1992-11-10	1995-01-03	CA	(null)	Democrat
7	F000469	F000469-0	rep	2019-01-03	2021-01-03	ID	1	Republican
8	K000367	K000367-0	sen	2007-01-04	2013-01-03	MN	(null)	Democrat
9	M000639	M000639-0	rep	1993-01-05	1995-01-03	NJ	13	Democrat
10	S000033	S000033-0	rep	1991-01-03	1993-01-03	VT	0	Independent
11	S000770	S000770-0	rep	1997-01-07	1999-01-03	MI	8	Democrat
12	T000464	T000464-0	sen	2007-01-04	2013-01-03	MT	(null)	Democrat
13	W000802	W000802-0	sen	2007-01-04	2013-01-03	RI	(null)	Democrat
14	B001300	B001300-0	rep	2017-01-03	2019-01-03	CA	44	Democrat
15	B001261	B001261-0	sen	2007-06-25	2013-01-03	WY	(null)	Republican
16	W000437	W000437-0	rep	1995-01-04	1997-01-03	MS	1	Republican
17	A000360	A000360-0	sen	2003-01-07	2009-01-03	TN	(null)	Republican
18	C001035	C001035-0	sen	1997-01-07	2003-01-03	ME	(null)	Republican
19	C001056	C001056-0	sen	2002-11-30	2003-01-03	TX	(null)	Republican

Figure 4-2. Sample of the legislators_terms table

Now that we have an understanding of what cohort analysis is and of the data set we'll be using for examples, let's get into how to write SQL for retention analysis. The key question SQL will help us answer is: once representatives take office, how long do they keep their jobs?

Retention

One of the most common types of cohort analysis is *retention analysis*. To retain is to keep or continue something. Many skills need to be practiced to be retained. Businesses usually want their customers to keep purchasing their products or using their services, since retaining customers is more profitable than acquiring new ones. Employers want to retain their employees, because recruiting replacements is expensive and time consuming. Elected officials seek reelection in order to continue working on the priorities of their constituents.

The main question in retention analysis is whether the starting size of the cohort— number of subscribers or employees, amount spent, or another key metric—will remain constant, decay, or increase over time. When there is an increase or a decrease, the amount and speed of change are also interesting questions. In most retention analyses, the starting size will tend to decay over time, since a cohort can lose but cannot gain new members once it is formed. Revenue is an interesting exception, since a cohort of customers can spend more in subsequent months than they did in the first month collectively, even if some of them churn.

Retention analysis uses the count of entities or sum of money or actions present in the data set for each period from the starting date, and it normalizes by dividing this number by the count or sum of entities, money, or actions in the first time period. The result is expressed as a percentage, and retention in the starting period is always 100%. Over time, retention based on counts generally declines and can never exceed 100%, whereas money- or action-based retention, while often declining, can increase and be greater than 100% in a time period. Retention analysis output is typically displayed in either table or graph form, which is referred to as a retention curve. We'll see a number of examples of retention curves later in this chapter.

Graphs of retention curves can be used to compare cohorts. The first characteristic to pay attention to is the shape of the curve in the initial few periods, where there is often an initial steep drop. For many consumer apps, losing half a cohort in the first few months is common. A cohort with a curve that is either more or less steep than others can indicate changes in the product or customer acquisition source that merit further investigation. A second characteristic to look for is whether the curve flattens after some number of periods or continues declining rapidly to zero. A flattening curve indicates that there is a point in time from which most of the cohort that remains stays indefinitely. A retention curve that inflects upward, sometimes called a smile curve, can occur if cohort members return or reactivate after falling out of the data set for some period. Finally, retention curves that measure subscription revenue are monitored for signs of increasing revenue per customer over time, a sign of a healthy SaaS software business.

This section will show how to create a retention analysis, add cohort groupings from the time series itself and other tables, and handle missing and sparse data that can occur in time series data. With this framework in hand, you'll learn in the subsequent section how to make modifications to create the other related types of cohort analysis. As a result, this section on retention will be the longest one in the chapter, as you build up code and develop your intuition about the calculations.

SQL for a Basic Retention Curve

For retention analysis, as with other cohort analyses, we need three components: the cohort definition, a time series of actions, and an aggregate metric that measures something relevant to the organization or process. In our case, the cohort members will be the legislators, the time series will be the terms in office for each legislator, and the metric of interest will be the count of those who are still in office each period from the starting date.

We'll start by calculating basic retention, before moving on to examples that include various cohort groupings. The first step is to find the first date each legislator took office (first_term). We will use this date to calculate the number of periods for each subsequent date in the time series. To do this, take the min of the term_start and *GROUP BY* each id_bioguide, the unique identifier for a legislator:

```
SELECT id_bioguide
,min(term_start) as first_term
FROM legislators_terms
GROUP BY 1
;

id_bioguide   first_term
-----------   ----------
A000118       1975-01-14
P000281       1933-03-09
K000039       1933-03-09
...           ...
```

The next step is to put this code into a subquery and *JOIN* it to the time series. The age function is applied to calculate the intervals between each term_start and the first_term for each legislator. Applying the date_part functions to the result, with year, transforms this into the number of yearly periods. Since elections happen every two or six years, we'll use years as the time interval to calculate the periods. We could use a shorter interval, but in this data set there is little fluctuation daily or weekly. The count of legislators with records for that period is the number retained:

```
SELECT date_part('year',age(b.term_start,a.first_term)) as period
,count(distinct a.id_bioguide) as cohort_retained
FROM
(
    SELECT id_bioguide, min(term_start) as first_term
```

```
    FROM legislators_terms
    GROUP BY 1
) a
JOIN legislators_terms b on a.id_bioguide = b.id_bioguide
GROUP BY 1
;

period  cohort_retained
------  ---------------
0.0     12518
1.0     3600
2.0     3619
...     ...
```

 In databases that support the datediff function, the date_part
and age construction can be replaced by this simpler function:

    datediff('year',first_term,term_start)

Some databases, such as Oracle, place the date_part last:

    datediff(first_term,term_start,'year'

Now that we have the periods and the number of legislators retained in each, the final
step is to calculate the total cohort_size and populate it in each row so that the
cohort_retained can be divided by it. The first_value window function returns
the first record in the *PARTITION BY* clause, according to the ordering set in the
ORDER BY, a convenient way to get the cohort size in each row. In this case, the
cohort_size comes from the first record in the entire data set, so the *PARTITION BY*
is omitted:

```
first_value(cohort_retained) over (order by period) as cohort_size
```

To find the percent retained, divide the cohort_retained value by this same
calculation:

```
SELECT period
,first_value(cohort_retained) over (order by period) as cohort_size
,cohort_retained
,cohort_retained /
 first_value(cohort_retained) over (order by period) as pct_retained
FROM
(
    SELECT date_part('year',age(b.term_start,a.first_term)) as period
    ,count(distinct a.id_bioguide) as cohort_retained
    FROM
    (
        SELECT id_bioguide, min(term_start) as first_term
        FROM legislators_terms
        GROUP BY 1
    ) a
    JOIN legislators_terms b on a.id_bioguide = b.id_bioguide
```

```
    GROUP BY 1
) aa
;

period  cohort_size  cohort_retained  pct_retained
------  -----------  ---------------  ------------
0.0     12518        12518            1.0000
1.0     12518        3600             0.2876
2.0     12518        3619             0.2891
...     ...          ...              ...
```

We now have a retention calculation, and we can see that there is a big drop-off between the 100% of legislators retained in period 0, or on their start date, and the share with another term record that starts a year later. Graphing the results, as in Figure 4-3, demonstrates how the curve flattens and eventually goes to zero, as even the longest-serving legislators eventually retire or die.

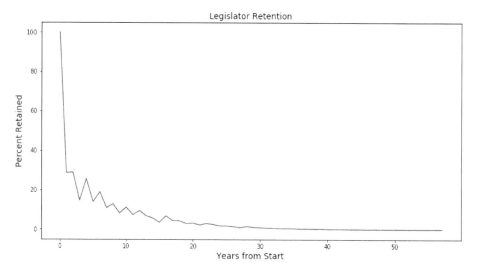

Figure 4-3. Retention from start of first term for US legislators

We can take the cohort retention result and reshape the data to show it in table format. Pivot and flatten the results using an aggregate function with a CASE statement; max is used in this example, but other aggregations such as min or avg would return the same result. Retention is calculated for years 0 through 4, but additional years can be added by following the same pattern:

```
SELECT cohort_size
,max(case when period = 0 then pct_retained end) as yr0
,max(case when period = 1 then pct_retained end) as yr1
,max(case when period = 2 then pct_retained end) as yr2
,max(case when period = 3 then pct_retained end) as yr3
,max(case when period = 4 then pct_retained end) as yr4
```

```
FROM
(
    SELECT period
    ,first_value(cohort_retained) over (order by period)
     as cohort_size
    ,cohort_retained
     / first_value(cohort_retained) over (order by period)
     as pct_retained
    FROM
    (
        SELECT
        date_part('year',age(b.term_start,a.first_term)) as period
        ,count(*) as cohort_retained
        FROM
        (
            SELECT id_bioguide, min(term_start) as first_term
            FROM legislators_terms
            GROUP BY 1
        ) a
        JOIN legislators_terms b on a.id_bioguide = b.id_bioguide
        GROUP BY 1
    ) aa
) aaa
GROUP BY 1
;

cohort_size  yr0     yr1     yr2     yr3     yr4
-----------  ------  ------  ------  ------  ------
12518        1.0000  0.2876  0.2891  0.1463  0.2564
```

Retention appears to be quite low, and from the graph we can see that it is jagged in the first few years. One reason for this is that a representative's term lasts two years, and senators' terms last six years, but the data set only contains records for the start of new terms; thus we are missing data for years in which a legislator was still in office but did not start a new term. Measuring retention each year is misleading in this case. One option is to measure retention only on a two- or six-year cycle, but there is also another strategy we can employ to fill in the "missing" data. I will cover this next before returning to the topic of forming cohort groups.

Adjusting Time Series to Increase Retention Accuracy

We discussed techniques for cleaning "missing" data in Chapter 2, and we will turn to those techniques in this section in order to arrive at a smoother and more truthful retention curve for the legislators. When working with time series data, such as in cohort analysis, it's important to consider not only the data that is present but also whether that data accurately reflects the presence or absence of entities at each time period. This is particularly a problem in contexts in which an event captured in the data leads to the entity persisting for some period of time that is not captured in the data. For example, a customer buying a software subscription is represented in the data at the time of the transaction, but that customer is entitled to use the software for months or years and is not necessarily represented in the data over that span. To correct for this, we need a way to derive the span of time in which the entity is still present, either with an explicit end date or with knowledge of the length of the subscription or term. Then we can say that the entity was present at any date in between those start and end dates.

In the legislators data set, we have a record for a term's start date, but we are missing the notion that this "entitles" a legislator to serve for two or six years, depending on the chamber. To correct for this and smooth out the curve, we need to fill in the "missing" values for the years that legislators are still in office between new terms. Since this data set includes a `term_end` value for each term, I'll show how to create a more accurate cohort retention analysis by filling in dates between the start and end values. Then I'll show how you can impute end dates when the data set does not include an end date.

Calculating retention using a start and end date defined in the data is the most accurate approach. For the following examples, we will consider legislators retained in a particular year if they were still in office as of the last day of the year, December 31. Prior to the Twentieth Amendment to the US Constitution, terms began on March 4, but afterward the start date moved to January 3, or to a subsequent weekday if the third falls on a weekend. Legislators can be sworn in on other days of the year due to special off-cycle elections or appointments to fill vacant seats. As a result, `term_start` dates cluster in January but are spread across the year. While we could pick another day, December 31 is a strategy for normalizing around these varying start dates.

The first step is to create a data set that contains a record for each December 31 that each legislator was in office. This can be accomplished by *JOIN*ing the subquery that found the `first_term` to the `legislators_terms` table to find the `term_start` and `term_end` for each term. A second *JOIN* to the `date_dim` retrieves the dates that fall between the start and end dates, restricting the returned values to c.month_name = 'December' and c.day_of_month = 31. The `period` is calculated as the years between the `date` from the `date_dim` and the `first_term`. Note that even though more than 11 months may have elapsed between being sworn in in January and December 31, the first year still appears as 0:

```
SELECT a.id_bioguide, a.first_term
,b.term_start, b.term_end
,c.date
,date_part('year',age(c.date,a.first_term)) as period
FROM
(
    SELECT id_bioguide, min(term_start) as first_term
    FROM legislators_terms
    GROUP BY 1
) a
```

```
JOIN legislators_terms b on a.id_bioguide = b.id_bioguide
LEFT JOIN date_dim c on c.date between b.term_start and b.term_end
and c.month_name = 'December' and c.day_of_month = 31
;

id_bioguide  first_term  term_start  term_end    date        period
-----------  ----------  ----------  ----------  ----------  ------
B000944      1993-01-05  1993-01-05  1995-01-03  1993-12-31  0.0
B000944      1993-01-05  1993-01-05  1995-01-03  1994-12-31  1.0
C000127      1993-01-05  1993-01-05  1995-01-03  1993-12-31  0.0
...          ...         ...         ...         ...         ...
```

If a date dimension is not available, you can create a subquery with
the necessary dates in a couple of ways. If your database supports
the generate_series, you can create a subquery that returns the
desired dates:

```
SELECT generate_series::date as date
FROM generate_series('1770-12-31','2020-12-
31',interval '1 year')
```

You may want to save this as a table or view for later use. Alternatively, you can query the data set or any other table in the database
that has a full set of dates. In this case, the table has all of the necessary years, but we will make a December 31 date for each year
using the make_date function:

```
SELECT distinct
make_date(date_part('year',term_start)::int,12,31)
FROM legislators_terms
```

There are a number of creative ways to get the series of dates
needed. Use whichever method is available and simplest within
your queries.

We now have a row for each date (year end) for which we would like to calculate
retention. The next step is to calculate the cohort_retained for each period, which is
done with a count of id_bioguide. A coalesce function is used on period to set a
default value of 0 when null. This handles the cases in which a legislator's term starts
and ends in the same year, giving credit for serving in that year:

```
SELECT
coalesce(date_part('year',age(c.date,a.first_term)),0) as period
,count(distinct a.id_bioguide) as cohort_retained
FROM
(
    SELECT id_bioguide, min(term_start) as first_term
    FROM legislators_terms
    GROUP BY 1
) a
JOIN legislators_terms b on a.id_bioguide = b.id_bioguide
```

```
LEFT JOIN date_dim c on c.date between b.term_start and b.term_end
and c.month_name = 'December' and c.day_of_month = 31
GROUP BY 1
;

period  cohort_retained
------  ---------------
0.0     12518
1.0     12328
2.0     8166
...     ...
```

The final step is to calculate the cohort_size and pct_retained as we did previously using first_value window functions:

```
SELECT period
,first_value(cohort_retained) over (order by period) as cohort_size
,cohort_retained
,cohort_retained * 1.0 /
 first_value(cohort_retained) over (order by period) as pct_retained
FROM
(
    SELECT coalesce(date_part('year',age(c.date,a.first_term)),0) as period
    ,count(distinct a.id_bioguide) as cohort_retained
    FROM
    (
        SELECT id_bioguide, min(term_start) as first_term
        FROM legislators_terms
        GROUP BY 1
    ) a
    JOIN legislators_terms b on a.id_bioguide = b.id_bioguide
    LEFT JOIN date_dim c on c.date between b.term_start and b.term_end
    and c.month_name = 'December' and c.day_of_month = 31
    GROUP BY 1
) aa
;

period  cohort_size  cohort_retained  pct_retained
------  -----------  ---------------  ------------
0.0     12518        12518            1.0000
1.0     12518        12328            0.9848
2.0     12518        8166             0.6523
...     ...          ...              ...
```

The results, graphed in Figure 4-4, are now much more accurate. Almost all legislators are still in office in year 1, and the first big drop-off occurs in year 2, when some representatives will fail to be reelected.

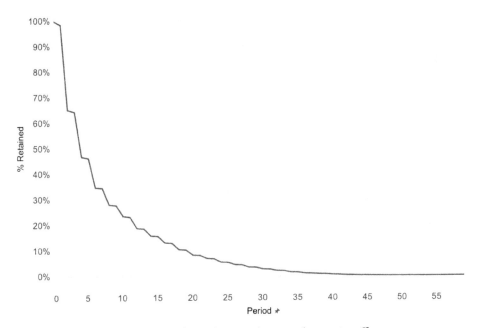

Figure 4-4. Legislator retention after adjusting for actual years in office

If the data set does not contain an end date, there are a couple of options for imputing one. One option is to add a fixed interval to the start date, when the length of a subscription or term is known. This can be done with date math by adding a constant interval to the `term_start`. Here, a CASE statement handles the addition for the two `term_types`:

```
SELECT a.id_bioguide, a.first_term
,b.term_start
,case when b.term_type = 'rep' then b.term_start + interval '2 years'
      when b.term_type = 'sen' then b.term_start + interval '6 years'
      end as term_end
FROM
(
    SELECT id_bioguide, min(term_start) as first_term
    FROM legislators_terms
    GROUP BY 1
) a
JOIN legislators_terms b on a.id_bioguide = b.id_bioguide
;

id_bioguide  first_term  term_start  term_end
-----------  ----------  ----------  ----------
B000944      1993-01-05  1993-01-05  1995-01-05
C000127      1993-01-05  1993-01-05  1995-01-05
```

```
C000141      1987-01-06  1987-01-06  1989-01-06
...           ...         ...         ...
```

This block of code can then be plugged into the retention code to derive the `period` and `pct_retained`. The drawback to this method is that it fails to capture instances in which a legislator did not complete a full term, which can happen in the event of death or appointment to a higher office.

A second option is to use the subsequent starting date, minus one day, as the `term_end` date. This can be calculated with the `lead` window function. This function is similar to the `lag` function we've used previously, but rather than returning a value from a row earlier in the partition, it returns a value from a row later in the partition, as determined in the *ORDER BY* clause. The default is one row, which we will use here, but the function has an optional argument indicating a different number of rows. Here we find the `term_start` date of the subsequent term using `lead` and then subtract the interval '1 day' to derive the `term_end`:

```
SELECT a.id_bioguide, a.first_term
,b.term_start
,lead(b.term_start) over (partition by a.id_bioguide
                          order by b.term_start)
 - interval '1 day' as term_end
FROM
(
    SELECT id_bioguide, min(term_start) as first_term
    FROM legislators_terms
    GROUP BY 1
) a
JOIN legislators_terms b on a.id_bioguide = b.id_bioguide
;

id_bioguide  first_term  term_start  term_end
-----------  ----------  ----------  ----------
A000001      1951-01-03  1951-01-03  (null)
A000002      1947-01-03  1947-01-03  1949-01-02
A000002      1947-01-03  1949-01-03  1951-01-02
...          ...         ...         ...
```

This code block can then be plugged into the retention code. This method has a couple of drawbacks. First, when there is no subsequent term, the `lead` function returns null, leaving that term without a `term_end`. A default value, such as a default interval shown in the last example, could be used in such cases. The second drawback is that this method assumes that terms are always consecutive, with no time spent out of office. Although most legislators tend to serve continuously until their congressional careers end, there are certainly examples of gaps between terms spanning several years.

Any time we make adjustments to fill in missing data, we need to be careful about the assumptions we make. In subscription- or term-based contexts, explicit start and end dates tend to be most accurate. Either of the two other methods shown—adding a fixed interval or setting the end date relative to the next start date—can be used when no end date is present and we have a reasonable expectation that most customers or users will stay for the duration assumed.

Now that we've seen how to calculate a basic retention curve and correct for missing dates, we can start adding in cohort groups. Comparing retention between different groups is one of the main reasons to do cohort analysis. Next, I'll discuss forming groups from the time series itself, and after that, I'll discuss forming cohort groups from data in other tables.

Cohorts Derived from the Time Series Itself

Now that we have SQL code to calculate retention, we can start to split the entities into cohorts. In this section, I will show how to derive cohort groupings from the time series itself. First I'll discuss time-based cohorts based on the first date, and I'll explain how to make cohorts based on other attributes from the time series.

The most common way to create the cohorts is based on the first or minimum date or time that the entity appears in the time series. This means that only one table is necessary for the cohort retention analysis: the time series itself. Cohorting by the first appearance or action is interesting because often groups that start at different times behave differently. For consumer services, early adopters are often more enthusiastic and retain differently than later adopters, whereas in SaaS software, later adopters may retain better because the product is more mature. Time-based cohorts can be grouped by any time granularity that is meaningful to the organization, though weekly, monthly, or yearly cohorts are common. If you're not sure what grouping to use, try running the cohort analysis with different groupings, without making the cohort sizes too small, to see where meaningful patterns emerge. Fortunately, once you know how to construct the cohorts and retention analysis, substituting different time granularities is straightforward.

The first example will use yearly cohorts, and then I will demonstrate swapping in centuries. The key question we will consider is whether the era in which a legislator first took office has any correlation with their retention. Political trends and the public mood do change over time, but by how much?

To calculate yearly cohorts, we first add the year of the `first_term` calculated previously to the query that finds the `period` and `cohort_retained`:

```
SELECT date_part('year',a.first_term) as first_year
,coalesce(date_part('year',age(c.date,a.first_term)),0) as period
,count(distinct a.id_bioguide) as cohort_retained
FROM
(
    SELECT id_bioguide, min(term_start) as first_term
    FROM legislators_terms
```

```
    GROUP BY 1
) a
JOIN legislators_terms b on a.id_bioguide = b.id_bioguide
LEFT JOIN date_dim c on c.date between b.term_start and b.term_end
and c.month_name = 'December' and c.day_of_month = 31
GROUP BY 1,2
;

first_year  period  cohort_retained
----------  ------  ---------------
1789.0      0.0     89
1789.0      2.0     89
1789.0      3.0     57
...         ...     ...
```

This query is then used as the subquery, and the cohort_size and pct_retained are calculated in the outer query as previously. In this case, however, we need a *PARTITION BY* clause that includes first_year so that the first_value is calculated only within the set of rows for that first_year, rather than across the whole result set from the subquery:

```
SELECT first_year, period
,first_value(cohort_retained) over (partition by first_year
                                    order by period) as cohort_size
,cohort_retained
,cohort_retained /
 first_value(cohort_retained) over (partition by first_year
                                    order by period) as pct_retained
FROM
(
    SELECT date_part('year',a.first_term) as first_year
    ,coalesce(date_part('year',age(c.date,a.first_term)),0) as period
    ,count(distinct a.id_bioguide) as cohort_retained
    FROM
    (
        SELECT id_bioguide, min(term_start) as first_term
        FROM legislators_terms
        GROUP BY 1
    ) a
    JOIN legislators_terms b on a.id_bioguide = b.id_bioguide
    LEFT JOIN date_dim c on c.date between b.term_start and b.term_end
    and c.month_name = 'December' and c.day_of_month = 31
    GROUP BY 1,2
) aa
;

first_year  period  cohort_size  cohort_retained  pct_retained
----------  ------  -----------  ---------------  ------------
1789.0      0.0     89           89               1.0000
1789.0      2.0     89           89               1.0000
1789.0      3.0     89           57               0.6404
...         ...     ...          ...              ...
```

This data set includes over two hundred starting years, too many to easily graph or examine in a table. Next we'll look at a less granular interval and cohort the legislators by the century of the first_term. This change is easily made by substituting century for year in the date_part function in subquery aa. Recall that century names are offset from the years they represent, so that the 18th century lasted from 1700 to 1799, the 19th century lasted from 1800 to 1899, and so on. The partitioning in the first_value function changes to the first_century field:

```
SELECT first_century, period
,first_value(cohort_retained) over (partition by first_century
                                    order by period) as cohort_size
,cohort_retained
,cohort_retained /
 first_value(cohort_retained) over (partition by first_century
                                    order by period) as pct_retained
FROM
(
    SELECT date_part('century',a.first_term) as first_century
    ,coalesce(date_part('year',age(c.date,a.first_term)),0) as period
    ,count(distinct a.id_bioguide) as cohort_retained
    FROM
    (
        SELECT id_bioguide, min(term_start) as first_term
        FROM legislators_terms
        GROUP BY 1
    ) a
    JOIN legislators_terms b on a.id_bioguide = b.id_bioguide
    LEFT JOIN date_dim c on c.date between b.term_start and b.term_end
    and c.month_name = 'December' and c.day_of_month = 31
    GROUP BY 1,2
) aa
ORDER BY 1,2
;
```

first_century	period	cohort_size	cohort_retained	pct_retained
18.0	0.0	368	368	1.0000
18.0	1.0	368	360	0.9783
18.0	2.0	368	242	0.6576
...	...	...	...	...

The results are graphed in Figure 4-5. Retention in the early years has been higher for those first elected in the 20th or 21st century. The 21st century is still underway, and thus many of those legislators have not had the opportunity to stay in office for five or more years, though they are still included in the denominator. We might want to consider removing the 21st century from the analysis, but I've left it here to demonstrate how the retention curve drops artificially due to this circumstance.

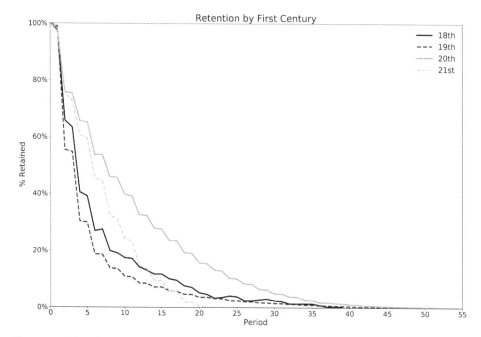

Figure 4-5. Legislator retention by century in which first term began

Cohorts can be defined from other attributes in a time series besides the first date, with options depending on the values in the table. The `legislators_terms` table has a `state` field, indicating which state the person is representing for that term. We can use this to create cohorts, and we will base them on the first state in order to ensure that anyone who has represented multiple states appears in the data only once.

> When cohorting on an attribute that can change over time, it's important to ensure that each entity is assigned only one value. Otherwise the entity may be represented in multiple cohorts, introducing bias into the analysis. Usually the value from the earliest record in the data set is used.

To find the first state for each legislator, we can use the `first_value` window function. In this example, we'll also turn the `min` function into a window function to avoid a lengthy *GROUP BY* clause:

```
SELECT distinct id_bioguide
,min(term_start) over (partition by id_bioguide) as first_term
,first_value(state) over (partition by id_bioguide
                          order by term_start) as first_state
FROM legislators_terms
;
```

```
id_bioguide    first_term    first_state
-----------    ----------    -----------
C000001        1893-08-07    GA
R000584        2009-01-06    ID
W000215        1975-01-14    CA
...            ...           ...
```

We can then plug this code into our retention code to find the retention by first_state:

```
SELECT first_state, period
,first_value(cohort_retained) over (partition by first_state
                                    order by period) as cohort_size
,cohort_retained
,cohort_retained /
 first_value(cohort_retained) over (partition by first_state
                                    order by period) as pct_retained
FROM
(
    SELECT a.first_state
    ,coalesce(date_part('year',age(c.date,a.first_term)),0) as period
    ,count(distinct a.id_bioguide) as cohort_retained
    FROM
    (
        SELECT distinct id_bioguide
        ,min(term_start) over (partition by id_bioguide) as first_term
        ,first_value(state) over (partition by id_bioguide order by term_start)
         as first_state
        FROM legislators_terms
    ) a
    JOIN legislators_terms b on a.id_bioguide = b.id_bioguide
    LEFT JOIN date_dim c on c.date between b.term_start and b.term_end
    and c.month_name = 'December' and c.day_of_month = 31
    GROUP BY 1,2
) aa
;
```

```
first_state    period    cohort_size    cohort_retained    pct_retained
-----------    ------    -----------    ---------------    ------------
AK             0.0       19             19                 1.0000
AK             1.0       19             19                 1.0000
AK             2.0       19             15                 0.7895
...            ...       ...            ...                ...
```

The retention curves for the five states with the highest total number of legislators are graphed in Figure 4-6. Those elected in Illinois and Massachusetts have the highest retention, while New Yorkers have the lowest retention. Determining the reasons why would be an interesting offshoot of this analysis.

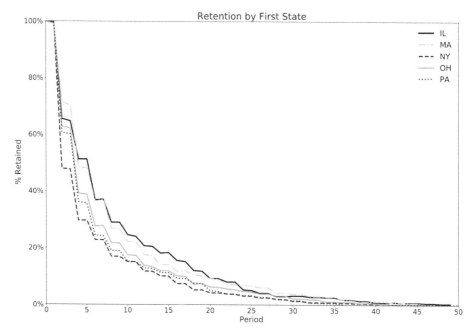

Figure 4-6. Legislator retention by first state: top five states by total legislators

Defining cohorts from the time series is relatively straightforward using a `min` date for each entity and then converting that date into a month, year, or century as appropriate for the analysis. Switching between month and year or other levels of granularity also is straightforward, allowing for multiple options to be tested in order to find a grouping that is meaningful for the organization. Other attributes can be used for cohorting with the `first_value` window function. Next, we'll turn to cases in which the cohorting attribute comes from a table other than that of the time series.

Defining the Cohort from a Separate Table

Often the characteristics that define a cohort exist in a table separate from the one that contains the time series. For example, a database might have a customer table with information such as acquisition source or registration date by which customers can be cohorted. Adding in attributes from other tables, or even subqueries, is relatively straightforward and can be done in retention analysis and related analyses discussed later in the chapter.

For this example, we'll consider whether the gender of the legislator has any impact on their retention. The `legislators` table has a `gender` field, where F means female and M means male, that we can use to cohort the legislators. To do this, we'll *JOIN* the legislators table in as alias d to add gender to the calculation of cohort_retained, in place of year or century:

```
SELECT d.gender
,coalesce(date_part('year',age(c.date,a.first_term)),0) as period
,count(distinct a.id_bioguide) as cohort_retained
FROM
(
    SELECT id_bioguide, min(term_start) as first_term
    FROM legislators_terms
    GROUP BY 1
) a
JOIN legislators_terms b on a.id_bioguide = b.id_bioguide
LEFT JOIN date_dim c on c.date between b.term_start and b.term_end
and c.month_name = 'December' and c.day_of_month = 31
JOIN legislators d on a.id_bioguide = d.id_bioguide
GROUP BY 1,2
;

gender  period  cohort_retained
------  ------  ---------------
F       0.0     366
M       0.0     12152
F       1.0     349
M       1.0     11979
...     ...     ...
```

It's immediately clear that many more males than females have served legislative terms. We can now calculate the percent_retained so we can compare the retention for these groups:

```
SELECT gender, period
,first_value(cohort_retained) over (partition by gender
                                    order by period) as cohort_size
,cohort_retained
,cohort_retained/
 first_value(cohort_retained) over (partition by gender
                                    order by period) as pct_retained
FROM
(
    SELECT d.gender
    ,coalesce(date_part('year',age(c.date,a.first_term)),0) as period
    ,count(distinct a.id_bioguide) as cohort_retained
    FROM
    (
        SELECT id_bioguide, min(term_start) as first_term
        FROM legislators_terms
        GROUP BY 1
    ) a
    JOIN legislators_terms b on a.id_bioguide = b.id_bioguide
    LEFT JOIN date_dim c on c.date between b.term_start and b.term_end
    and c.month_name = 'December' and c.day_of_month = 31
```

```
    JOIN legislators d on a.id_bioguide = d.id_bioguide
    GROUP BY 1,2
) aa
;

gender  period  cohort_size  cohort_retained  pct_retained
------  ------  -----------  ---------------  ------------
F       0.0     366          366              1.0000
M       0.0     12152        12152            1.0000
F       1.0     366          349              0.9536
M       1.0     12152        11979            0.9858
...     ...     ...          ...              ...
```

We can see from the results graphed in Figure 4-7 that retention is higher for female legislators than for their male counterparts for periods 2 through 29. The first female legislator did not take office until 1917, when Jeannette Rankin joined the House as a Republican representative from Montana. As we saw earlier, retention has increased in more recent centuries.

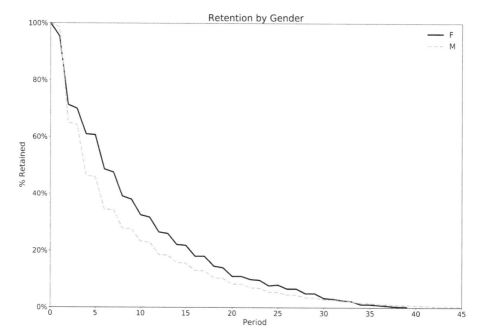

Figure 4-7. Legislator retention by gender

To make a more fair comparison, we might restrict the legislators included in the analysis to only those whose first_term started since there have been women in Congress. We can do this by adding a *WHERE* filter to subquery aa. Here the results are also restricted to those who started before 2000, to ensure the cohorts have had at least 20 possible years to stay in office:

```
SELECT gender, period
,first_value(cohort_retained) over (partition by gender
                                    order by period) as cohort_size
,cohort_retained
,cohort_retained /
 first_value(cohort_retained) over (partition by gender
                                    order by period) as pct_retained
FROM
(
    SELECT d.gender
    ,coalesce(date_part('year',age(c.date,a.first_term)),0) as period
    ,count(distinct a.id_bioguide) as cohort_retained
    FROM
    (
        SELECT id_bioguide, min(term_start) as first_term
        FROM legislators_terms
        GROUP BY 1
    ) a
    JOIN legislators_terms b on a.id_bioguide = b.id_bioguide
    LEFT JOIN date_dim c on c.date between b.term_start and b.term_end
    and c.month_name = 'December' and c.day_of_month = 31
    JOIN legislators d on a.id_bioguide = d.id_bioguide
    WHERE a.first_term between '1917-01-01' and '1999-12-31'
    GROUP BY 1,2
) aa
;
```

gender	period	cohort_size	cohort_retained	pct_retained
F	0.0	200	200	1.0000
M	0.0	3833	3833	1.0000
F	1.0	200	187	0.9350
M	1.0	3833	3769	0.9833
...	...	...	...	...

Male legislators still outnumber female legislators, but by a smaller margin. The retention for the cohorts is graphed in Figure 4-8. With the revised cohorts, male legislators have higher retention through year 7, but starting in year 12, female legislators have higher retention. The difference between the two gender-based cohort analyses underscores the importance of setting up appropriate cohorts and ensuring that they have comparable amounts of time to be present or complete other actions of interest. To further improve this analysis, we could cohort by both starting year or decade *and* gender, in order to control for additional changes in retention through the 20th century and into the 21st century.

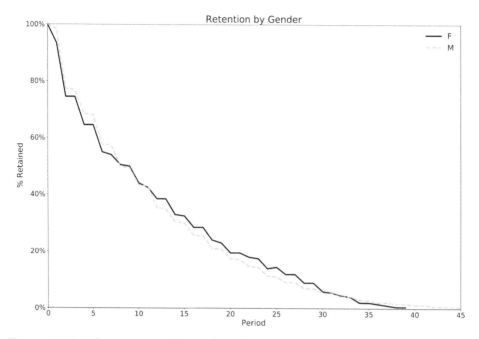

Figure 4-8. Legislator retention by gender: cohorts from 1917 to 1999

Cohorts can be defined in multiple ways, from the time series and from other tables. With the framework we've developed, subqueries, views, or other derived tables can be swapped in, opening up a whole range of calculations to be the basis of a cohort. Multiple criteria, such as starting year and gender, can be used. One caution when dividing populations into cohorts based on multiple criteria is that this can lead to sparse cohorts, where some of the defined groups are too small and are not represented in the data set for all time periods. The next section will discuss methods for overcoming this challenge.

Dealing with Sparse Cohorts

In the ideal data set, every cohort has some action or record in the time series for every period of interest. We've already seen how "missing" dates can occur due to subscriptions or terms lasting over multiple periods, and we looked at how to correct for them using a date dimension to infer intermediate dates. Another issue can arise when, due to grouping criteria, the cohort becomes too small and as a result is represented only sporadically in the data. A cohort may disappear from the result set, when we would prefer it to appear with a zero retention value. This problem is called *sparse cohorts*, and it can be worked around with the careful use of *LEFT JOINs*.

To demonstrate this, let's attempt to cohort female legislators by the first state they represented to see if there are any differences in retention. We've already seen that there have been relatively few female legislators. Cohorting them further by state is highly likely to create some sparse cohorts in which there are very few members. Before making code adjustments, let's add `first_state` (calculated in the section on deriving cohorts from the time series) into our previous gender example and look at the results:

```
SELECT first_state, gender, period
,first_value(cohort_retained) over (partition by first_state, gender
                                    order by period) as cohort_size
,cohort_retained
,cohort_retained /
 first_value(cohort_retained) over (partition by first_state, gender
                                    order by period) as pct_retained
FROM
(
    SELECT a.first_state, d.gender
    ,coalesce(date_part('year',age(c.date,a.first_term)),0) as period
    ,count(distinct a.id_bioguide) as cohort_retained
    FROM
    (
        SELECT distinct id_bioguide
        ,min(term_start) over (partition by id_bioguide) as first_term
        ,first_value(state) over (partition by id_bioguide
                                  order by term_start) as first_state
        FROM legislators_terms
    ) a
    JOIN legislators_terms b on a.id_bioguide = b.id_bioguide
    LEFT JOIN date_dim c on c.date between b.term_start and b.term_end
    and c.month_name = 'December' and c.day_of_month = 31
    JOIN legislators d on a.id_bioguide = d.id_bioguide
    WHERE a.first_term between '1917-01-01' and '1999-12-31'
    GROUP BY 1,2,3
) aa
;
```

first_state	gender	period	cohort_size	cohort_retained	pct_retained
AZ	F	0.0	2	2	1.0000
AZ	M	0.0	26	26	1.0000
AZ	F	1.0	2	2	1.0000
...	...	...	...	...	...

Graphing the results for the first 20 periods, as in Figure 4-9, reveals the sparse cohorts. Alaska did not have any female legislators, while Arizona's female retention curve disappears after year 3. Only California, a large state with many legislators, has complete retention curves for both genders. This pattern repeats for other small and large states.

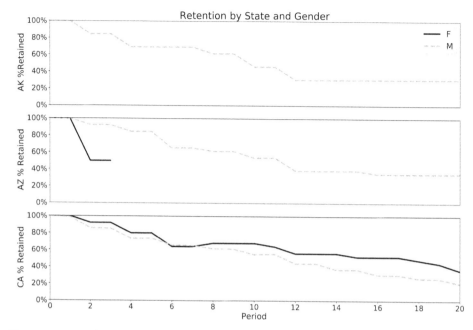

Figure 4-9. Legislator retention by gender and first state

Now let's look at how to ensure a record for every period so that the query returns zero values for retention instead of nulls. The first step is to query for all combinations of `periods` and cohort attributes, in this case `first_state` and `gender`, with the starting `cohort_size` for each combination. This can be done by *JOIN*ing subquery `aa`, which calculates the cohort, with a `generate_series` subquery that returns all integers from 0 to 20, with the criteria on `1 = 1`. This is a handy way to force a Cartesian *JOIN* when the two subqueries don't have any fields in common:

```
SELECT aa.gender, aa.first_state, cc.period, aa.cohort_size
FROM
(
    SELECT b.gender, a.first_state
    ,count(distinct a.id_bioguide) as cohort_size
    FROM
    (
        SELECT distinct id_bioguide
        ,min(term_start) over (partition by id_bioguide) as first_term
        ,first_value(state) over (partition by id_bioguide
                                    order by term_start) as first_state
        FROM legislators_terms
    ) a
    JOIN legislators b on a.id_bioguide = b.id_bioguide
    WHERE a.first_term between '1917-01-01' and '1999-12-31'
    GROUP BY 1,2
```

```
) aa
JOIN
(
    SELECT generate_series as period
    FROM generate_series(0,20,1)
) cc on 1 = 1
;

gender  state  period  cohort
------  -----  ------  ------
F       AL     0       3
F       AL     1       3
F       AL     2       3
...     ...    ...     ...
```

The next step is to *JOIN* this back to the actual periods in office, with a *LEFT JOIN* to ensure all the time periods remain in the final result:

```
SELECT aaa.gender, aaa.first_state, aaa.period, aaa.cohort_size
,coalesce(ddd.cohort_retained,0) as cohort_retained
,coalesce(ddd.cohort_retained,0) / aaa.cohort_size as pct_retained
FROM
(
    SELECT aa.gender, aa.first_state, cc.period, aa.cohort_size
    FROM
    (
        SELECT b.gender, a.first_state
        ,count(distinct a.id_bioguide) as cohort_size
        FROM
        (
            SELECT distinct id_bioguide
            ,min(term_start) over (partition by id_bioguide)
             as first_term
            ,first_value(state) over (partition by id_bioguide
                                order by term_start)
                                as first_state
            FROM legislators_terms
        ) a
        JOIN legislators b on a.id_bioguide = b.id_bioguide
        WHERE a.first_term between '1917-01-01' and '1999-12-31'
        GROUP BY 1,2
    ) aa
    JOIN
    (
        SELECT generate_series as period
        FROM generate_series(0,20,1)
    ) cc on 1 = 1
) aaa
LEFT JOIN
(
    SELECT d.first_state, g.gender
    ,coalesce(date_part('year',age(f.date,d.first_term)),0) as period
    ,count(distinct d.id_bioguide) as cohort_retained
```

```
FROM
(
    SELECT distinct id_bioguide
    ,min(term_start) over (partition by id_bioguide) as first_term
    ,first_value(state) over (partition by id_bioguide
                                  order by term_start) as first_state
    FROM legislators_terms
) d
JOIN legislators_terms e on d.id_bioguide = e.id_bioguide
LEFT JOIN date_dim f on f.date between e.term_start and e.term_end
 and f.month_name = 'December' and f.day_of_month = 31
JOIN legislators g on d.id_bioguide = g.id_bioguide
WHERE d.first_term between '1917-01-01' and '1999-12-31'
GROUP BY 1,2,3
) ddd on aaa.gender = ddd.gender and aaa.first_state = ddd.first_state
and aaa.period = ddd.period
;


gender  first_state  period  cohort_size  cohort_retained  pct_retained
------  -----------  ------  -----------  ---------------  ------------
F       AL           0       3            3                1.0000
F       AL           1       3            1                0.3333
F       AL           2       3            0                0.0000
...     ...          ...     ...          ...              ...
```

We can then pivot the results and confirm that a value exists for each cohort for each period:

```
gender  first_state  yr0     yr2     yr4     yr6     yr8     yr10
------  -----------  -----   ------  ------  ------  ------  ------
F       AL           1.000   0.0000  0.0000  0.0000  0.0000  0.0000
F       AR           1.000   0.8000  0.2000  0.4000  0.4000  0.4000
F       CA           1.000   0.9200  0.8000  0.6400  0.6800  0.6800
...     ...          ...     ...     ...     ...     ...     ...
```

Notice that at this point, the SQL code has gotten quite long. One of the harder parts of writing SQL for cohort retention analysis is keeping all of the logic straight and the code organized, a topic I'll discuss more in Chapter 8. When building up retention code, I find it helpful to go step-by-step, checking results along the way. I also spot-check individual cohorts to validate that the final result is accurate.

Cohorts can be defined in many ways. So far, we've normalized all our cohorts to the first date they appear in the time series data. This isn't the only option, however, and interesting analysis can be done starting in the middle of an entity's life span. Before concluding our work on retention analysis, let's take a look at this additional way to define cohorts.

Defining Cohorts from Dates Other Than the First Date

Usually time-based cohorts are defined from the entity's first appearance in the time series or from some other earliest date, such as a registration date. However, cohorting on a different date can be useful and insightful. For example, we might want to look at retention across all customers using a service as of a particular date. This type of analysis can be used to understand whether product or marketing changes have had a long-term impact on existing customers.

When using a date other than the first date, we need to take care to precisely define the criteria for inclusion in each cohort. One option is to pick entities present on a particular calendar date. This is relatively straightforward to put into SQL code, but it can be problematic if a large share of the regular user population doesn't show up every day, causing retention to vary depending on the exact day chosen. One option to correct for this is to calculate retention for several starting dates and then average the results.

Another option is to use a window of time such as a week or month. Any entity that appears in the data set during that window is included in the cohort. While this approach is often more representative of the business or process, the trade-off is that the SQL code will become more complex, and the query time may be slower due to more intense database calculations. Finding the right balance between query performance and accuracy of results is something of an art.

Let's take a look at how to calculate such midstream analysis with the legislators data set by considering retention for legislators who were in office in the year 2000. We'll cohort by the `term_type`, which has values of "sen" for senators and "rep" for representatives. The definition will include any legislator in office at any time during the year 2000: those who started prior to 2000 and whose terms ended during or after 2000 qualify, as do those who started a term in 2000. We can hardcode any date in 2000 as the `first_term`, since we will later check whether they were in office at some point during 2000. The `min_start` of the terms falling in this window is also calculated for use in a later step:

```
SELECT distinct id_bioguide, term_type, date('2000-01-01') as first_term
,min(term_start) as min_start
FROM legislators_terms
WHERE term_start <= '2000-12-31' and term_end >= '2000-01-01'
GROUP BY 1,2,3
;

id_bioguide  term_type  first_term  min_start
-----------  ---------  ----------  ---------
C000858      sen        2000-01-01  1997-01-07
G000333      sen        2000-01-01  1995-01-04
M000350      rep        2000-01-01  1999-01-06
...          ...        ...         ...
```

We can then plug this into our retention code, with two adjustments. First, an additional *JOIN* criteria between subquery a and the legislators_terms table is added in order to return only terms that started on or after the min_start date. Second, an additional filter is added to the date_dim so that it only returns dates in 2000 or later:

```
SELECT term_type, period
,first_value(cohort_retained) over (partition by term_type order by period)
 as cohort_size
,cohort_retained
,cohort_retained /
 first_value(cohort_retained) over (partition by term_type order by period)
 as pct_retained
FROM
(
    SELECT a.term_type
    ,coalesce(date_part('year',age(c.date,a.first_term)),0) as period
    ,count(distinct a.id_bioguide) as cohort_retained
    FROM
    (
        SELECT distinct id_bioguide, term_type
        ,date('2000-01-01') as first_term
        ,min(term_start) as min_start
        FROM legislators_terms
        WHERE term_start <= '2000-12-31' and term_end >= '2000-01-01'
        GROUP BY 1,2,3
    ) a
    JOIN legislators_terms b on a.id_bioguide = b.id_bioguide
    and b.term_start >= a.min_start
    LEFT JOIN date_dim c on c.date between b.term_start and b.term_end
    and c.month_name = 'December' and c.day_of_month = 31
    and c.year >= 2000
    GROUP BY 1,2
) aa
;
```

term_type	period	cohort_size	cohort_retained	pct_retained
rep	0.0	440	440	1.0000
sen	0.0	101	101	1.0000
rep	1.0	440	392	0.8909
sen	1.0	101	89	0.8812
...	...	...	...	...

Figure 4-10 shows that despite longer terms for senators, retention among the two cohorts was similar, and was actually worse for senators after 10 years. A further analysis comparing the different years they were first elected, or other cohort attributes, might yield some interesting insights.

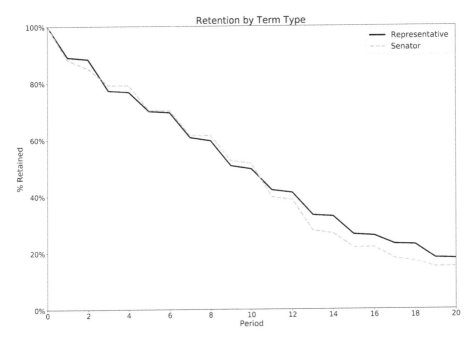

Figure 4-10. Retention by term type for legislators in office during the year 2000

A common use case for cohorting on a value other than a starting value is when trying to analyze retention after an entity has reached a threshold, such as a certain number of purchases or a certain amount spent. As with any cohort, it's important to take care in defining what qualifies an entity to be in a cohort and which date will be used as the starting date.

Cohort retention is a powerful way to understand the behavior of entities in a time series data set. We've seen how to calculate retention with SQL and how to cohort based on the time series itself or on other tables, and from points in the middle of entity life span. We also looked at how to use functions and *JOIN*s to adjust dates within time series and compensate for sparse cohorts. There are several types of analyses that are related to cohort retention: analysis, survivorship, returnship, and cumulative calculations, all of which build off of the SQL code that we've developed for retention. Let's turn to them next.

Related Cohort Analyses

In the last section, we learned how to write SQL for cohort retention analysis. Retention captures whether an entity was in a time series data set on a specific date or window of time. In addition to presence on a specific date, analysis is often interested in questions of how long an entity lasted, whether an entity did multiple actions, and how many of those actions occurred. These can all be answered with code that is similar to retention and is well suited to just about any cohorting criteria you like. Let's take a look at the first of these, survivorship.

Survivorship

Survivorship, also called *survival analysis*, is concerned with questions about how long something lasts, or the duration of time until a particular event such as churn or death. Survivorship analysis can answer questions about the share of the population that is likely to remain past a certain amount of time. Cohorts can help identify or at least provide hypotheses about which characteristics or circumstances increase or decrease the survival likelihood.

This is similar to a retention analysis, but instead of calculating whether an entity was present in a certain period, we calculate whether the entity is present in that period or later in the time series. Then the share of the total cohort is calculated. Typically one or more periods are chosen depending on the nature of the data set analyzed. For example, if we want to know the share of game players who survive for a week or longer, we can check for actions that occur after a week from starting and consider those players still surviving. On the other hand, if we are concerned about the number of students who are still in school after a certain number of years, we could look for the absence of a graduation event in a data set. The number of periods can be *SELECT*ed either by calculating an average or typical life span or by choosing time periods that are meaningful to the organization or process analyzed, such as a month, year, or longer time period.

In this example, we'll look at the share of legislators who survived in office for a decade or more after their first term started. Since we don't need to know the specific dates of each term, we can start by calculating the first and last `term_start` dates, using `min` and `max` aggregations:

```
SELECT id_bioguide
,min(term_start) as first_term
,max(term_start) as last_term
FROM legislators_terms
GROUP BY 1
;

id_bioguide   first_term   last_term
-----------   ----------   ---------
A000118       1975-01-14   1977-01-04
P000281       1933-03-09   1937-01-05
K000039       1933-03-09   1951-01-03
...           ...          ...
```

Next, we add to the query a `date_part` function to find the century of the `min` `term_start`, and we calculate the `tenure` as the number of years between the `min` and `max` `term_starts` found with the `age` function:

```
SELECT id_bioguide
,date_part('century',min(term_start)) as first_century
,min(term_start) as first_term
,max(term_start) as last_term
,date_part('year',age(max(term_start),min(term_start))) as tenure
FROM legislators_terms
GROUP BY 1
;
```

```
id_bioguide  first_century  first_term  last_term   tenure
-----------  -------------  ----------  ----------  ------
A000118      20.0           1975-01-14  1977-01-04  1.0
P000281      20.0           1933-03-09  1937-01-05  3.0
K000039      20.0           1933-03-09  1951-01-03  17.0
...          ...            ...         ...         ...
```

Finally, we calculate the `cohort_size` with a `count` of all the legislators, as well as calculating the number who survived for at least 10 years by using a CASE statement and `count` aggregation. The percent who survived is found by dividing these two values:

```
SELECT first_century
,count(distinct id_bioguide) as cohort_size
,count(distinct case when tenure >= 10 then id_bioguide
                end) as survived_10
,count(distinct case when tenure >= 10 then id_bioguide end)
 / count(distinct id_bioguide) as pct_survived_10
FROM
(
    SELECT id_bioguide
    ,date_part('century',min(term_start)) as first_century
    ,min(term_start) as first_term
    ,max(term_start) as last_term
    ,date_part('year',age(max(term_start),min(term_start))) as tenure
    FROM legislators_terms
    GROUP BY 1
) a
GROUP BY 1
;
```

```
century  cohort  survived_10  pct_survived_10
-------  ------  -----------  ---------------
18       368     83           0.2255
19       6299    892          0.1416
20       5091    1853         0.3640
21       760     119          0.1566
```

Since terms may or may not be consecutive, we can also calculate the share of legislators in each century who survived for five or more total terms. In the subquery, add a count to find the total number of terms per legislator. Then in the outer query, divide the number of legislators with five or more terms by the total cohort size:

```
SELECT first_century
,count(distinct id_bioguide) as cohort_size
,count(distinct case when total_terms >= 5 then id_bioguide end)
 as survived_5
,count(distinct case when total_terms >= 5 then id_bioguide end)
 / count(distinct id_bioguide) as pct_survived_5_terms
FROM
(
    SELECT id_bioguide
    ,date_part('century',min(term_start)) as first_century
    ,count(term_start) as total_terms
    FROM legislators_terms
    GROUP BY 1
) a
GROUP BY 1
;
```

century	cohort	survived_5	pct_survived_5_terms
18	368	63	0.1712
19	6299	711	0.1129
20	5091	2153	0.4229
21	760	205	0.2697

Ten years or five terms is somewhat arbitrary. We can also calculate the survivorship for each number of years or periods and display the results in graph or table form. Here, we calculate the survivorship for each number of terms from 1 to 20. This is accomplished through a Cartesian *JOIN* to a subquery that contains those integers derived by the `generate_series` function:

```
SELECT a.first_century, b.terms
,count(distinct id_bioguide) as cohort
,count(distinct case when a.total_terms >= b.terms then id_bioguide
                end) as cohort_survived
,count(distinct case when a.total_terms >= b.terms then id_bioguide
                end)
 / count(distinct id_bioguide) as pct_survived
FROM
(
    SELECT id_bioguide
    ,date_part('century',min(term_start)) as first_century
    ,count(term_start) as total_terms
    FROM legislators_terms
    GROUP BY 1
) a
JOIN
```

```
(
    SELECT generate_series as terms
    FROM generate_series(1,20,1)
) b on 1 = 1
GROUP BY 1,2
;

century  terms  cohort  cohort_survived  pct_survived
-------  -----  ------  ---------------  ------------
18       1      368     368              1.0000
18       2      368     249              0.6766
18       3      368     153              0.4157
...      ...    ...     ...              ...
```

The results are graphed in Figure 4-11. Survivorship was highest in the 20th century, a result that agrees with results we saw previously in which retention was also highest in the 20th century.

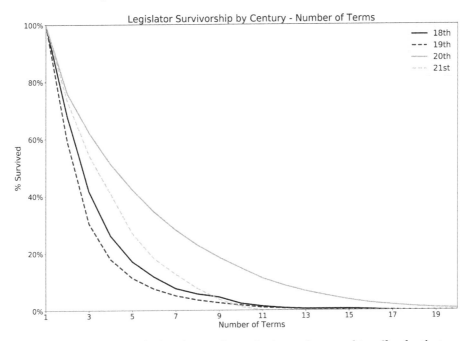

Figure 4-11. Survivorship for legislators: share of cohort who stayed in office for that many terms or longer

Survivorship is closely related to retention. While retention counts entities present in a specific number of periods from the start, survivorship considers only whether an entity was present as of a specific period or later. As a result, the code is simpler since it needs only the first and last dates in the time series, or a count of dates. Cohorting is done similar to cohorting for retention, and cohort definitions can come from within the time series or be derived from another table or subquery.

Next we'll consider another type of analysis that is in some ways the inverse of survivorship. Rather than calculating whether an entity is present in the data set at a certain time or later, we will calculate whether an entity returns or repeats an action at a certain period or earlier. This is called returnship or repeat purchase behavior.

Returnship, or Repeat Purchase Behavior

Survivorship is useful for understanding how long a cohort is likely to stick around. Another useful type of cohort analysis seeks to understand whether a cohort member can be expected to return within a given window of time and the intensity of activity during that window. This is called *returnship* or *repeat purchase behavior*.

For example, an ecommerce site might want to know not only how many new buyers were acquired via a marketing campaign but also whether those buyers have become repeat buyers. One way to figure this out is to simply calculate total purchases per customer. However, comparing customers acquired two years ago with those acquired a month ago isn't fair, since the former have had a much longer time in which to return. The older cohort would almost certainly appear more valuable than the newer one. Although this is true in a sense, it gives an incomplete picture of how the cohorts are likely to behave across their entire life span.

To make fair comparisons between cohorts with different starting dates, we need to create an analysis based on a *time box*, or a fixed window of time from the first date, and consider whether cohort members returned within that window. This way, every cohort has an equal amount of time under consideration, so long as we include only those cohorts for which the full window has elapsed. Returnship analysis is common for retail organizations, but it can also be applied in other domains. For example, a university might want to see how many students enrolled in a second course, or a hospital might be interested in how many patients need follow-up medical treatments after an initial incident.

To demonstrate returnship analysis, we can ask a new question of the legislators data set: how many legislators have more than one term type, and specifically, what share of them start as representatives and go on to become senators (some senators later become representatives, but that is much less common). Since relatively few make this transition, we'll cohort legislators by the century in which they first became a representative.

The first step is to find the cohort size for each century, using the subquery and date_part calculations seen previously, for only those with term_type = 'rep':

```
SELECT date_part('century',a.first_term) as cohort_century
,count(id_bioguide) as reps
```

```
FROM
(
    SELECT id_bioguide, min(term_start) as first_term
    FROM legislators_terms
    WHERE term_type = 'rep'
    GROUP BY 1
) a
GROUP BY 1
;

cohort_century  reps
--------------  ----
18              299
19              5773
20              4481
21              683
```

Next we'll perform a similar calculation, with a *JOIN* to the `legislators_terms` table, to find the representatives who later became senators. This is accomplished with the clauses `b.term_type = 'sen'` and `b.term_start > a.first_term`:

```
SELECT date_part('century',a.first_term) as cohort_century
,count(distinct a.id_bioguide) as rep_and_sen
FROM
(
    SELECT id_bioguide, min(term_start) as first_term
    FROM legislators_terms
    WHERE term_type = 'rep'
    GROUP BY 1
) a
JOIN legislators_terms b on a.id_bioguide = b.id_bioguide
and b.term_type = 'sen' and b.term_start > a.first_term
GROUP BY 1
;

cohort_century  rep_and_sen
--------------  -----------
18              57
19              329
20              254
21              25
```

Finally, we *JOIN* these two subqueries together and calculate the percent of representatives who became senators. A *LEFT JOIN* is used; this clause is typically recommended to ensure that all cohorts are included whether or not the subsequent event happened. If there is a century in which no representatives became senators, we still want to include that century in the result set:

```
SELECT aa.cohort_century
,bb.rep_and_sen / aa.reps as pct_rep_and_sen
FROM
(
```

```
SELECT date_part('century',a.first_term) as cohort_century
,count(id_bioguide) as reps
FROM
(
    SELECT id_bioguide, min(term_start) as first_term
    FROM legislators_terms
    WHERE term_type = 'rep'
    GROUP BY 1
) a
GROUP BY 1
) aa
LEFT JOIN
(
    SELECT date_part('century',b.first_term) as cohort_century
    ,count(distinct b.id_bioguide) as rep_and_sen
    FROM
    (
        SELECT id_bioguide, min(term_start) as first_term
        FROM legislators_terms
        WHERE term_type = 'rep'
        GROUP BY 1
    ) b
    JOIN legislators_terms c on b.id_bioguide = b.id_bioguide
    and c.term_type = 'sen' and c.term_start > b.first_term
    GROUP BY 1
) bb on aa.cohort_century = bb.cohort_century
;

cohort_century  pct_rep_and_sen
--------------  ---------------
18              0.1906
19              0.0570
20              0.0567
21              0.0366
```

Representatives from the 18th century were most likely to become senators. However, we have not yet applied a time box to ensure a fair comparison. While we can safely assume that all legislators who served in the 18th and 19th centuries are no longer living, many of those who were first elected in the 20th and 21st centuries are still in the middle of their careers. Adding the filter WHERE age(c.term_start, b.first_term) <= interval '10 years' to subquery bb creates a time box of 10 years. Note that the window can easily be made larger or smaller by changing the constant in the interval. An additional filter applied to subquery a, WHERE first_term <= '2009-12-31', excludes those who were less than 10 years into their careers when the data set was assembled:

```
SELECT aa.cohort_century
,bb.rep_and_sen * 100.0 / aa.reps as pct_10_yrs
FROM
(
    SELECT date_part('century',a.first_term)::int as cohort_century
```

```
        ,count(id_bioguide) as reps
        FROM
        (
            SELECT id_bioguide, min(term_start) as first_term
            FROM legislators_terms
            WHERE term_type = 'rep'
            GROUP BY 1
        ) a
        WHERE first_term <= '2009-12-31'
        GROUP BY 1
) aa
LEFT JOIN
(
    SELECT date_part('century',b.first_term)::int as cohort_century
    ,count(distinct b.id_bioguide) as rep_and_sen
    FROM
    (
        SELECT id_bioguide, min(term_start) as first_term
        FROM legislators_terms
        WHERE term_type = 'rep'
        GROUP BY 1
    ) b
    JOIN legislators_terms c on b.id_bioguide = c.id_bioguide
    and c.term_type = 'sen' and c.term_start > b.first_term
    WHERE age(c.term_start, b.first_term) <= interval '10 years'
    GROUP BY 1
) bb on aa.cohort_century = bb.cohort_century
;


Cohort_century  pct_10_yrs
--------------  ----------
18              0.0970
19              0.0244
20              0.0348
21              0.0764
```

With this new adjustment, the 18th century still had the highest share of representatives becoming senators within 10 years, but the 21st century has the second-highest share, and the 20th century had a higher share than the 19th.

Since 10 years is somewhat arbitrary, we might also want to compare several time windows. One option is to run the query several times with different intervals and note the results. Another option is to calculate multiple windows in the same result set by using a set of CASE statements inside of count distinct aggregations to form the intervals, rather than specifying the interval in the *WHERE* clause:

```
SELECT aa.cohort_century
,bb.rep_and_sen_5_yrs * 1.0 / aa.reps as pct_5_yrs
,bb.rep_and_sen_10_yrs * 1.0 / aa.reps as pct_10_yrs
,bb.rep_and_sen_15_yrs * 1.0 / aa.reps as pct_15_yrs
FROM
(
```

```
SELECT date_part('century',a.first_term) as cohort_century
,count(id_bioguide) as reps
FROM
(
    SELECT id_bioguide, min(term_start) as first_term
    FROM legislators_terms
    WHERE term_type = 'rep'
    GROUP BY 1
) a
WHERE first_term <= '2009-12-31'
GROUP BY 1
) aa
LEFT JOIN
(
    SELECT date_part('century',b.first_term) as cohort_century
    ,count(distinct case when age(c.term_start,b.first_term)
                        <= interval '5 years'
                    then b.id_bioguide end) as rep_and_sen_5_yrs
    ,count(distinct case when age(c.term_start,b.first_term)
                        <= interval '10 years'
                    then b.id_bioguide end) as rep_and_sen_10_yrs
    ,count(distinct case when age(c.term_start,b.first_term)
                        <= interval '15 years'
                    then b.id_bioguide end) as rep_and_sen_15_yrs
    FROM
    (
        SELECT id_bioguide, min(term_start) as first_term
        FROM legislators_terms
        WHERE term_type = 'rep'
        GROUP BY 1
    ) b
    JOIN legislators_terms c on b.id_bioguide = c.id_bioguide
    and c.term_type = 'sen' and c.term_start > b.first_term
    GROUP BY 1
) bb on aa.cohort_century = bb.cohort_century
;

cohort_century  pct_5_yrs  pct_10_yrs  pct_15_yrs
--------------  ---------  ----------  ----------
18              0.0502     0.0970      0.1438
19              0.0088     0.0244      0.0409
20              0.0100     0.0348      0.0478
21              0.0400     0.0764      0.0873
```

With this output, we can see how the share of representatives who became senators evolved over time, both within each cohort and across cohorts. In addition to the table format, graphing the output often reveals interesting trends. In Figure 4-12, the cohorts based on century are replaced with cohorts based on the first decade, and the trends over 10 and 20 years are shown. Conversion of representatives to senators during the first few decades of the new US legislature was clearly different from patterns in the years since.

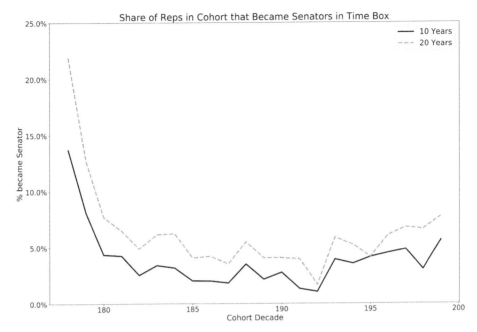

Figure 4-12. Trend of the share of representatives for each cohort, defined by starting decade, who later became senators

Finding the repeat behavior within a fixed time box is a useful tool for comparing cohorts. This is particularly true when the behaviors are intermittent in nature, such as purchase behavior or content or service consumption. In the next section, we'll look at how to calculate not only whether an entity had a subsequent action but also how many subsequent actions they had, and we'll aggregate them with cumulative calculations.

Cumulative Calculations

Cumulative cohort analysis can be used to establish *cumulative lifetime value*, also called *customer lifetime value* (the acronyms CLTV and LTV are used interchangeably), and to monitor newer cohorts in order to be able to predict what their full LTV will be. This is possible because early behavior is often highly correlated with long-term behavior. Users of a service who return frequently in their first days or weeks of using it tend to be the most likely to stay around over the long term. Customers who buy a second or third time early on are likely to continue purchasing over a longer time period. Subscribers who renew after the first month or year are often likely to stick around over many subsequent months or years.

In this section, I'll mainly talk about the revenue-generating activities of customers, but this analysis can also be applied to situations in which customers or entities incur costs, such as through product returns, support interactions, or use of health-care services.

With cumulative calculations, we're less concerned about whether an entity did an action on a particular date and more about the total as of a particular date. The cumulative calculations used in this type of analysis are most often counts or sums. We will again use the time box concept to ensure apples-to-apples comparisons between cohorts. Let's look at the number of terms started within 10 years of the first term_start, cohorting the legislators by century and type of first term:

```
SELECT date_part('century',a.first_term) as century
,first_type
,count(distinct a.id_bioguide) as cohort
,count(b.term_start) as terms
FROM
(
    SELECT distinct id_bioguide
    ,first_value(term_type) over (partition by id_bioguide
                                  order by term_start) as first_type
    ,min(term_start) over (partition by id_bioguide) as first_term
    ,min(term_start) over (partition by id_bioguide)
    + interval '10 years' as first_plus_10
    FROM legislators_terms
) a
LEFT JOIN legislators_terms b on a.id_bioguide = b.id_bioguide
and b.term_start between a.first_term and a.first_plus_10
GROUP BY 1,2
;
```

century	first_type	cohort	terms
18	rep	297	760
18	sen	71	101
19	rep	5744	12165
19	sen	555	795
20	rep	4473	16203
20	sen	618	1008
21	rep	683	2203
21	sen	77	118

The largest cohort is that of representatives first elected in the 19th century, but the cohort with the largest number of terms started within 10 years is that of representatives first elected in the 20th century. This type of calculation can be useful for understanding the overall contribution of a cohort to an organization. Total sales or total repeat purchases can be valuable metrics. Usually, though, we want to normalize to understand the contribution on a per-entity basis. Calculations we might want to make include average actions per person, average order value (AOV), items per order, and orders per customer. To normalize by the cohort size, simply divide by the starting cohort, which we've done previously with retention, survivorship, and returnship. Here we do that and also pivot the results into table form for easier comparisons:

```
SELECT century
,max(case when first_type = 'rep' then cohort end) as rep_cohort
,max(case when first_type = 'rep' then terms_per_leg end)
 as avg_rep_terms
,max(case when first_type = 'sen' then cohort end) as sen_cohort
,max(case when first_type = 'sen' then terms_per_leg end)
 as avg_sen_terms
FROM
(
    SELECT date_part('century',a.first_term) as century
    ,first_type
    ,count(distinct a.id_bioguide) as cohort
    ,count(b.term_start) as terms
    ,count(b.term_start)
     / count(distinct a.id_bioguide) as terms_per_leg
    FROM
    (
        SELECT distinct id_bioguide
        ,first_value(term_type) over (partition by id_bioguide
                                      order by term_start
                                      ) as first_type
        ,min(term_start) over (partition by id_bioguide) as first_term
        ,min(term_start) over (partition by id_bioguide)
         + interval '10 years' as first_plus_10
        FROM legislators_terms
    ) a
    LEFT JOIN legislators_terms b on a.id_bioguide = b.id_bioguide
    and b.term_start between a.first_term and a.first_plus_10
    GROUP BY 1,2
) aa
GROUP BY 1
;
```

century	rep_cohort	avg_rep_terms	sen_cohort	avg_sen_terms
18	297	2.6	71	1.4
19	5744	2.1	555	1.4
20	4473	3.6	618	1.6
21	683	3.2	77	1.5

With the cumulative terms normalized by the cohort size, we can now confirm that representatives first elected in the 20th century had the highest average number of terms, while those who started in the 19th century had the fewest number of terms on average. Senators have fewer but longer terms than their representative peers, and again those who started in the 20th century have had the highest number of terms on average.

Cumulative calculations are often used in customer lifetime value calculations. LTV is usually calculated using monetary measures, such as total dollars spent by a customer, or the gross margin (revenue minus costs) generated by a customer across their lifetime. To facilitate comparisons between cohorts, the "lifetime" is often chosen to reflect average customer lifetime, or periods that are convenient to analyze, such as 3, 5, or 10 years. The legislators data set doesn't contain financial metrics, but swapping in dollar values in any of the preceding SQL code would be straightforward. Fortunately, SQL is a flexible enough language that we can adapt these templates to address a wide variety of analytical questions.

Cohort analysis includes a set of techniques that can be used to answer questions related to behavior over time and how various attributes may contribute to differences between groups. Survivorship, returnship, and cumulative calculations all shed light on these questions. With a good understanding of how cohorts behave, we often have to turn our attention back to the composition or mix of cohorts over time, understanding how that can impact total retention, survivorship, returnship, or cumulative values such that these measures differ surprisingly from the individual cohorts.

Cross-Section Analysis, Through a Cohort Lens

So far in this chapter, we've been looking at cohort analysis. We've followed the behavior of cohorts across time with retention, survivorship, returnship, and cumulative behavior analyses. One of the challenges with these analyses, however, is that even as they make changes within cohorts easy to spot, it can be difficult to spot changes in the overall composition of a customer or user base.

Mix shifts, which are changes in the composition of the customer or user base over time, can also occur, making later cohorts different from earlier ones. Mix shifts may be due to international expansion, shifting between organic and paid acquisition strategies, or moving from a niche enthusiast audience to a broader mass market one. Creating additional cohorts, or segments, along any of these suspected lines can help diagnose whether a mix shift is happening.

Cohort analysis can be contrasted with cross-sectional analysis, which compares individuals or groups at a single point in time. Cross-sectional studies can correlate years of education with current income, for example. On the positive side, collecting data sets for cross-sectional analysis is often easier since no time series is necessary. Cross-sectional analysis can be insightful, generating hypotheses for further investigation. On the negative side, a form of selection bias called survivorship bias usually exists, which can lead to false conclusions.

Survivorship Bias

"Let's look at our best customers and see what they have in common." This seemingly innocent and well-intentioned idea can lead to some very problematic conclusions. *Survivorship bias* is the logical error of focusing on the people or things that made it past some selection process, while ignoring those that did not. Commonly this is because the entities no longer exist in the data set at the time of selection, because they have failed, churned, or left the population for some other reason. Concentrating only on the remaining population can lead to overly optimistic conclusions, because failures are ignored.

Much has been written about a few people who dropped out of college and started wildly successful technology companies. This doesn't mean you should immediately leave college, since the vast majority of people who drop out do not go on to be successful CEOs. That part of the population doesn't make for nearly as sensational headlines, so it's easy to forget about that reality.

In the successful customer context, survivorship bias might show up as an observation that the best customers tend to live in California or Texas and tend to be 18 to 30 years old. This is a large population to start with, and it may turn out that these characteristics are shared by many customers who churned prior to the analysis date. Going back to the original population might reveal that other demographics, such as 41-to-50-year-olds in Vermont, actually stick around and spend more over time, even though there are fewer of them in absolute terms. Cohort analysis helps distinguish and reduce survivorship bias.

Cohort analysis is a way to overcome survivorship bias by including all members of a starting cohort in the analysis. We can take a series of cross sections from a cohort analysis to understand how the mix of entities may have changed over time. On any given date, users from a variety of cohorts are present. We can use cross-sectional analysis to examine them, like layers of sediment, to reveal new insights. In the next example, we'll create a time series of the share of legislators from each cohort for each year in the data set.

The first step is to find the number of legislators in office each year by *JOIN*ing the legislators table to the date_dim, *WHERE* the date from the date_dim is between the start and end dates of each term. Here we use December 31 for each year to find the legislators in office at each year's end:

```
SELECT b.date, count(distinct a.id_bioguide) as legislators
FROM legislators_terms a
JOIN date_dim b on b.date between a.term_start and a.term_end
and b.month_name = 'December' and b.day_of_month = 31
and b.year <= 2019
GROUP BY 1
;
```

```
date        legislators
----------  -----------
1789-12-31  89
1790-12-31  95
1791-12-31  99
...         ...
```

Next, we add in the century cohorting criteria by *JOIN*ing to a subquery with the first_term calculated:

```
SELECT b.date
,date_part('century',first_term) as century
,count(distinct a.id_bioguide) as legislators
FROM legislators_terms a
JOIN date_dim b on b.date between a.term_start and a.term_end
 and b.month_name = 'December' and b.day_of_month = 31
 and b.year <= 2019
JOIN
(
    SELECT id_bioguide, min(term_start) as first_term
    FROM legislators_terms
    GROUP BY 1
) c on a.id_bioguide = c.id_bioguide
GROUP BY 1,2
;

date        century legislators
----------  ------- -----------
1789-12-31  18      89
1790-12-31  18      95
1791-12-31  18      99
...         ...     ...
```

Finally, we calculate the percent of total legislators in each year that the century cohort represents. This can be done in a couple of ways, depending on the shape of output desired. The first way is to keep a row for each date and century combination and use a sum window function in the denominator of the percentage calculation:

```
SELECT date
,century
,legislators
,sum(legislators) over (partition by date) as cohort
,legislators / sum(legislators) over (partition by date)
 as pct_century
FROM
(
    SELECT b.date
    ,date_part('century',first_term) as century
    ,count(distinct a.id_bioguide) as legislators
    FROM legislators_terms a
    JOIN date_dim b on b.date between a.term_start and a.term_end
```

```
    and b.month_name = 'December' and b.day_of_month = 31
    and b.year <= 2019
    JOIN
    (
        SELECT id_bioguide, min(term_start) as first_term
        FROM legislators_terms
        GROUP BY 1
    ) c on a.id_bioguide = c.id_bioguide
    GROUP BY 1,2
) a
;
```

```
date        century  legislators  cohort  pct_century
----------  -------  -----------  ------  -----------
2018-12-31  20       122          539     0.2263
2018-12-31  21       417          539     0.7737
2019-12-31  20       97           537     0.1806
2019-12-31  21       440          537     0.8194
...         ...      ...          ...     ...
```

The second approach results in one row per year, with a column for each century, a table format that may be easier to scan for trends:

```
SELECT date
,coalesce(sum(case when century = 18 then legislators end)
        / sum(legislators),0) as pct_18
,coalesce(sum(case when century = 19 then legislators end)
        / sum(legislators),0) as pct_19
,coalesce(sum(case when century = 20 then legislators end)
        / sum(legislators),0) as pct_20
,coalesce(sum(case when century = 21 then legislators end)
        / sum(legislators),0) as pct_21
FROM
(
    SELECT b.date
    ,date_part('century',first_term) as century
    ,count(distinct a.id_bioguide) as legislators
    FROM legislators_terms a
    JOIN date_dim b on b.date between a.term_start and a.term_end
     and b.month_name = 'December' and b.day_of_month = 31
     and b.year <= 2019
    JOIN
    (
        SELECT id_bioguide, min(term_start) as first_term
        FROM legislators_terms
        GROUP BY 1
    ) c on a.id_bioguide = c.id_bioguide
    GROUP BY 1,2
) aa
GROUP BY 1
;
```

date	pct_18	pct_19	pct_20	pct_21
2017-12-31	0	0	0.2305	0.7695
2018-12-31	0	0	0.2263	0.7737
2019-12-31	0	0	0.1806	0.8193
...	...	...	...	...

We can graph the output, as in Figure 4-13, to see how newer cohorts of legislators gradually overtake older cohorts, until they themselves are replaced by new cohorts.

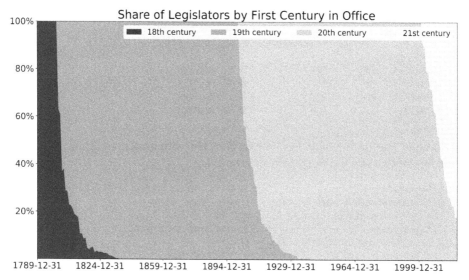

Figure 4-13. Percent of legislators each year, by century first elected

Rather than cohorting on `first_term`, we can cohort on tenure instead. Finding the share of customers who are relatively new, are of medium tenure, or are long-term customers at various points in time can be insightful. Let's take a look at how the tenure of legislators in Congress has changed over time.

The first step is to calculate, for each year, the cumulative number of years in office for each legislator. Since there can be gaps between terms when legislators are voted out or leave office for other reasons, we'll first find each year in which the legislator was in office at the end of the year, in the subquery. Then we'll use a `count` window function, with the window covering the rows `unbounded preceding`, or all prior rows for that legislator, and `current row`:

```
SELECT id_bioguide, date
,count(date) over (partition by id_bioguide
                   order by date rows between
                   unbounded preceding and current row
                   ) as cume_years
```

```
FROM
(
    SELECT distinct a.id_bioguide, b.date
    FROM legislators_terms a
    JOIN date_dim b on b.date between a.term_start and a.term_end
     and b.month_name = 'December' and b.day_of_month = 31
     and b.year <= 2019
) aa
;
```

```
id_bioguide  date        cume_years
-----------  ----------  ----------
A000001      1951-12-31  1
A000001      1952-12-31  2
A000002      1947-12-31  1
A000002      1948-12-31  2
A000002      1949-12-31  3
...          ...         ...
```

Next, count the number of legislators for each combination of date and cume_years to create a distribution:

```
SELECT date, cume_years
,count(distinct id_bioguide) as legislators
FROM
(
SELECT id_bioguide, date
,count(date) over (partition by id_bioguide
                   order by date rows between
                   unbounded preceding and current row
                   ) as cume_years
FROM
(
    SELECT distinct a.id_bioguide, b.date
    FROM legislators_terms a
    JOIN date_dim b on b.date between a.term_start and a.term_end
     and b.month_name = 'December' and b.day_of_month = 31
     and b.year <= 2019
    GROUP BY 1,2
    ) aa
) aaa
GROUP BY 1,2
;
```

```
date        cume_years  legislators
----------  ----------  ----------
1789-12-31  1           89
1790-12-31  1           6
1790-12-31  2           89
1791-12-31  1           37
...         ...         ...
```

Before calculating the percentage for each tenure per year and adjusting the presentation format, we might want to consider grouping the tenures. A quick profiling of our results so far reveals that in some years, almost 40 different tenures are represented. This will likely be difficult to visualize and interpret:

```
SELECT date, count(*) as tenures
FROM
(
    SELECT date, cume_years
    ,count(distinct id_bioguide) as legislators
    FROM
    (
        SELECT id_bioguide, date
        ,count(date) over (partition by id_bioguide
                            order by date rows between
                            unbounded preceding and current row
                            ) as cume_years
        FROM
        (
            SELECT distinct a.id_bioguide, b.date
            FROM legislators_terms a
            JOIN date_dim b
             on b.date between a.term_start and a.term_end
             and b.month_name = 'December' and b.day_of_month = 31
             and b.year <= 2019
            GROUP BY 1,2
        ) aa
    ) aaa
    GROUP BY 1,2
) aaaa
GROUP BY 1
;

date          tenures
-----------   -------
1998-12-31    39
1994-12-31    39
1996-12-31    38
...           ...
```

As a result, we may want to group the values. There is no single right way to group tenures. If there are organizational definitions of tenure groups, go ahead and use them. Otherwise, I usually try to break them up into three to five groups of roughly equal size. Here we'll group the tenures into four cohorts, where cume_years is less than or equal to 4 years, between 5 and 10 years, between 11 and 20 years, and equal to or more than 21 years:

```
SELECT date, tenure
,legislators / sum(legislators) over (partition by date)
 as pct_legislators
FROM
(
    SELECT date
    ,case when cume_years <= 4 then '1 to 4'
         when cume_years <= 10 then '5 to 10'
         when cume_years <= 20 then '11 to 20'
         else '21+' end as tenure
    ,count(distinct id_bioguide) as legislators
    FROM
    (
        SELECT id_bioguide, date
        ,count(date) over (partition by id_bioguide
                           order by date rows between
                           unbounded preceding and current row
                           ) as cume_years
        FROM
        (
            SELECT distinct a.id_bioguide, b.date
            FROM legislators_terms a
            JOIN date_dim b
             on b.date between a.term_start and a.term_end
             and b.month_name = 'December' and b.day_of_month = 31
             and b.year <= 2019
            GROUP BY 1,2
        ) a
    ) aa
    GROUP BY 1,2
) aaa
;

date        tenure   pct_legislators
----------  -------  ---------------
2019-12-31  1 to 4   0.2998
2019-12-31  5 to 10  0.3203
2019-12-31  11 to 20 0.2011
2019-12-31  21+      0.1788
...         ...      ...
```

The graphing of the results in Figure 4-14 shows that in the early years of the country, most legislators had very little tenure. In more recent years, the share of legislators with 21 or more years in office has been increasing. There are also interesting periodic increases in 1-to-4-year-tenure legislators that may reflect shifts in political trends.

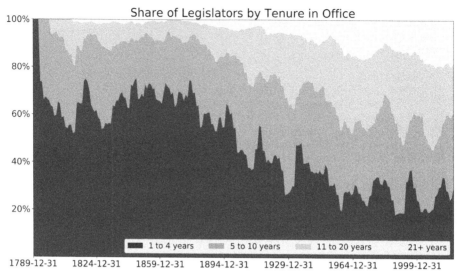

Figure 4-14. Percent of legislators by number of years in office

A cross section of a population at any point in time is made up of members from multiple cohorts. Creating a time series of these cross sections is another interesting way of analyzing trends. Combining this with insights from retention can provide a more robust picture of trends in any organization.

Conclusion

Cohort analysis is a useful way to investigate how groups change over time, whether it be from the perspective of retention, repeat behavior, or cumulative actions. Cohort analysis is retrospective, looking back at populations using intrinsic attributes or attributes derived from behavior. Interesting and hopefully useful correlations can be found through this type of analysis. However, as the saying goes, correlation does not imply causation. To determine actual causality, randomized experiments are the gold standard. Chapter 7 will go into depth on experiment analysis.

Before we turn to experimentation, however, we have a few other types of analysis to cover. Next we'll cover text analysis: components of text analysis often show up in other analyses, and it's an interesting facet of analysis in itself.

CHAPTER 5

Text Analysis

In the last two chapters, we explored applications of dates and numbers with time series analysis and cohort analysis. But data sets are often more than just numeric values and associated timestamps. From qualitative attributes to free text, character fields are often loaded with potentially interesting information. Although databases excel at numeric calculations such as counting, summing, and averaging things, they are also quite good at performing operations on text data.

I'll begin this chapter by providing an overview of the types of text analysis tasks that SQL is good for, and of those for which another programming language is a better choice. Next, I'll introduce our data set of UFO sightings. Then we'll get into coding, covering text characteristics and profiling, parsing data with SQL, making various transformations, constructing new text from parts, and finally finding elements within larger blocks of text, including with regular expressions.

Why Text Analysis with SQL?

Among the huge volumes of data generated every day, a large portion consists of text: words, sentences, paragraphs, and even longer documents. Text data used for analysis can come from a variety of sources, including descriptors populated by humans or computer applications, log files, support tickets, customer surveys, social media posts, or news feeds. Text in databases ranges from *structured* (where data is in different table fields with distinct meanings) to *semistructured* (where the data is in separate columns but may need parsing or cleaning to be useful) or mostly *unstructured* (where long VARCHAR or BLOB fields hold arbitrary length strings that require extensive structuring before further analysis). Fortunately, SQL has a number of useful functions that can be combined to accomplish a range of text-structuring and analysis tasks.

What Is Text Analysis?

Text analysis is the process of deriving meaning and insight from text data. There are two broad categories of text analysis, which can be distinguished by whether the output is qualitative or quantitative. *Qualitative analysis*, which may also be called *textual analysis*, seeks to understand and synthesize the meaning from a single text or a set of texts, often applying other knowledge or unique conclusions. This work is often done by journalists, historians, and user experience researchers. *Quantitative analysis* of text also seeks to synthesize information from text data, but the output is quantitative. Tasks include categorization and data extraction, and analysis is usually in the form of counts or frequencies, often trended over time. SQL is much more suited to quantitative analysis, so that is what the rest of this chapter is concerned with. If you have the opportunity to work with a counterpart who specializes in the first type of text analysis, however, do take advantage of their expertise. Combining the qualitative with the quantitative is a great way to derive new insights and persuade reluctant colleagues.

Text analysis encompasses several goals or strategies. The first is text extraction, where a useful piece of data must be pulled from surrounding text. Another is categorization, where information is extracted or parsed from text data in order to assign tags or categories to rows in a database. Another strategy is sentiment analysis, where the goal is to understand the mood or intent of the writer on a scale from negative to positive.

Although text analysis has been around for a while, interest and research in this area have taken off with the advent of machine learning and the computing resources that are often needed to work with large volumes of text data. *Natural language processing* (NLP) has made huge advances in recognizing, classifying, and even generating brand-new text data. Human language is incredibly complex, with different languages and dialects, grammars, and slang, not to mention the thousands and thousands of words, some that have overlapping meanings or subtly modify the meaning of other words. As we'll see, SQL is good at some forms of text analysis, but for other, more advanced tasks, there are languages and tools that are better suited.

Why SQL Is a Good Choice for Text Analysis

There are a number of good reasons to use SQL for text analysis. One of the most obvious is when the data is already in a database. Modern databases have a lot of computing power that can be leveraged for text tasks in addition to the other tasks we've discussed so far. Moving data to a flat file for analysis with another language or tool is time consuming, so doing as much work as possible with SQL within the database has advantages.

If the data is not already in a database, for relatively large data sets, moving the data to a database may be worthwhile. Databases are more powerful than spreadsheets for processing transformations on many records. SQL is less error-prone than spreadsheets, since no copying and pasting is required, and the original data stays intact. Data could potentially be altered with an *UPDATE* command, but this is hard to do accidentally.

SQL is also a good choice when the end goal is quantification of some sort. Counting how many support tickets contain a key phrase and parsing categories out of larger text that will be used to group records are good examples of when SQL shines. SQL is good at cleaning and structuring text fields. *Cleaning* includes removing extra characters or whitespace, fixing capitalization, and standardizing spellings. *Structuring* involves creating new columns from elements extracted or derived from other fields or constructing new fields from parts stored in different places. String functions can be nested or applied to the results of other functions, allowing for almost any manipulations that might be needed.

SQL code for text analysis can be simple or complex, but it is always rule based. In a rule-based system, the computer follows a set of rules or instructions—no more, no less. This can be contrasted with machine learning, in which the computer adapts based on the data. Rules are good because they are easy for humans to understand. They are written down in code form and can be checked to ensure they produce the desired output. The downside of rules is that they can become long and complicated, particularly when there are a lot of different cases to handle. This can also make them difficult to maintain. If the structure or type of data entered into the column changes, the rule set needs to be updated. On more than one occasion, I've started with what seemed like a simple CASE statement with 4 or 5 lines, only to have it grow to 50 or 100 lines as the application changed. Rules might still be the right approach, but keeping in sync with the development team on changes is a good idea.

Finally, SQL is a good choice when you know in advance what you are looking for. There are a number of powerful functions, including regular expressions, that allow you to search for, extract, or replace specific pieces of information. "How many reviewers mention 'short battery life' in their reviews?" is a question SQL can help you answer. On the other hand, "Why are these customers angry?" is not going to be as easy.

When SQL Is Not a Good Choice

SQL essentially allows you to harness the power of the database to apply a set of rules, albeit often powerful rules, to a set of text to make it more useful for analysis. SQL is certainly not the only option for text analysis, and there are a number of use cases for which it's not the best choice. It's useful to be aware of these.

The first category encompasses use cases for which a human is more appropriate. When the data set is very small or very new, hand labeling can be faster and more informative. Additionally, if the goal is to read all the records and come up with a qualitative summary of key themes, a human is a better choice.

The second category is when there's a need to search for and retrieve specific records that contain text strings with low latency. Tools like Elasticsearch or Splunk have been developed to index strings for these use cases. Performance will often be an issue with SQL and databases; this is one of the main reasons that we usually try to structure the data into discrete columns that can more easily be searched by the database engine.

The third category comprises tasks in the broader NLP category, where machine learning approaches and the languages that run them, such as Python, are a better choice. Sentiment analysis, used to analyze ranges of positive or negative feelings in texts, can be handled only in a simplistic way with SQL. For example, "love" and "hate" could be extracted and used to categorize records, but given the range of words that can express positive and negative emotions, as well as all the ways to negate those words, it would be nearly impossible to create a rule set with SQL to handle them all. Part-of-speech tagging, where words in a text are labeled as nouns, verbs, and so on, is better handled with libraries available in Python. Language generation, or creating brand-new text based on learnings from example texts, is another example best handled in other tools. We will see how we can create new text by concatenating pieces of data together, but SQL is still bound by rules and won't automatically learn from and adapt to new examples in the data set.

Now that we've discussed the many good reasons to use SQL for text analysis, as well as the types of use cases to avoid, let's take a look at the data set we'll be using for the examples before launching into the SQL code itself.

The UFO Sightings Data Set

For the examples in this chapter, we'll use a data set of UFO sightings compiled by the National UFO Reporting Center (*http://www.nuforc.org*). The data set consists of approximately 95,000 reports posted between 2006 and 2020. Reports come from individuals who can enter information through an online form.

The table we will work with is ufo, and it has only two columns. The first is a composite column called sighting_report that contains information about when the sighting occurred, when it was reported, and when it was posted. It also contains metadata about the location, shape, and duration of the sighting event. The second column is a text field called description that contains the full description of the event. Figure 5-1 shows a sample of the data.

Figure 5-1. Sample of the ufo table

Through the examples and discussion in this chapter, I will show how to parse the first column into structured dates and descriptors. I will also show how to perform various analyses on the description field. If I were working with this data on a continual basis, I might consider creating an ETL pipeline, a job that processes the data in the same way on a regular basis, and storing the resulting structured data in a new table. For the examples in this chapter, however, we'll stick with the raw table.

Let's get into the code, starting with SQL to explore and characterize the text from the sightings.

Text Characteristics

The most flexible data type in a database is VARCHAR, because almost any data can be put in fields of this type. As a result, text data in databases comes in a variety of shapes and sizes. As with other data sets, profiling and characterizing the data is one of the first things we do. From there we can develop a game plan for the kinds of cleaning and parsing that may be necessary for the analysis.

One way we can get to know the text data is to find the number of characters in each value, which can be done with the length function (or len in some databases). This function takes the string or character field as an argument and is similar to functions found in other languages and spreadsheet programs:

```
SELECT length('Sample string');

length
------
13
```

We can create a distribution of field lengths to get a sense of the typical length and of whether there are any extreme outliers that might need to be handled in special ways:

```
SELECT length(sighting_report), count(*) as records
FROM ufo
GROUP BY 1
ORDER BY 1
;

length  records
------  -------
90      1
91      4
92      8
...     ...
```

We can see in Figure 5-2 that most of the records are between roughly 150 and 180 characters long, and very few are less than 140 or more than 200 characters. The lengths of the description field range from 5 to 64,921 characters. We can assume that there is much more variety in this field, even before doing any additional profiling.

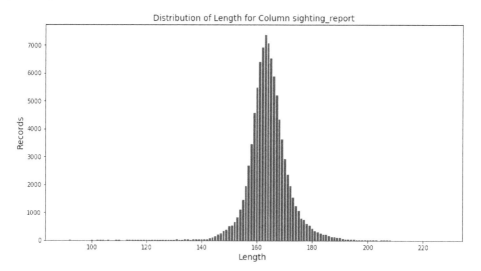

Figure 5-2. Distribution of field lengths in the first column of the ufo table

Let's take a look at a few sample rows of the sighting_report column. In a query tool, I might scroll through a hundred or so rows to get familiar with the contents, but these are representative of the values in the column:

```
Occurred : 3/4/2018 19:07 (Entered as : 03/04/18 19:07)Reported: 3/6/2018 7:05:12
PM 19:05Posted: 3/8/2018Location: Colorado Springs, COShape: LightDuration:3
minutes
Occurred : 10/16/2017 21:42 (Entered as : 10/16/2017 21:42)Reported: 3/6/2018
5:09:47 PM 17:09Posted: 3/8/2018Location: North Dayton, OHShape: SphereDuration:~5
minutes
Occurred : 2/15/2018 00:10 (Entered as : 2/15/18 0:10)Reported: 3/6/2018
6:19:54 PM 18:19Posted: 3/8/2018Location: Grand Forks, NDShape: SphereDuration:
5 seconds
```

This data is what I would call semistructured, or overstuffed. It can't be used in an analysis as is, but there are clearly distinct pieces of information stored here, and the pattern is similar between rows. For example, each row has the word "Occurred" followed by what looks like a timestamp, "Location" followed by a place, and "Duration" followed by an amount of time.

 Data can end up in overstuffed fields for a variety of reasons, but there are two common ones I see. One is when there aren't enough fields available in the source system or application to store all the attributes required, so multiple attributes are entered into the same field. Another is when the data is stored in a JSON blob in an application in order to accommodate sparse attributes or frequent additions of new attributes. Although both scenarios are less than ideal from an analysis perspective, as long as there is a consistent structure, we can usually handle these with SQL.

Our next step is to make this field more usable by parsing it into several new fields, each of which contains a single piece of information. The steps in this process are:

- Plan the field(s) desired as output
- Apply parsing functions
- Apply transformations, including data type conversions
- Check the results when applied to the entire data set, since there will often be some records that don't conform to the pattern
- Repeat these steps until the data is in the desired columns and formats

The new columns we will parse out of sighting_report are occurred, entered_as, reported, posted, location, shape, and duration. Next, we will learn about parsing functions and work on structuring the ufo data set.

Text Parsing

Parsing data with SQL is the process of extracting pieces of a text value to make them more useful for analysis. Parsing splits the data into the part that we want and "everything else," though typically our code returns only the part we want.

The simplest parsing functions return a fixed number of characters from either the beginning or the end of a string. The `left` function returns characters from the left side or beginning of the string, while the `right` function returns characters from the right side or end of the string. They otherwise work in the same way, taking the value to parse as the first argument and the number of characters as the second. Either argument can be a database field or calculation, allowing for dynamic results:

```
SELECT left('The data is about UFOs',3) as left_digits
,right('The data is about UFOs',4) as right_digits
;

left_digits  right_digits
-----------  -----
The          UFOs
```

In the `ufo` data set, we can parse out the first word, "Occurred," using the `left` function:

```
SELECT left(sighting_report,8) as left_digits
,count(*)
FROM ufo
GROUP BY 1
;

left_digits  count
-----------  -----
Occurred     95463
```

We can confirm that all records start with this word, which is good news because it means at least this part of the pattern is consistent. However, what we really want is the values for what occurred, not the word itself, so let's try again. In the first example record, the end of the occurred timestamp is at character 25. In order to remove "Occurred" and retain only the actual timestamp, we can return the rightmost 14 characters using the `right` function. Note that the `right` and `left` functions are nested—the first argument of the `right` function is the result of the `left` function:

```
SELECT right(left(sighting_report,25),14) as occurred
FROM ufo
;

occurred
--------------
3/4/2018 19:07
10/16/2017 21:
```

Although this returns the correct result for the first record, it unfortunately can't handle the records that have two-digit month or day values. We could increase the number of characters returned by the left and right functions, but the result would then include too many characters for the first record.

The left and right functions are useful for extracting fixed-length parts of a string, as in our extraction of the word "Occurred," but for more complex patterns, a function called split_part is more useful. The idea behind this function is to split a string into parts based on a delimiter and then allow you to select a specific part. A *delimiter* is one or more characters that are used to specify the boundary between regions of text or other data. The comma delimiter and tab delimiter are probably the most common, as these are used in text files (with extensions such as *.csv*, *.tsv*, or *.txt*) to indicate where columns start and end. However, any sequence of characters can be used, which will come in handy for our parsing task. The form of the function is:

```
split_part(string or field name, delimiter, index)
```

The index is the position of the text to be returned, relative to the delimiter. So index = 1 returns all of the text to the left of the first instance of the delimiter, index = 2 returns the text between the first and second instance of the delimiter (or all of the text to the right of the delimiter if the delimiter appears only once), and so on. There is no zero index, and the values must be positive integers:

```
SELECT split_part('This is an example of an example string'
                ,'an example'
                ,1);

split_part
----------
This is

SELECT split_part('This is an example of an example string'
                ,'an example'
                ,2);

split_part
----------
 of
```

MySQL has a substring_index function instead of split_part. SQL Server does not have a split_part function at all

Note that spaces in the text will be retained unless specified as part of the delimiter. Let's take a look at how we can parse the elements of the `sighting_report` column. As a reminder, a sample value looks like this:

```
Occurred : 6/3/2014 23:00 (Entered as : 06/03/14 11:00)Reported: 6/3/2014 10:33:24
PM 22:33Posted: 6/4/2014Location: Bethesda, MDShape: LightDuration:15 minutes
```

The value we want our query to return is the text between "Occurred : " and " (Entered". That is, we want the string "6/3/2014 23:00". Checking the sample text, "Occurred :" and "(Entered" both appear only once. A colon (:) appears several times, both to separate the label from the value and in the middle of timestamps. This might make parsing using the colon tricky. The open parenthesis character appears only once. We have some choices as to what to specify as the delimiter, choosing either longer strings or only the fewest characters required to split the string accurately. I tend to be a little more verbose to ensure that I get exactly the piece that I want, but it really depends on the situation.

First, split `sighting_report` on "Occurred : " and check the result:

```
SELECT split_part(sighting_report,'Occurred : ',2) as split_1
FROM ufo
;

split_1
--------------------------------------------------------------
6/3/2014 23:00 (Entered as : 06/03/14 11:00)Reported: 6/3/2014 10:33:24 PM
22:33Posted: 6/4/2014Location: Bethesda, MDShape: LightDuration:15 minutes
```

We have successfully removed the label, but we still have a lot of extra text remaining. Let's check the result when we split on " (Entered":

```
SELECT split_part(sighting_report,' (Entered',1) as split_2
FROM ufo
;

split_2
-------------------------
Occurred : 6/3/2014 23:00
```

This is closer, but it still has the label in the result. Fortunately, nesting `split_part` functions will return only the desired date and time value:

```
SELECT split_part(
         split_part(sighting_report,' (Entered',1)
         ,'Occurred : ',2) as occurred
FROM ufo
;

occurred
---------------
6/3/2014 23:00
```

```
4/25/2014 21:15
5/25/2014
```

Now the result includes the desired values. Reviewing a few additional lines shows that two-digit day and month values are handled appropriately, as are dates that do not have a time value. It turns out that some records omit the "Entered as" value, so one additional split is required to handle records where the "Reported" label marks the end of the desired string:

```
SELECT
split_part(
  split_part(
    split_part(sighting_report,' (Entered',1)
    ,'Occurred : ',2)
    ,'Reported',1) as occurred
FROM ufo
;

occurred
---------------
6/24/1980 14:00
4/6/2006 02:05
9/11/2001 09:00
...
```

The most common occurred values parsed out with the SQL code are graphed in Figure 5-3.

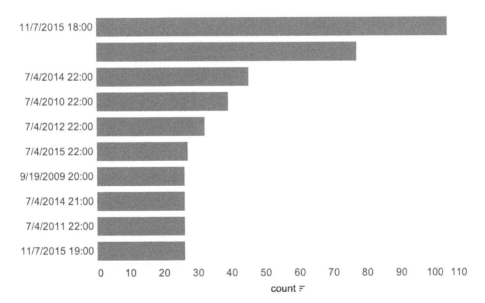

Figure 5-3. Top 10 most common occurred *values for UFO sightings*

Finding a set of functions that works for all values in the data set is one of the hardest parts of text parsing. It often takes several rounds of trial and error and profiling the results along the way to get it right.

The next step is to apply similar parsing rules to extract the other desired fields, using beginning and ending delimiters to isolate just the relevant part of the string. The final query uses split_part several times, with different arguments for each value:

```
SELECT
  split_part(
    split_part(
      split_part(sighting_report,' (Entered',1)
      ,'Occurred : ',2)
    ,'Reported',1) as occurred
,split_part(
  split_part(sighting_report,')',1)
    ,'Entered as : ',2) as entered_as
,split_part(
  split_part(
    split_part(
      split_part(sighting_report,'Post',1)
      ,'Reported: ',2)
    ,' AM',1)
  ,' PM',1) as reported
,split_part(split_part(sighting_report,'Location',1),'Posted: ',2)
  as posted
,split_part(split_part(sighting_report,'Shape',1),'Location: ',2)
  as location
,split_part(split_part(sighting_report,'Duration',1),'Shape: ',2)
  as shape
,split_part(sighting_report,'Duration:',2) as duration
FROM ufo
;
```

occurred	entered_as	reported	posted	location	shape	duration
7/4/2...	07/04/2...	7/5...	7/5/...	Columbus...	Formation	15 minutes
7/4/2...	07/04/2...	7/5...	7/5/...	St. John...	Circle	2-3 minutes
7/4/2...	07/7/1...	7/5...	7/5/...	Royal Pa...	Circle	3 minutes
...	...	...	...	...	...	...

With this SQL parsing, the data is now in a much more structured and usable format. Before we finish, however, there are a few transformations that will clean up the data a little further. We'll take a look at these string transformation functions next.

Text Transformations

Transformations change string values in some way. We saw a number of date and timestamp transformation functions in Chapter 3. There is a set of functions in SQL that specifically work on string values. These are useful for working with parsed data, but also for any text data in a database that needs to be adjusted or cleaned for analysis.

Among the most common transformations are the ones that change capitalization. The upper function converts all letters to their uppercase form, while the lower function converts all letters to their lowercase form. For example:

```
SELECT upper('Some sample text');

upper
----------------
SOME SAMPLE TEXT

SELECT lower('Some sample text');

lower
----------------
some sample text
```

These are useful for standardizing values that may have been entered in different ways. For example, any human will recognize that "California," "caLiforNia," and "CALIFORNIA" all refer to the same state, but a database will treat them as distinct values. If we were to count UFO sightings by states with these values, we would end up with three records for California, resulting in incorrect analysis conclusions. Converting them to all uppercase or all lowercase letters would solve this problem. Some databases, including Postgres, have an initcap function that capitalizes the first letter of each word in a string. This is useful for proper nouns, such as state names:

```
SELECT initcap('caLiforNia'), initcap('golden gate bridge');

initcap     initcap
----------  ------------------
California  Golden Gate Bridge
```

The shape field in the data set we parsed contains one value that is in all capitals, "TRIANGULAR." To clean this and standardize it with the other values, which all have only their first letter capitalized, apply the initcap function:

```
SELECT distinct shape, initcap(shape) as shape_clean
FROM
(
    SELECT split_part(
            split_part(sighting_report,'Duration',1)
            ,'Shape: ',2) as shape
    FROM ufo
) a
;

shape       shape_clean
----------  -----------
...         ...
Sphere      Sphere
TRIANGULAR  Triangular
Teardrop    Teardrop
...         ...
```

The number of sightings for each shape is shown in Figure 5-4. Light is by far the most common shape, followed by circle and triangle. Some sightings do not report a shape, so a count for null value appears in the graph as well.

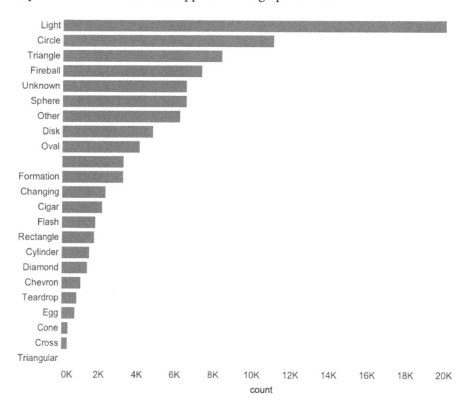

Figure 5-4. Frequency of shapes in UFO sightings

Another useful transformation function is one called `trim` that removes blank spaces at the beginning and end of a string. Extra whitespace characters are a common problem when parsing values out of longer strings, or when data is created by human entry or by copying data from one application to another. As an example, we can remove the leading spaces before "California" in the following string by using the `trim` function:

```
SELECT trim(' California ');

trim
----------
California
```

The `trim` function has a few optional parameters that make it flexible for a variety of data-cleaning challenges. First, it can remove characters from the start of a string or from the end of a string, or both. Trimming from both ends is the default, but the other options can be specified with `leading` or `trailing`. Additionally, `trim` can remove any character, not just whitespace. So, for example, if an application placed a dollar sign ($) at the beginning of each state name for some reason, we could remove this with `trim`:

```
SELECT trim(leading '$' from '$California');
```

A few of the values in the `duration` field have leading spaces, so applying `trim` will result in a cleaner output:

```
SELECT duration, trim(duration) as duration_clean
FROM
(
    SELECT split_part(sighting_report,'Duration:',2) as duration
    FROM ufo
) a
;

duration                duration_clean
--------------------    --------------------
 ~2 seconds              ~2 seconds
 15 minutes              15 minutes
 20 minutes (ongoing)    20 minutes (ongoing)
```

The number of sightings for the most common durations are graphed in Figure 5-5. Sightings lasting between 1 and 10 minutes are common. Some sightings do not report a duration, so a count for null value appears in the graph.

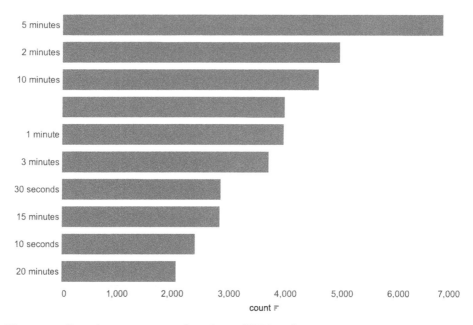

Figure 5-5. Top 10 most common durations of UFO sightings

The next type of transformation is a data type conversion. This type of transformation, discussed in Chapter 2, will be useful for ensuring that the results of our parsing have the intended data type. In our case, there are two fields that should be treated as timestamps—the `occurred` and `reported` columns—and the `posted` column should be a date type. The data types can be changed with casting, using either the double colon (::) operator or the `CAST field as type` syntax. We'll leave the `entered_as`, `location`, `shape`, and `duration` values as VARCHAR:

```
SELECT occurred::timestamp
,reported::timestamp as reported
,posted::date as posted
FROM
(
    SELECT
    split_part(
      split_part(
        split_part(sighting_report,' (Entered',1)
        ,'Occurred : ',2)
       ,'Reported',1)
      as occurred
    ,split_part(
      split_part(
        split_part(
          split_part(sighting_report,'Post',1)
          ,'Reported: ',2)
```

```
        ,' AM',1),' PM',1)
       as reported
     ,split_part(
       split_part(sighting_report,'Location',1)
       ,'Posted: ',2)
       as posted
     FROM ufo
 ) a
 ;

 occurred              reported              posted
 ------------------    ------------------    ----------
 2015-05-24 19:30:00   2015-05-25 10:07:21   2015-05-29
 2015-05-24 22:40:00   2015-05-25 09:09:09   2015-05-29
 2015-05-24 22:30:00   2015-05-24 10:49:43   2015-05-29
 ...                   ...                   ...
```

A sample of the data converts to the new formats. Notice that the database adds the seconds to the timestamp, even though there were no seconds in the original value, and correctly recognizes dates that were in month/day/year (mm/dd/yyyy) format.[1] There is a problem when applying these transformations to the entire data set, however. A few records do not have values at all, appearing as an empty string, and some have the time value but no date associated with them. Although an empty string and null seem to contain the same information—nothing—databases treat them differently. An empty string is still a string and can't be converted to another data type. Setting all the nonconforming records to null with a CASE statement allows the type conversion to work properly. Since we know that dates must contain at least eight characters (four digits for year, one or two digits each for month and day, and two "-" or "/" characters), one way to accomplish this is by setting any record with LENGTH less than 8 equal to null with a CASE statement:

```
SELECT
case when occurred = '' then null
     when length(occurred) < 8 then null
     else occurred::timestamp
     end as occurred
,case when length(reported) < 8 then null
      else reported::timestamp
      end as reported
,case when posted = '' then null
      else posted::date
      end as posted
FROM
(
```

---

1 Since the data set was created in the United States, it is in mm/dd/yyyy format. Many other parts of the world use the dd/mm/yyyy format instead. It's always worth checking your source and adjusting your code as needed.

```
SELECT
split_part(
  split_part(
    split_part(sighting_report,'(Entered',1)
    ,'Occurred : ',2)
  ,'Reported',1) as occurred
,split_part(
  split_part(
    split_part(
      split_part(sighting_report,'Post',1)
      ,'Reported: ',2)
    ,' AM',1)
  ,' PM',1) as reported
,split_part(
  split_part(sighting_report,'Location',1)
  ,'Posted: ',2) as posted
FROM ufo
) a
;

occurred             reported             posted
-------------------  -------------------  ----------
1991-10-01 14:00:00  2018-03-06 08:54:22  2018-03-08
2018-03-04 19:07:00  2018-03-06 07:05:12  2018-03-08
2017-10-16 21:42:00  2018-03-06 05:09:47  2018-03-08
...                  ...                  ...
```

The final transformation I'll discuss in this section is the `replace` function. Sometimes there is a word, phrase, or other string within a field that we would like to change to another string or remove entirely. The `replace` function comes in handy for this task. It takes three arguments—the original text, the string to find, and the string to substitute in its place:

```
replace(string or field, string to find, string to substitute)
```

So, for example, if we want to change references of "unidentified flying objects" to "UFOs," we can use the `replace` function:

```
SELECT replace('Some unidentified flying objects were noticed
above...','unidentified flying objects','UFOs');

replace
-----------------------------
Some UFOs were noticed above...
```

This function will find and replace every instance of the string in the second argument, regardless of where it appears. An empty string can be used as the third argument, which is a good way to remove parts of a string that are not wanted. Like other string functions, `replace` can be nested, with the output from one `replace` becoming the input for another.

In the parsed UFO-sighting data set we've been working with, some of the location values include qualifiers indicating that the sighting took place "near," "close to," or "outside of" a city or town. We can use replace to standardize these to "near":

```
SELECT location
,replace(replace(location,'close to','near')
        ,'outside of','near') as location_clean
FROM
(
    SELECT split_part(split_part(sighting_report,'Shape',1)
                    ,'Location: ',2) as location
    FROM ufo
) a
;

location                      location_clean
--------------------------    ---------------------
Tombstone (outside of), AZ    Tombstone (near), AZ
Terrell (close to), TX        Terrell (near), TX
Tehachapie (outside of), CA   Tehachapie (near), CA
...                           ...
```

The top 10 sighting locations are graphed in Figure 5-6.

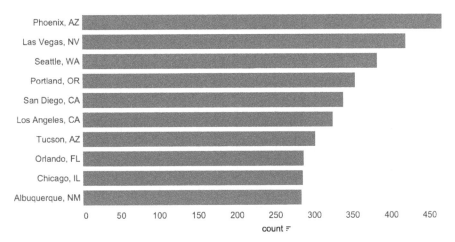

Figure 5-6. Most common locations of UFO sightings

Now we have parsed and cleaned all the elements of the sighting_report field into distinct, appropriately typed columns. The final code looks like this:

```
SELECT
case when occurred = '' then null
     when length(occurred) < 8 then null
     else occurred::timestamp
     end as occurred
```

```
,entered_as
,case when length(reported) < 8 then null
      else reported::timestamp
      end as reported
,case when posted = '' then null
      else posted::date
      end as posted
,replace(replace(location,'close to','near'),'outside of','near')
 as location
,initcap(shape) as shape
,trim(duration) as duration
FROM
(
    SELECT
    split_part(
       split_part(split_part(sighting_report,' (Entered',1)
          ,'Occurred : ',2)
          ,'Reported',1) as occurred
    ,split_part(
      split_part(sighting_report,')',1)
         ,'Entered as : ',2) as entered_as
    ,split_part(
      split_part(
        split_part(
          split_part(sighting_report,'Post',1)
          ,'Reported: ',2)
        ,' AM',1)
      ,' PM',1) as reported
    ,split_part(
       split_part(sighting_report,'Location',1)
       ,'Posted: ',2) as posted
    ,split_part(
       split_part(sighting_report,'Shape',1)
       ,'Location: ',2) as location
    ,split_part(
       split_part(sighting_report,'Duration',1)
       ,'Shape: ',2) as shape
    ,split_part(sighting_report,'Duration:',2) as duration
    FROM ufo
) a
;

occurred   entered_as  reported  posted   location     shape      duration
--------   ----------  --------  ------   ----------   -------    ----------
1988-...   8-8-198...  2018-...  2018...  Amity, ...   Unknown    4 minutes
2018-...   07/41/1...  2018-...  2018...  Bakersf...   Triangle   15 minutes
2018-...   08/01/1...  2018-...  2018...  Naples,...   Light      10 seconds
...        ...         ...       ...      ...          ...        ...
```

This piece of SQL code can be reused in other queries, or it can be used to copy the raw UFO data into a new, cleaned-up table. Alternatively, it could be turned into a view or put into a common table expression for reuse. Chapter 8 will discuss these strategies in more detail.

We've seen how to apply parsing and transformation functions to clean and improve the analysis value of text data that has some amount of structure in it. Next, we'll look at the other field in the UFO sightings data set, the free text `description` field, and learn how to use SQL functions to search for specific elements.

Finding Elements Within Larger Blocks of Text

Parsing and transformations are common operations applied to text data to prepare it for analysis. Another common operation with text data is finding strings within larger blocks of text. This can be done to filter results, categorize records, or replace the searched-for strings with alternate values.

Wildcard Matches: LIKE, ILIKE

SQL has several functions for matching patterns within strings. The LIKE operator matches the specified pattern within the string. In order to allow it to match a pattern and not just find an exact match, wildcard symbols can be added before, after, or in the middle of the pattern. The "%" wildcard matches zero or more characters, while the "_" wildcard matches exactly one character. If the goal is to match the "%" or "_" itself, place the backslash escape symbol ("\") in front of that character:

```
SELECT 'this is an example string' like '%example%';

true

SELECT 'this is an example string' like '%abc%';

false

SELECT 'this is an example string' like '%this_is%';

true
```

The LIKE operator can be used in a number of clauses within the SQL statement. It can be used to filter records in the *WHERE* clause. For example, some reporters mention that they were with a spouse at the time, and so we might want to find out how many reports mention the word "wife." Since we want to find the string anywhere in the description text, we'll place the "%" wildcard before and after "wife":

```
SELECT count(*)
FROM ufo
WHERE description like '%wife%'
;
```

```
count
-----
6231
```

We can see that more than six thousand reports mention "wife." However, this will return only matches on the lowercase string. What if some reporters mention "Wife," or they left Caps Lock on and typed in "WIFE" instead? There are two options for making the search case insensitive. One option is to transform the field to be searched using either the upper or lower function discussed in the previous section, which has the effect of making the search case insensitive since characters are all either uppercase or lowercase:

```
SELECT count(*)
FROM ufo
WHERE lower(description) like '%wife%'
;

count
-----
6439
```

Another way to accomplish this is with the ILIKE operator, which is effectively a case-insensitive LIKE operator. The drawback is that it is not available in every database; notably, MySQL and SQL Server do not support it. However, it's a nice, compact syntax option if you are working in a database that does support it:

```
SELECT count(*)
FROM ufo
WHERE description ilike '%wife%'
;

count
-----
6439
```

Any of these variations of LIKE and ILIKE can be negated with NOT. So, for example, to find the records that do not mention "wife," we can use NOT LIKE:

```
SELECT count(*)
FROM ufo
WHERE lower(description) not like '%wife%'
;

count
-----
89024
```

Filtering on multiple strings is possible with AND and OR operators:

```
SELECT count(*)
FROM ufo
WHERE lower(description) like '%wife%'
```

```
or lower(description) like '%husband%'
;

count
-----
10571
```

Be careful to use parentheses to control the order of operations when using OR in conjunction with AND operators, or you might get unexpected results. For example, these *WHERE* clauses do not return the same result since OR is evaluated before AND:

```
SELECT count(*)
FROM ufo
WHERE lower(description) like '%wife%'
or lower(description) like '%husband%'
and lower(description) like '%mother%'
;

count
-----
6610

SELECT count(*)
FROM ufo
WHERE (lower(description) like '%wife%'
        or lower(description) like '%husband%'
        )
and lower(description) like '%mother%'
;

count
-----
382
```

In addition to filtering in *WHERE* or *JOIN...ON* clauses, LIKE can be used in the *SELECT* clause to categorize or aggregate certain records. Let's start with categorization. The LIKE operator can be used within a CASE statement to label and group records. Some of the descriptions mention an activity the observer was doing during or prior to the sighting, such as driving or walking. We can find out how many descriptions contain such terms by using a CASE statement with LIKE:

```
SELECT
case when lower(description) like '%driving%' then 'driving'
     when lower(description) like '%walking%' then 'walking'
     when lower(description) like '%running%' then 'running'
     when lower(description) like '%cycling%' then 'cycling'
     when lower(description) like '%swimming%' then 'swimming'
     else 'none' end as activity
,count(*)
FROM ufo
GROUP BY 1
```

```
ORDER BY 2 desc
;

activity  count
--------  -----
none      77728
driving   11675
walking   4516
running   1306
swimming  196
cycling   42
```

The most common activity was driving, whereas not many people report sightings while swimming or cycling. This is perhaps not surprising, since these activities are simply less common than driving.

 Although values derived through text-parsing transformation functions can be used in *JOIN* criteria, database performance is often a problem. Consider parsing and/or transforming in a sub-query and then joining the result with an exact match in the *JOIN* clause.

Note that this CASE statement labels each description with only one of the activities and evaluates whether each record matches the pattern in the order in which the statement is written. A description that contains both "driving" and "walking" will be labeled as "driving." This is appropriate in many cases, but particularly when analyzing longer text such as from reviews, survey comments, or support tickets, the ability to label records with multiple categories is important. For this type of use case, a series of binary or BOOLEAN flag columns is called for.

We saw earlier that LIKE can be used to generate a BOOLEAN response of TRUE or FALSE, and we can use this to label rows. In the data set, a number of descriptions mention the direction in which the object was detected, such as north or south, and some mention more than one direction. We might want to label each record with a field indicating whether the description mentions each direction:

```
SELECT description ilike '%south%' as south
,description ilike '%north%' as north
,description ilike '%east%' as east
,description ilike '%west%' as west
,count(*)
FROM ufo
GROUP BY 1,2,3,4
ORDER BY 1,2,3,4
;
```

south	north	east	west	count
false	false	false	false	43757
false	false	false	true	3963
false	false	true	false	5724
false	false	true	true	4202
false	true	false	false	4048
false	true	false	true	2607
false	true	true	false	3299
false	true	true	true	2592
true	false	false	false	3687
true	false	false	true	2571
true	false	true	false	3041
true	false	true	true	2491
true	true	false	false	3440
true	true	false	true	2064
true	true	true	false	2684
true	true	true	true	5293

The result is a matrix of BOOLEANs that can be used to find the frequency of various combinations of directions, or to find when a direction is used without any of the other directions in the same description.

All of the combinations are useful in some contexts, particularly in building data sets that will be used by others to explore the data, or in a BI or visualization tool. However, sometimes it is more useful to summarize the data further and perform an aggregation on the records that contain a string pattern. Here we will count the records, but other aggregations such as sum and average can be used if the data set contains other numerical fields, such as sales figures:

```
SELECT
count(case when description ilike '%south%' then 1 end) as south
,count(case when description ilike '%north%' then 1 end) as north
,count(case when description ilike '%west%' then 1 end) as west
,count(case when description ilike '%east%' then 1 end) as east
FROM ufo
;
```

south	north	west	east
25271	26027	25783	29326

We now have a much more compact summary of the frequency of direction terms in the description field, and we can see that "east" is mentioned more often than other directions. The results are graphed in Figure 5-7.

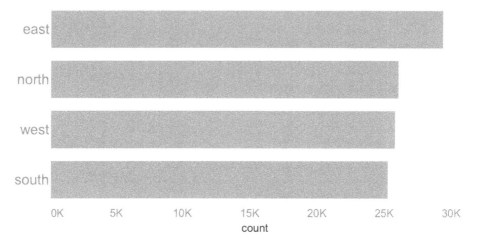

Figure 5-7. Frequency of compass directions mentioned in UFO sighting reports

In the preceding query, we still allow a record that contains more than one direction to be counted more than once. However, there is no longer visibility into which specific combinations exist. Complexity can be added into the query as needed to handle such cases, with a statement such as:

```
count(case when description ilike '%east%'
and description ilike '%north%' then 1 end) as east
```

Pattern matching with LIKE, NOT LIKE, and ILIKE is flexible and can be used in various places in a SQL query to filter, categorize, and aggregate data for a variety of output needs. These operators can be used in combination with the text-parsing and transformation functions we discussed earlier for even more flexibility. Next, I'll discuss handling multiple elements when the matches are exact before returning to more patterns in a discussion of regular expressions.

Exact Matches: IN, NOT IN

Before we move on to more complex pattern matching with regular expressions, it's worth looking at a couple of additional operators that are useful in text analysis. Although not strictly about pattern matching, they are often useful in combination with LIKE and its relatives in order to come up with a rule set that includes exactly the right set of results. The operators are IN and its negation, NOT IN. These allow you to specify a list of matches, resulting in more compact code.

Let's imagine we are interested in categorizing the sightings based on the first word of the description. We can find the first word using the split_part function, with a space character as the delimiter. Many reports start with a color as the first word. We might want to filter the records in order to take a look at reports that start by naming a color. This can be done by listing each color with an OR construction:

```
SELECT first_word, description
FROM
(
    SELECT split_part(description,' ',1) as first_word
    ,description
    FROM ufo
) a
WHERE first_word = 'Red'
or first_word = 'Orange'
or first_word = 'Yellow'
or first_word = 'Green'
or first_word = 'Blue'
or first_word = 'Purple'
or first_word = 'White'
;

first_word  description
----------  --------------------------------------------------
Blue        Blue Floating LightSaw blue light hovering...
White       White dot of light traveled across the sky, very...
Blue        Blue Beam project known seen from the high desert...
...         ...
```

Using an IN list is more compact and often less error-prone, particularly when there are other elements in the *WHERE* clause. IN takes a comma-separated list of items to match. The data type of elements should match the data type of the column. If the data type is numeric, the elements should be numbers; if the data type is text, the elements should be quoted as text (even if the element is a number):

```
SELECT first_word, description
FROM
(
    SELECT split_part(description,' ',1) as first_word
    ,description
    FROM ufo
) a
WHERE first_word in ('Red','Orange','Yellow','Green','Blue','Purple','White')
;

first_word  description
----------  --------------------------------------------------
Red         Red sphere with yellow light in middleMy Grandson...
Blue        Blue light fireball shape shifted into several...
Orange      Orange lights.Strange orange-yellow hovering not...
...         ...
```

The two forms are identical in their results, and the frequencies are shown in Figure 5-8.

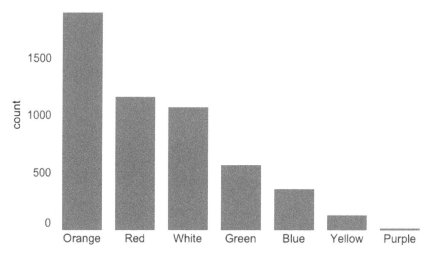

Figure 5-8. Frequency of select colors used as the first word in UFO sighting descriptions

The main benefit of IN and NOT IN is that they make code more compact and readable. This can come in handy when creating more complex categorizations in the *SELECT* clause. For example, imagine we wanted to categorize and count the records by the first word into colors, shapes, movements, or other possible words. We might come up with something like the following that combines elements of parsing, transformations, pattern matching, and IN lists:

```
SELECT
case when lower(first_word) in ('red','orange','yellow','green',
'blue','purple','white') then 'Color'
when lower(first_word) in ('round','circular','oval','cigar')
then 'Shape'
when first_word ilike 'triang%' then 'Shape'
when first_word ilike 'flash%' then 'Motion'
when first_word ilike 'hover%' then 'Motion'
when first_word ilike 'pulsat%' then 'Motion'
else 'Other'
end as first_word_type
,count(*)
FROM
(
    SELECT split_part(description,' ',1) as first_word
    ,description
    FROM ufo
) a
GROUP BY 1
ORDER BY 2 desc
;
```

```
first_word_type  count
---------------  -----
Other            85268
Color            6196
Shape            2951
Motion           1048
```

Of course, given the nature of this data set, it would likely take many more lines of code and rules to accurately categorize the reports by first word. SQL allows you to create a variety of complex and nuanced expressions to deal with text data. Next, we'll turn to some even more sophisticated ways to work with text data in SQL, using regular expressions.

Regular Expressions

There are a number of ways to match patterns in SQL. One of the most powerful methods, though it is also confusing, is the use of regular expressions (regex). I will admit to finding regular expressions intimidating, and I avoided using them for a long time in my data analysis career. In a pinch, I was lucky enough to have colleagues who were willing to share code snippets and get my work unstuck. It was only when I ended up with a big text analysis project that I decided it was finally time to learn about them.

Regular expressions are sequences of characters, many with special meanings, that define search patterns. The main challenge in learning regex, and in using and maintaining code that contains it, is that the syntax is not particularly intuitive. Code snippets don't read anything like a human language, or even like computer languages such as SQL or Python. With a working knowledge of the special characters, however, the code can be written and deciphered. Like the code for all our queries, it's a good idea to start simple, build in complexity as needed, and check results as you go. And leave comments liberally, both for other analysts and for future you.

Regex is a language, but it's one that is used only within other languages. For example, regular expressions can be called within Java, Python, and SQL, but there is no independent way to program with them. All major databases have some implementation of regex. The syntax isn't always exactly the same, but as with other functions, once you have a sense of the possibilities, adjusting syntax to your environment should be possible.

A full explanation, and all of the syntax and ways to use regex, is beyond the scope of this book, but I'll show you enough for you to get started and accomplish a number of common tasks in SQL. For a more thorough introduction, *Learning Regular Expressions (https://oreil.ly/5aYkb)* by Ben Forta (O'Reilly) is a good choice. Here I'll start by introducing the ways to indicate to the database that you are using a regex, and then I'll introduce the syntax, before moving on to some examples of how regex can be useful in the UFO sighting reports analysis.

Regex can be used in SQL statements in a couple of ways. The first is with POSIX comparators, and the second is with regex functions. POSIX stands for Portable Operating System Interface and refers to a set of IEEE standards, but you don't need to know any more than that to use POSIX comparators in your SQL code. The first comparator is the ~ (tilde) symbol, which compares two statements and returns TRUE if one string is contained in the other. As a simple example, we can check to see whether the string "The data is about UFOs" contains the string "data":

```
SELECT 'The data is about UFOs' ~ 'data' as comparison;

comparison
----------
true
```

The return value is a BOOLEAN, TRUE or FALSE. Note that, although it doesn't contain any special syntax, "data" is a regex. Regular expressions can also contain normal text strings. This example is similar to what could be accomplished with a LIKE operator. The ~ comparator is case sensitive. To make it case insensitive, similar to ILIKE, use ~* (the tilde followed by an asterisk):

```
SELECT 'The data is about UFOs' ~* 'DATA' as comparison;

comparison
----------
true
```

To negate the comparator, place an ! (exclamation point) before the tilde or tilde-asterisk combination:

```
SELECT 'The data is about UFOs' !~ 'alligators' as comparison;

comparison
----------
true
```

Table 5-1 summarizes the four POSIX comparators.

Table 5-1. POSIX comparators

Syntax	What it does	Case sensitive?
~	Compares two statements and returns TRUE if one is contained in the other	Yes
~*	Compares two statements and returns TRUE if one is contained in the other	No
!~	Compares two statements and returns FALSE if one is contained in the other	Yes
!~*	Compares two statements and returns FALSE if one is contained in the other	No

Now that we have a way to introduce regex into our SQL, let's get familiar with some of the special pattern-matching syntax it offers. The first special character to know is the . (period) symbol, a wildcard that is used to match any single character:

```
SELECT
'The data is about UFOs' ~ '. data' as comparison_1
,'The data is about UFOs' ~ '.The' as comparison_2
;

comparison_1  comparison_2
-----------   -----------
true          false
```

Let's break this down in order to understand what's going on and develop our intuition about how regex works. In the first comparison, the pattern tries to match any character, indicated by the period, a space, and then the word "data." This pattern matches the string "e data" in the example sentence, so TRUE is returned. If this seems counterintuitive, since there are additional characters before the letter "e" and after the word "data," remember that the comparator is only looking for this pattern somewhere within the string, similar to a LIKE operator. In the second comparison, the pattern tries to match any character followed by "The." Since in the example sentence "The" is the start of the string and there are no characters before it, the value FALSE is returned.

To match multiple characters, use the * (asterisk) symbol. This will match zero or more characters, similar to using the % (percent) symbol in a LIKE statement. This use of the asterisk is different from placing it immediately after the tilde (~*), which makes the match case insensitive. Notice, however, that in this case "%" is not a wildcard and is instead treated as a literal character to be matched:

```
SELECT 'The data is about UFOs' ~ 'data *' as comparison_1
,'The data is about UFOs' ~ 'data %' as comparison_2
;

comparison_1  comparison_2
-----------   -----------
true          false
```

The next special characters to know are [and] (left and right brackets). These are used to enclose a set of characters, any one of which must match. The brackets match a single character even though multiple characters can be between them, though we'll see shortly how to match more than one time. One use for the brackets is to make part of a pattern case insensitive by enclosing the uppercase and lowercase letters within the brackets (do not use a comma, as that would match the comma character itself):

```
SELECT 'The data is about UFOs' ~ '[Tt]he' as comparison;

comparison
----------
true
```

In this example, the pattern will match either "the" or "The"; since this string starts the example sentence, the statement returns the value TRUE. This isn't quite the same thing as the case-insensitive match ~*, because in this case variations such as "tHe" and "THE" do not match the pattern:

```
SELECT 'The data is about UFOs' ~ '[Tt]he' as comparison_1
,'the data is about UFOs' ~ '[Tt]he' as comparison_2
,'tHe data is about UFOs' ~ '[Tt]he' as comparison_3
,'THE data is about UFOs' ~ '[Tt]he' as comparison_4
;

comparison_1  comparison_2  comparison_3  comparison_4
------------  ------------  ------------  ------------
true          true          false         false
```

Another use of the bracket set match is to match a pattern that includes a number, allowing for any number. For example, imagine we wanted to match any description that mentions "7 minutes," "8 minutes," or "9 minutes." This could be accomplished with a CASE statement with several LIKE operators, but with regex the pattern syntax is more compact:

```
SELECT 'sighting lasted 8 minutes' ~ '[789] minutes' as comparison;

comparison
----------
true
```

To match any number, we could enclose all the digits between the brackets:

```
[0123456789]
```

However, regex allows a range of characters to be entered with a - (dash) separator. All of the numbers can be indicated by [0-9]. Any smaller range of numbers can be used as well, such as [0-3] or [4-9]. This pattern, with a range, is equivalent to the last example that listed out each number:

```
SELECT 'sighting lasted 8 minutes' ~ '[7-9] minutes' as comparison;

comparison
----------
true
```

Ranges of letters can be matched in a similar way. Table 5-2 summarizes the range patterns that are most useful in SQL analysis. Nonnumber and nonletter values can also be placed between brackets, as in [$%@].

Table 5-2. Regex range patterns

Range pattern	Purpose
[0-9]	Match any number
[a-z]	Match any lowercase letter
[A-Z]	Match any uppercase letter
[A-Za-z0-9]	Match any lower- or uppercase letter, or any number
[A-z]	Match any ASCII character; generally not used because it matches everything, including symbols

If the desired pattern match contains more than one instance of a particular value or type of value, one option is to include as many ranges as needed, one after the other. For example, we can match a three-digit number by repeating the number range notation three times:

```
SELECT 'driving on 495 south' ~ 'on [0-9][0-9][0-9]' as comparison;

comparison
----------
true
```

Another option is to use one of the optional special syntaxes for repeating a pattern multiple times. This can be useful when you don't know exactly how many times the pattern will repeat, but be careful to check the results to make sure you don't accidentally return more matches than intended. To match one or more times, place the + (plus) symbol after the pattern:

```
SELECT
'driving on 495 south' ~ 'on [0-9]+' as comparison_1
,'driving on 1 south' ~ 'on [0-9]+' as comparison_2
,'driving on 38east' ~ 'on [0-9]+' as comparison_3
,'driving on route one' ~ 'on [0-9]+' as comparison_4
;

comparison_1  comparison_2  comparison_3  comparison_4
------------  ------------  ------------  ------------
true          true          true          false
```

Table 5-3 summarizes the other options for indicating the number of times to repeat a pattern.

Table 5-3. Regex patterns for matching a character set multiple times; in each case, the symbol or symbols are placed immediately after the set expression

Symbol	Purpose
+	Match the character set one or more times
*	Match the character set zero or more times
?	Match the character set zero or one time
{}	Match the character set the number of times specified between the curly braces; for example, {3} matches exactly three times
{,}	Match the character set any number of times in a range specified by the comma-separated numbers between the curly braces; for example, {3,5} matches between three and five times

Sometimes rather than matching a pattern, we want to find items that do *not* match a pattern. This can be done by placing the ^ (caret) symbol before the pattern, which serves to negate the pattern:

```
SELECT
'driving on 495 south' ~ 'on [0-9]+' as comparison_1
,'driving on 495 south' ~ 'on ^[0-9]+' as comparison_2
,'driving on 495 south' ~ '^on [0-9]+' as comparison_3
;

comparison_1   comparison_2   comparison_3
------------   ------------   ------------
true           false          false
```

We might want to match a pattern that includes one of the special characters, so we need a way to tell the database to check for that literal character and not treat it as special. To do this, we need an escape character, which is the \ (backslash) symbol in regex:

```
SELECT
'"Is there a report?" she asked' ~ '\?' as comparison_1
,'it was filed under ^51.' ~ '^[0-9]+' as comparison_2
,'it was filed under ^51.' ~ '\^[0-9]+' as comparison_3
;

comparison_1   comparison_2   comparison_3
------------   ------------   ------------
true           false          true
```

In the first line, omitting the backslash before the question mark causes the database to return an "invalid regular expression" error (the exact wording of the error may be different depending on the database type). In the second line, even though ^ is followed by one or more digits ([0-9]+), the database interprets the ^ in the comparison '^[0-9]+' to be a negation and will evaluate whether the string does not include the specified digits. The third line escapes the caret with a backslash, and the database now interprets this as the literal ^ character.

Text data usually includes whitespace characters. These range from the space, which our eyes notice, to the subtle and sometimes unprinted tab and newline characters. We will see later how to replace these with regex, but for now let's stick to how to match them in a regex. Tabs are matched with \t. Newlines are matched with \r for a carriage return or \n for a line feed, and depending on the operating system, sometimes both are required: \r\n. Experiment with your environment by running a few simple queries to see what returns the desired result. To match any whitespace character, use \s, but note that this also matches the space character:

```
SELECT
'spinning
flashing
and whirling' ~ '\n' as comparison_1
,'spinning
flashing
and whirling' ~ '\s' as comparison_2
,'spinning flashing' ~ '\s' as comparison_3
,'spinning' ~ '\s' as comparison_4
;


comparison_1  comparison_2  comparison_3  comparison_4
------------  ------------  ------------  ------------
true          true          true          false
```

 SQL query tools or SQL query parsers may have trouble interpreting new lines typed directly into them and thus may return an error. If this is the case, try copying and pasting the text from the source rather than typing it in. All SQL query tools should be able to work with newlines that exist in a database table, however.

Similar to mathematical expressions, parentheses can be used to enclose expressions that should be treated together. For example, we might want to match a somewhat complex pattern that repeats several times:

```
SELECT
'valid codes have the form 12a34b56c' ~ '([0-9]{2}[a-z]){3}'
  as comparison_1
,'the first code entered was 123a456c' ~ '([0-9]{2}[a-z]){3}'
  as comparison_2
,'the second code entered was 99x66y33z' ~ '([0-9]{2}[a-z]){3}'
  as comparison_3
;


comparison_1  comparison_2  comparison_3
------------  ------------  ------------
true          false         true
```

All three lines use the same regex pattern, '([0-9]{2}[a-z]){3}', for matching. The pattern inside the parentheses, [0-9]{2}[a-z], looks for two digits followed by a lowercase letter. Outside of the parentheses, {3} indicates that the whole pattern should be repeated three times. The first line follows this pattern, since it contains the string 12a34b56c. The second line does not match the pattern; it does have two digits followed by a lowercase letter (23a) and then two more digits (23a45), but this second repetition is followed by a third digit rather than by another lowercase letter (23a456), so there is no match. The third line has a matching pattern, 99x66y33z.

As we've just seen, regex can be used in any number of combinations with other expressions, both regex and normal text, to create pattern-matching code. In addition to specifying *what* to match, regex can be used to specify *where* to match. Use the special character \y to match a pattern starting at the beginning or end of a word (in some databases, this might be \b instead). As an example, imagine we were interested in finding the word "car" in the UFO sighting reports. We could write an expression like this:

```
SELECT
'I was in my car going south toward my home' ~ 'car' as comparison;

comparison
----------
true
```

It finds "car" in the string and returns TRUE as expected. However, let's look at a few more strings from the data set, looking for the same expression:

```
SELECT
'I was in my car going south toward my home' ~ 'car'
  as comparison_1
,'UFO scares cows and starts stampede breaking' ~ 'car'
  as comparison_2
,'I''m a carpenter and married father of 2.5 kids' ~ 'car'
  as comparison_3
,'It looked like a brown boxcar way up into the sky' ~ 'car'
  as comparison_4
;

comparison_1  comparison_2  comparison_3  comparison_4
------------  ------------  ------------  ------------
true          true          true          true
```

All of these strings match the pattern "car" as well, even though "scares," "carpenter," and "boxcar" aren't exactly what was intended when we went looking for mentions of cars. To fix this, we can add \y to the beginning and end of the "car" pattern in our expression:

```
SELECT
'I was in my car going south toward my home' ~ '\ycar\y'
  as comparison_1
,'UFO scares cows and starts stampede breaking' ~ '\ycar\y'
  as comparison_2
```

```
,'I''m a carpenter and married father of 2.5 kids' ~ '\ycar\y'
  as comparison_3
,'It looked like a brown boxcar way up into the sky' ~ '\ycar\y'
  as comparison_4
;

comparison_1  comparison_2  comparison_3  comparison_4
------------  ------------  ------------  ------------
true          false         false         false
```

Of course, in this simple example, we could have simply added spaces before and
after the word "car" with the same result. The benefit of the pattern is that it will also
pick up cases in which the pattern is at the beginning of a string and thus does not
have a leading space:

```
SELECT 'Car lights in the sky passing over the highway' ~* '\ycar\y'
  as comparison_1
,'Car lights in the sky passing over the highway' ~* ' car '
  as comparison_2
;

comparison_1  comparison_2
------------  ------------
true          false
```

The pattern '\ycar\y' makes a case-insensitive match when "Car" is the first word,
but the pattern ' car ' does not. To match the beginning of an entire string, use the
\A special character, and to match the end of a string, use \Z:

```
SELECT
'Car lights in the sky passing over the highway' ~* '\Acar\y'
  as comparison_1
,'I was in my car going south toward my home' ~* '\Acar\y'
  as comparison_2
,'An object is sighted hovering in place over my car' ~* '\ycar\Z'
  as comparison_3
,'I was in my car going south toward my home' ~* '\ycar\Z'
  as comparison_4
;

comparison_1  comparison_2  comparison_3  comparison_4
------------  ------------  ------------  ------------
true          false         true          false
```

In the first line, the pattern matches "Car" at the beginning of the string. The second
line starts with "I," so the pattern does not match. In the third line, the pattern is
looking for "car" at the end of the string and does match it. Finally, in the fourth line,
the last word is "home," so the pattern does not match.

If this is your first time working with regular expressions, it may take a few read-
throughs and some experimentation in your SQL editor to get the hang of them.

There's nothing like working with real examples to help solidify learning, so next I'll go through some applications to our UFO sightings analysis, and I'll also introduce a couple of specific regex SQL functions.

 Regular expression implementations vary widely by database vendor. The POSIX operators in this section work in Postgres and in databases derived from Postgres such as Amazon Redshift, but not necessarily in others.

An alternative to the ~ operator is the `rlike` or `regexp_like` function (depending on the database). These have the following format:

```
regexp_like(string, pattern, optional_parameters)
```

The first example in this section would be written as:

```
SELECT regexp_like('The data is about UFOs','data')
  as comparison;
```

The optional parameters control matching type, such as whether the match is case insensitive.

Many of these databases have additional functions not covered here, such as `regexp_substr` to find matching substrings, and `regexp_count` to find the number of times a pattern is matched. Postgres supports POSIX but unfortunately does not support these other functions. Organizations that expect to do a lot of text analysis will do well to choose a database type with a robust set of regular expression functions.

Finding and replacing with regex

In the previous section, we discussed regular expressions and how to construct patterns with regex to match parts of strings in our data sets. Let's apply this technique to the UFO sightings data set to see how it works in practice. Along the way, I'll also introduce some additional regex SQL functions.

The sighting reports contain a variety of details, such as what the reporter was doing at the time of the sighting and when and where they were doing it. Another detail commonly mentioned is seeing some number of lights. As a first example, let's find the descriptions that contain a number and the word "light" or "lights." For the sake of display in this book, I'll just check the first 100 characters, but this code can also work across the entire description field:

```
SELECT left(description,50)
FROM ufo
WHERE left(description,50) ~ '[0-9]+ light[s ,.]'
;

left
------------------------------------------------
```

```
Was walking outside saw 5 lights in a line changed
2 lights about 5 mins apart, goin from west to eas
Black triangular aircraft with 3 lights hovering a
...
```

The regular expression pattern matches any number of digits ([0-9]+), followed by a space, then the string "light", and finally either a letter "s," a space, a comma, or a period. In addition to finding the relevant records, we might want to split out just the part that refers to the number and the word "lights." To do this, we'll use the regex function regexp_matches.

 Regex function support varies widely by database vendor and sometimes by database software version. SQL Server does not support the functions, while MySQL has minimal support for them. Analytic databases such as Redshift, Snowflake, and Vertica support a variety of useful functions. Postgres has only match and replace functions. Explore the documentation for your database for specific function availability.

The regexp_matches function takes two arguments: a string to search and a regex match pattern. It returns an array of the string(s) that matched the pattern. If there are no matches, a null value is returned. Since the return value is an array, we'll use an index of [1] to return just a single value as a VARCHAR, which will allow for additional string manipulation as needed. If you are working in another type of database, the regexp_substr function is similar to regexp_matches, but it returns a VARCHAR value, so there is no need to add the [1] index.

 An *array* is a collection of objects stored together in the computer's memory. In databases, arrays are enclosed in { } (curly braces), and this is a good way to spot that something in the database is not one of the regular data types we've been working with so far. Arrays have some advantages when storing and retrieving data, but they are not as easy to work with in SQL since they require special syntax. Elements in an array are accessed using [ ] (square brackets) notation. For our purposes here, it's enough to know that the first element is found with [1], the second with [2], and so on.

Building on our example, we can parse the desired value, the number, and the word "light(s)" from the description field and then *GROUP BY* this value and the most common variations:

```
SELECT (regexp_matches(description,'[0-9]+ light[s ,.]'))[1]
,count(*)
FROM ufo
WHERE description ~ '[0-9]+ light[s ,.]'
```

```
GROUP BY 1
ORDER BY 2 desc
;

regexp_matches  count
--------------  -----
3 lights        1263
2 lights        565
4 lights        549
...             ...
```

The top 10 results are graphed in Figure 5-9.

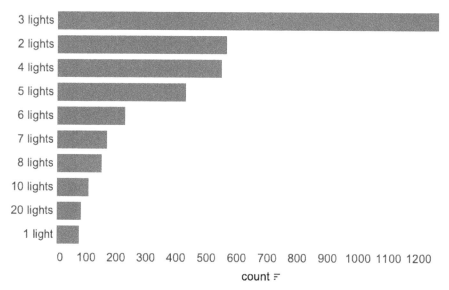

Figure 5-9. Number of lights mentioned at the beginning of UFO sighting descriptions

Reports mentioning three lights are more than twice as common as the second most often mentioned number of lights, and from two to six lights are most commonly seen. To find the full range of the number of lights, we can parse the matched text and then find the min and max values:

```
SELECT min(split_part(matched_text,' ',1)::int) as min_lights
,max(split_part(matched_text,' ',1)::int) as max_lights
FROM
(
    SELECT (regexp_matches(description
                          ,'[0-9]+ light[s ,.]')
                          )[1] as matched_text
    ,count(*)
    FROM ufo
    WHERE description ~ '[0-9]+ light[s ,.]'
    GROUP BY 1
```

```
) a
;

min_lights  max_lights
----------  -----
0           2000
```

At least one report mentions two thousand lights, and the minimum value of zero lights is also mentioned. We might want to review these reports further to see if there is anything else interesting or unusual about these extreme values.

In addition to finding matches, we might want to replace the matched text with some alternate text. This is particularly useful when trying to clean a data set of text that has multiple spellings for the same underlying thing. The regexp_replace function can accomplish this. It is similar to the replace function discussed earlier in the chapter, but it can take a regular expression argument as the pattern to match. The syntax is similar to the replace function:

```
regexp_replace(field or string, pattern, replacement value)
```

Let's put this to work to try to clean up the duration field that we parsed out of the sighting_report column earlier. This appears to be a free text entry field, and there are more than eight thousand different values. However, inspection reveals that there are common themes—most refer to some combination of seconds, minutes, and hours:

```
SELECT split_part(sighting_report,'Duration:',2) as duration
,count(*) as reports
FROM ufo
GROUP BY 1
;

duration    reports
--------    -------
10 minutes  4571
1 hour      1599
10 min      333
10 mins     150
>1 hour     113
...         ...
```

Within this sample, the durations of "10 minutes," "10 min," and "10 mins" all represent the same amount of time, but the database doesn't know to combine them because the spellings are slightly different. We could use a series of nested replace functions to convert all these different spellings. However, we would also have to take into account other variations, such as capitalizations. Regex is handy in this situation, allowing us to create more compact code. The first step is to develop a pattern that matches the desired string, which we can do with the regexp_matches function. It's a good idea to review this intermediate step to make sure we're matching the correct text:

```
SELECT duration
,(regexp_matches(duration
                ,'\m[Mm][Ii][Nn][A-Za-z]*\y')
                )[1] as matched_minutes
FROM
(
    SELECT split_part(sighting_report,'Duration:',2) as duration
    ,count(*) as reports
    FROM ufo
    GROUP BY 1
) a
;

duration        matched_minutes
------------    ---------------
10 min.         min
10 minutes+     minutes
10 min          min
10 minutes +    minutes
10 minutes?     minutes
10 minutes      minutes
10 mins         mins
...             ...
```

Let's break this down. In the subquery, the `duration` value is split out of the `sighting_report` field. Then the `regexp_matches` function looks for strings that match the pattern:

```
'\m[Mm][Ii][Nn][A-Za-z]*\y'
```

This pattern starts at the beginning of a word (\m) and then looks for any sequence of the letters "m," "i," and "n," regardless of capitalization ([Mm] and so on). Next, it looks for zero or more instances of any other lowercase or uppercase letter ([A-Za-z]*), and then it finally checks for the end of a word (\y) so that only the word that includes the variation of "minutes" is included and not the rest of the string. Notice that the "+" and "?" characters are not matched. With this pattern, we can now replace all these variations with the standard value "min":

```
SELECT duration
,(regexp_matches(duration
                ,'\m[Mm][Ii][Nn][A-Za-z]*\y')
                )[1] as matched_minutes
,regexp_replace(duration
                ,'\m[Mm][Ii][Nn][A-Za-z]*\y'
                ,'min') as replaced_text
FROM
(
    SELECT split_part(sighting_report,'Duration:',2) as duration
```

```
      ,count(*) as reports
      FROM ufo
      GROUP BY 1
) a
;
```

```
duration        matched_minutes   replaced_text
-----------     ---------------   -------------
10 min.         min               10 min.
10 minutes+     minutes           10 min+
10 min          min               10 min
10 minutes +    minutes           10 min +
10 minutes?     minutes           10 min?
10 minutes      minutes           10 min
10 mins         mins              10 min
...             ...               ...
```

The values in the replaced_text column are much more standardized now. The period, plus, and question mark characters could also be replaced by enhancing the regex. From an analytical standpoint, however, we might want to consider how to represent the uncertainty that the plus and question mark represent. The regexp_replace functions can be nested in order to achieve replacement of different parts or types of strings. For example, we can standardize both the minutes and the hours:

```
SELECT duration
,(regexp_matches(duration
                ,'\m[Hh][Oo][Uu][Rr][A-Za-z]*\y')
                )[1] as matched_hour
,(regexp_matches(duration
                ,'\m[Mm][Ii][Nn][A-Za-z]*\y')
                )[1] as matched_minutes
,regexp_replace(
        regexp_replace(duration
                    ,'\m[Mm][Ii][Nn][A-Za-z]*\y'
                    ,'min')
        ,'\m[Hh][Oo][Uu][Rr][A-Za-z]*\y'
        ,'hr') as replaced_text
FROM
(
    SELECT split_part(sighting_report,'Duration:',2) as duration
    ,count(*) as reports
    FROM ufo
    GROUP BY 1
) a
;
```

```
duration              matched_hour   matched_minutes   replaced_text
------------------    ------------   ---------------   -------------
1 Hour 15 min         Hour           min               1 hr 15 min
1 hour & 41 minutes   hour           minutes           1 hr & 41 min
```

1 hour 10 mins	hour	mins	1 hr 10 min
1 hour 10 minutes	hour	minutes	1 hr 10 min
...	...	...	...

The regex for hours is similar to the one for minutes, looking for case-insensitive matches of "hour" at the beginning of a word, followed by zero or more other letter characters before the end of the word. The intermediate hour and minutes matches may not be needed in the final result, but I find them helpful to review as I'm developing my SQL code to prevent errors later. A full cleaning of the duration column would likely involve many more lines of code, and it's all too easy to lose track and introduce a typo.

The regexp_replace function can be nested any number of times, or it can be combined with the basic replace function. Another use for regexp_replace is in CASE statements, for targeted replacement when conditions in the statement are met. Regex is a powerful and flexible tool within SQL that, as we've seen, can be used in a number of ways within an overall SQL query.

In this section, I've introduced a number of ways to search for, find, and replace specific elements within longer texts, from wildcard matches with LIKE to IN lists and more complex pattern matching with regex. All of these, along with the text-parsing and transformation functions introduced earlier, allow us to create customized rule sets with as much complexity as needed to handle the data sets in hand. It's worth keeping in mind the balance between complexity and maintenance burden, however. For one-time analysis of a data set, it can be worth the trouble to create complex rule sets that perfectly clean the data. For ongoing reporting and monitoring, it's usually worthwhile to explore options for receiving cleaner data from data sources. Next, we'll turn to several ways to construct new text strings with SQL: using constants, existing strings, and parsed strings.

Constructing and Reshaping Text

We've seen how to parse, transform, find, and replace elements of strings in order to perform a variety of cleaning and analysis tasks with SQL. In addition to these, SQL can be used to generate new combinations of text. In this section, I'll first discuss *concatenation*, which allows different fields and types of data to be consolidated into a single field. Then I'll discuss changing text shape with functions that combine multiple columns into a single row, as well as the opposite: breaking up a single string into multiple rows.

Concatenation

New text can be created with SQL with concatenation. Any combination of constant or hardcoded text, database fields, and calculations on those fields can be joined together. There are a few ways to concatenate. Most databases support the `concat` function, which takes as arguments the fields or values to be concatenated:

```
concat(value1, value2)
concat(value1, value2, value3...)
```

Some databases support the `concat_ws` (concatenate with separator) function, which takes a separator value as the first argument, followed by the list of values to concatenate. This is useful when there are multiple values that you want to put together, using a comma, dash, or similar element to separate them:

```
concat_ws(separator, value1, value2...)
```

Finally, || (double pipe) can be used in many databases to concatenate strings (SQL Server uses + instead):

```
value1 || value2
```

 If any of the values in a concatenation are null, the database will return null. Be sure to use `coalesce` or CASE to replace null values with a default if you suspect they can occur.

Concatenation can bring together a field and a constant string. For example, imagine we wanted to label the shapes as such and add the word "reports" to the count of reports for each shape. The subquery parses the name of the shape from the `sight ing_report` field and counts the number of records. The outer query concatenates the shapes with the string ' (shape)' and the `reports` with the string ' reports':

```
SELECT concat(shape, ' (shape)') as shape
,concat(reports, ' reports') as reports
FROM
(
    SELECT split_part(
                split_part(sighting_report,'Duration',1)
                ,'Shape: ',2) as shape
    ,count(*) as reports
    FROM ufo
    GROUP BY 1
) a
;

Shape              reports
----------------   -----------
Changing (shape)   2295 reports
Chevron (shape)    1021 reports
Cigar (shape)      2119 reports
...                ...
```

We can also combine two fields together, optionally with a string separator. For example, we could unite the shape and location values into a single field:

```
SELECT concat(shape,' - ',location) as shape_location
,reports
FROM
(
    SELECT
    split_part(split_part(sighting_report,'Shape',1)
      ,'Location: ',2) as location
    ,split_part(split_part(sighting_report,'Duration',1)
      ,'Shape: ',2) as shape
    ,count(*) as reports
    FROM ufo
    GROUP BY 1,2
) a
;

shape_location              reports
----------------------      -------
Light - Albuquerque, NM     58
Circle - Albany, OR         11
Fireball - Akron, OH        8
...                         ...
```

The top 10 combinations are graphed in Figure 5-10.

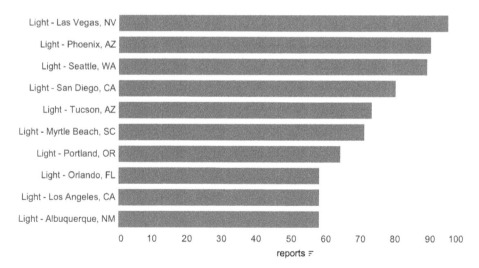

Figure 5-10. Top combinations of shape and location in UFO sightings

We saw earlier that "light" is the most common shape, so it's not surprising that it appears in each of the top results. Phoenix is the most common location, while Las Vegas is the second most common overall.

In this case, since we went to so much trouble to parse out the different fields, it might not make as much sense to concatenate them back together. However, it can be useful to rearrange text or combine values into a single field for display in another tool. By combining various fields and text, we can also generate sentences that can function as summaries of the data, for use in emails or automated reports. In this example, subquery a parses the occurred and shape fields, as we've seen previously, and counts the records. Then in subquery aa, the min and max of occurred are calculated, along with the total number of reports, and the results are *GROUPed BY* shape. Rows with occurred fields shorter than eight characters are excluded, to remove ones that don't have properly formed dates and avoid errors in the min and max calculations. Finally, in the outer query, the final text is assembled with the con cat function. The format of the dates is changed to read as long dates (April 9, 1957) for the earliest and latest dates:

```
SELECT
concat('There were '
        ,reports
        ,' reports of '
        ,lower(shape)
        ,' objects. The earliest sighting was '
        ,trim(to_char(earliest,'Month'))
        , ' '
        , date_part('day',earliest)
        , ', '
        , date_part('year',earliest)
        ,' and the most recent was '
        ,trim(to_char(latest,'Month'))
        , ' '
        , date_part('day',latest)
        , ', '
        , date_part('year',latest)
        ,'.'
        )
FROM
(
    SELECT shape
    ,min(occurred::date) as earliest
    ,max(occurred::date) as latest
    ,sum(reports) as reports
    FROM
    (
        SELECT split_part(
                    split_part(
                        split_part(sighting_report,' (Entered',1)
                        ,'Occurred : ',2)
                    ,'Reported',1) as occurred
        ,split_part(
                split_part(sighting_report,'Duration',1)
                ,'Shape: ',2) as shape
```

```
        ,count(*) as reports
        FROM ufo
        GROUP BY 1,2
    ) a
    WHERE length(occurred) >= 8
    GROUP BY 1
) aa
;

concat
--------------------------------------------------------------------
There were 820 reports of teardrop objects. The earliest sighting was
April 9, 1957 and the most recent was October 3, 2020.
There were 7331 reports of fireball objects. The earliest sighting was
June 30, 1790 and the most recent was October 5, 2020.
There were 1020 reports of chevron objects. The earliest sighting was
July 15, 1954 and the most recent was October 3, 2020.
```

We could get even more creative with formatting the number of reports or adding coalesce or CASE statements to handle blank shape names, for example. Although these sentences are repetitive and are therefore no match for human (or AI) writers, they will be dynamic if the data source is frequently updated and thus can be useful in reporting applications.

Along with functions and operators for creating new text with concatenation, SQL has some special functions for reshaping text, which we'll turn to next.

Reshaping Text

As we saw in Chapter 2, changing the shape of the data—either pivoting from rows to columns or the reverse, changing the data from columns to rows—is sometimes useful. We saw how to do that with *GROUP BY* and aggregations, or with *UNION* statements. In SQL there are some special functions for reshaping text, however.

One use case for reshaping text is when there are multiple rows with different text values for an entity and we would like to combine them into a single value. Combining values can make them more difficult to analyze, of course, but sometimes the use case requires a single record per entity in the output. Combining the individual values into a single field allows us to retain the detail. The string_agg function takes two arguments, a field or an expression, and a separator, which is commonly a comma but can be any separator character desired. The function aggregates only values that are not null, and the order can be controlled with an *ORDER BY* clause within the function as needed:

```
SELECT location
,string_agg(shape,', ' order by shape asc) as shapes
FROM
(
    SELECT
```

```
        case when split_part(
                    split_part(sighting_report,'Duration',1)
                    ,'Shape: ',2) = '' then 'Unknown'
            when split_part(
                    split_part(sighting_report,'Duration',1)
                    ,'Shape: ',2) = 'TRIANGULAR' then 'Triangle'
            else split_part(
                    split_part(sighting_report,'Duration',1),'Shape: ',2)
            end as shape
        ,split_part(
            split_part(sighting_report,'Shape',1)
            ,'Location: ',2) as location
        ,count(*) as reports
        FROM ufo
        GROUP BY 1,2
) a
GROUP BY 1
;

location        shapes
--------------  -----------------------------------
Macungie, PA    Fireball, Formation, Light, Unknown
Kingsford, MI   Circle, Light, Triangle
Olivehurst, CA  Changing, Fireball, Formation, Oval
...             ...
```

Since `string_agg` is an aggregate function, it requires a *GROUP BY* clause on the other fields in the query. In MySQL, an equivalent function is `group_concat`, and analytic databases such as Redshift and Snowflake have a similar function called `listagg`.

Another use case is to do just the opposite of `string_agg` and instead split out a single field into multiple rows. There is a lot of inconsistency in how this is implemented in different databases, and even whether a function exists for this at all. Postgres has a function called `regexp_split_to_table`, while certain other databases have a `split_to_table` function that operates similarly (check documentation for availability and syntax in your database). The `regexp_split_to_table` function takes two arguments, a string value and a delimiter. The delimiter can be a regular expression, but keep in mind that a regex can also be a simple string such as a comma or space character. The function then splits the values into rows:

```
SELECT
regexp_split_to_table('Red, Orange, Yellow, Green, Blue, Purple'
                    ,', ');

regexp_split_to_table
--------------------
Red
Orange
Yellow
```

```
Green
Blue
Purple
```

The string to be split can include anything and doesn't necessarily need to be a list. We can use the function to split up any string, including sentences. We can then use this to find the most common words used in text fields, a potentially useful tool for text analysis work. Let's take a look at the most common words used in UFO sighting report descriptions:

```
SELECT word, count(*) as frequency
FROM
(
    SELECT regexp_split_to_table(lower(description),'\s+') as word
    FROM ufo
) a
GROUP BY 1
ORDER BY 2 desc
;

word   frequency
----   ---------
the    882810
and    477287
a      450223
```

The subquery first transforms the description into lowercase, since case variations are not interesting for this example. Next, the string is split using the regex '\s+', which splits on any one or more whitespace characters.

The most commonly used words are not surprising; however, they are not particularly useful since they are just commonly used words in general. To find a more meaningful list, we can remove what are called *stop words*. These are simply the most commonly used words in a language. Some databases have built-in lists in what are called dictionaries, but the implementations are not standard. There is also no single agreed-upon correct list of stop words, and it is common to adjust the particular list for the desired application; however, there are a number of lists of common stop words on the internet. For this example, I loaded a list of 421 common words into a table called stop_words, available on the book's GitHub site (*https://oreil.ly/94jIS*). The stop words are removed from the result set with a *LEFT JOIN* to the stop_words table, filtered to results that are not in that table:

```
SELECT word, count(*) as frequency
FROM
(
    SELECT regexp_split_to_table(lower(description),'\s+') as word
    FROM ufo
) a
LEFT JOIN stop_words b on a.word = b.stop_word
WHERE b.stop_word is null
```

```
GROUP BY 1
ORDER BY 2 desc
;

word    frequency
------  ---------
light   97071
lights  89537
object  80785
...     ...
```

The top 10 most common words are graphed in Figure 5-11.

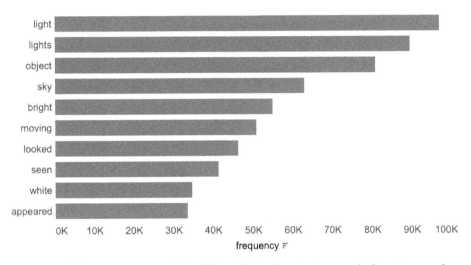

Figure 5-11. Most common words in UFO sighting descriptions, excluding stop words

We could continue to get more sophisticated by adding additional common words to the stop_words table or by *JOIN*ing the results with the descriptions to tag them with the interesting words they contain. Note that regexp_split_to_table and similar functions in other databases can be slow, depending on the length and number of records analyzed.

Constructing and reshaping text with SQL can be done in as simple or complex a way or ways as needed. Concatenation, string aggregation, and string-splitting functions can be used alone, in combination with each other, and with other SQL functions and operators to achieve the desired data output.

Conclusion

Although SQL isn't always the first tool mentioned when it comes to text analysis, it has many powerful functions and operators for accomplishing a variety of tasks. From parsing and transformations, to finding and replacing, to constructing and reshaping text, SQL can be used to both clean and prepare text data as well as perform analysis.

In the next chapter, we'll turn to using SQL for anomaly detection, another topic in which SQL isn't always the first tool mentioned but for which it has surprising capabilities.

CHAPTER 6

Anomaly Detection

An *anomaly* is something that is different from other members of the same group. In data, an anomaly is a record, an observation, or a value that differs from the remaining data points in a way that raises concerns or suspicions. Anomalies go by a number of different names, including *outliers*, *novelties*, *noise*, *deviations*, and *exceptions*, to name a few. I'll use the terms *anomaly* and *outlier* interchangeably throughout this chapter, and you may see the other terms used in discussions of this topic as well. Anomaly detection can be the end goal of an analysis or a step within a broader analysis project.

Anomalies typically have one of two sources: real events that are extreme or otherwise unusual, or errors introduced during data collection or processing. While many of the steps used to detect outliers are the same regardless of the source, how we choose to handle a particular anomaly depends on the root cause. As a result, understanding the root cause and distinguishing between the two types of causes is important to the analysis process.

Real events can generate outliers for a variety of reasons. Anomalous data can signal fraud, network intrusion, structural defects in a product, loopholes in policies, or product use that wasn't intended or envisioned by the developers. Anomaly detection is widely used to root out financial fraud, and cybersecurity also makes use of this type of analysis. Sometimes anomalous data results not because a bad actor is trying to exploit a system but because a customer is using a product in an unexpected way. For example, I knew someone who used a fitness-tracking app, which was intended for running, cycling, walking, and similar activities, to record data from his outings at the auto race track. He hadn't found a better option and wasn't thinking about how anomalous the speed and distance values for a car on a track are compared to those recorded for bike rides or running. When anomalies can be tracked to a real process, deciding what to do with them requires a good understanding of the analysis to be done, as well as domain knowledge, terms of use, and sometimes the legal system that governs the product.

Data can also contain anomalies because of errors in collection or processing. Manually entered data is notorious for typos and incorrect data. Changes to forms, fields, or validation rules can introduce unexpected values, including nulls. Behavior tracking of web and mobile applications is common; however, any change to how and when this logging is done can introduce anomalies. I've spent enough hours diagnosing changes in metrics that I've learned to ask up front whether any logging was recently changed. Data processing can introduce outliers when some values are filtered erroneously, processing steps fail to complete, or data is loaded multiple times, creating duplicates. When anomalies result from data processing, we can generally be more confident in correcting or discarding those values. Of course, fixing the upstream data entry or processing is always a good idea, if possible, to prevent future quality problems.

In this chapter, I'll first discuss some of the reasons to use SQL for this type of analysis and places in which it falls short. Then I'll introduce the earthquakes data set that will be used in the examples in the rest of the chapter. After that, I'll introduce the basic tools that we have at our disposal in SQL for detecting outliers. Then I'll discuss the various forms of outliers that we can apply the tools to find. Once we've detected and understood anomalies, the next step is to decide what to do with them. Anomalies need not always be problematic, as they are in fraud detection, cyberattack detection, and health system monitoring. The techniques in this chapter can also be used to detect unusually good customers or marketing campaigns, or positive shifts in customer behavior. Sometimes the goal of anomaly detection is to pass the anomalies on to other humans or machines to deal with, but often this is a step in a wider analysis, so I'll wrap up with various options for correcting anomalies.

Capabilities and Limits of SQL for Anomaly Detection

SQL is a versatile and powerful language for many data analysis tasks, though it can't do everything. When performing anomaly detection, SQL has a number of strengths, as well as some drawbacks that make other languages or tools better choices for some tasks.

SQL is worth considering when the data set is already in a database, as we previously saw with time series and text analysis in Chapters 3 and 5, respectively. SQL leverages the computational power of the database to perform calculations over many records quickly. Particularly with large tables of data, transferring out of a database and into another tool is time consuming. Working within a database makes even more sense when anomaly detection is a step in a larger analysis that will be done in SQL. Code written in SQL can be examined to understand why particular records were flagged as outliers, and SQL will remain consistent over time even as the data flowing into a database changes.

On the negative side, SQL does not have the statistical sophistication that is available in packages developed for languages like R and Python. SQL has several standard statistical functions, but additional, more complex statistical calculations may be too slow or intense for some databases. For use cases requiring very rapid response, such as fraud or intrusion detection, analyzing data in a database may simply not be appropriate, since there is often lag in loading data, particularly to analytics databases. A common workflow is to use SQL to do the initial analysis and determine typical minimum, maximum, and average values and then develop more real-time monitoring using a streaming service or special real-time data stores. Detecting types of outlier patterns and then implementing in streaming services or special real-time data stores can be an option, however. Finally, SQL code is rule based, as we saw in Chapter 5. It is very good for handling a known set of conditions or criteria, but SQL will not automatically adjust for the types of changing patterns seen with rapidly changing adversaries. Machine learning approaches, and the languages associated with them, are often a better choice for these applications.

Now that we've discussed the advantages of SQL and when to use it instead of another language or tool, let's take a look at the data we'll be using for examples in this chapter before moving on to the code itself.

The Data Set

The data for the examples in this chapter is a set of records for all earthquakes recorded by the US Geological Survey (USGS) from 2010 to 2020. The USGS provides the data in a number of formats, including real-time feeds, at *https://earthquake.usgs.gov/ earthquakes/feed*.

The data set contains approximately 1.5 million records. Each record represents a single earthquake event and includes information such as the timestamp, location, magnitude, depth, and source of the information. A sample of the data is shown in Figure 6-1. A full data dictionary (*https://oreil.ly/NjgCt*) is available on the USGS site.

*	time	latitude	longitude	depth	mag	net	place	type	status
1	2011-03-11 05:46:24	38.297	142.373	29	9.1	official	2011 Great Tohoku Earthquake, Japan	earthquake	reviewed
2	2010-02-27 06:34:11	-36.122	-72.898	22.9	8.8	official	offshore Bio-Bio, Chile	earthquake	reviewed
3	2012-04-11 08:38:36	2.327	93.063	20	8.6	official	off the west coast of northern Sumatra	earthquake	reviewed
4	2015-09-16 22:54:32	-31.5729	-71.6744	22.44	8.3	us	48km W of Illapel, Chile	earthquake	reviewed
5	2013-05-24 05:44:48	54.892	153.221	598.1	8.3	us	Sea of Okhotsk	earthquake	reviewed
6	2012-04-11 10:43:10	0.802	92.463	25.1	8.2	us	off the west coast of northern Sumatra	earthquake	reviewed
7	2017-09-08 04:49:19	15.0222	-93.8993	47.39	8.2	us	101km SSW of Tres Picos, Mexico	earthquake	reviewed
8	2014-04-01 23:46:47	-19.6097	-70.7691	25	8.2	us	94km NW of Iquique, Chile	earthquake	reviewed
9	2018-08-19 00:19:40	-18.1125	-178.153	600	8.2	us	286km NNE of Ndoi Island, Fiji	earthquake	reviewed
10	2019-05-26 07:41:15	-5.8119	-75.2697	122.57	8	us	78km SE of Lagunas, Peru	earthquake	reviewed
11	2013-02-06 01:12:25	-10.799	165.114	24	8	us	76km W of Lata, Solomon Islands	earthquake	reviewed
12	2011-03-11 06:15:40	36.281	141.111	42.6	7.9	us	near the east coast of Honshu, Japan	earthquake	reviewed
13	2017-01-22 04:30:22	-6.2464	155.1718	135	7.9	us	35km WNW of Panguna, Papua New Guinea	earthquake	reviewed
14	2018-01-23 09:31:40	56.0039	-149.1658	14.06	7.9	us	280km SE of Kodiak, Alaska	earthquake	reviewed
15	2016-12-17 10:51:10	-4.5049	153.5216	94.54	7.9	us	54km E of Taron, Papua New Guinea	earthquake	reviewed
16	2014-06-23 20:53:09	51.8486	178.7352	109	7.9	us	19km SE of Little Sitkin Island, Alaska	earthquake	reviewed
17	2018-09-06 15:49:18	-18.4743	179.3502	670.81	7.9	us	102km ESE of Suva, Fiji	earthquake	reviewed
18	2016-12-08 17:38:46	-10.6812	161.3273	40	7.8	us	69km WSW of Kirakira, Solomon Islands	earthquake	reviewed
19	2016-11-13 11:02:56	-42.7373	173.054	15.11	7.8	us	54km NNE of Amberley, New Zealand	earthquake	reviewed
20	2015-05-30 11:23:02	27.8386	140.4931	664	7.8	us	189km WNW of Chichi-shima, Japan	earthquake	reviewed
21	2020-07-22 06:12:44	55.0715	-158.596	28	7.8	us	99 km SSE of Perryville, Alaska	earthquake	reviewed
22	2010-04-06 22:15:01	2.383	97.048	31	7.8	us	northern Sumatra, Indonesia	earthquake	reviewed

Figure 6-1. Sample of the earthquakes data

Earthquakes are caused by sudden slips along faults in the tectonic plates that exist on the outer surface of the earth. Locations on the edges of these plates experience many more, and more dramatic, earthquakes than other places. The so-called Ring of Fire is a region along the rim of the Pacific Ocean in which many earthquakes occur. Various locations within this region, including California, Alaska, Japan, and Indonesia, will appear frequently in our analysis.

Magnitude is a measure of the size of an earthquake at its source, as measured by its seismic waves. Magnitude is recorded on a logarithmic scale, meaning that the amplitude of a magnitude 5 earthquake is 10 times that of a magnitude 4 earthquake. The actual measurement of earthquakes is fascinating but beyond the scope of this book. The USGS website (*https://earthquake.usgs.gov*) is a good place to start if you want to learn more.

Detecting Outliers

Although the idea of an anomaly or outlier—a data point that is very different from the rest—seems straightforward, actually finding one in any particular data set poses some challenges. The first challenge has to do with knowing when a value or data point is common or rare, and the second is setting a threshold for marking values on either side of this dividing line. As we go through the earthquakes data, we'll profile the depths and magnitudes in order to develop an understanding of which values are normal and which are unusual.

Generally, the larger or more complete the data set, the easier it is to make a judgment on what is truly anomalous. In some instances, we have labeled or "ground truth" values to which we can refer. A label is generally a column in the data set that indicates whether the record is normal or an outlier. Ground truth can be obtained from industry or scientific sources or from past analysis and might tell us, for example, that any earthquake greater than magnitude 7 is an anomaly. In other cases, we must look to the data itself and apply reasonable judgment. For the remainder of the chapter, we'll assume that we have a large enough data set to do just that, though of course there are outside references we could consult on typical and extreme earthquake magnitudes.

Our tools for detecting outliers using the data set itself fall into a few categories. First, we can sort or *ORDER BY* the values in the data. This can optionally be combined with various *GROUP BY* clauses to find outliers by frequency. Second, we can use SQL's statistical functions to find extreme values at either end of a value range. Finally, we can graph data and inspect it visually.

Sorting to Find Anomalies

One of the basic tools we have for finding outliers is sorting the data, accomplished with the *ORDER BY* clause. The default behavior of *ORDER BY* is to sort ascending (*ASC*). To sort in descending order, add *DESC* after the column. An *ORDER BY* clause can include one or more columns, and each column can be sorted ascending or descending, independently of the others. Sorting starts with the first column specified. If a second column is specified, the results of the first sort are then sorted by the second column (retaining the first sort), and so on through all the columns in the clause.

 Since ordering happens after the database has calculated the rest of the query, many databases allow you to reference the query columns by number instead of by name. SQL Server is an exception; it requires the full name. I prefer the numbering syntax because it results in more compact code, particularly when query columns include lengthy calculations or function syntax.

For example, we can sort the earthquakes table by mag, the magnitude:

```
SELECT mag
FROM earthquakes
ORDER BY 1 desc
;

mag
------
(null)
(null)
(null)
...
```

This returns a number of rows of nulls. Let's make a note that the data set can contain null values for magnitude—a possible outlier in itself. We can exclude the null values:

```
SELECT mag
FROM earthquakes
WHERE mag is not null
ORDER BY 1 desc
;

mag
---
9.1
8.8
8.6
8.3
```

There is only one value greater than 9, and there are only two additional values greater than 8.5. In many contexts, these would not appear to be particularly large values. However, with a little domain knowledge about earthquakes, we can recognize that these values are in fact both very large and unusual. The USGS provides a list of the 20 largest earthquakes in the world (*https://oreil.ly/gHUhy*). All of them are magnitude 8.4 or larger, while only five are magnitude 9.0 or larger, and three occurred between 2010 and 2020, the time period covered by our data set.

Another way to consider whether values are anomalies within a data set is to calculate their frequency. We can count the id field and *GROUP BY* the mag to find the number of earthquakes per magnitude. The number of earthquakes per magnitude is then divided by the total number of earthquakes, which can be found using a sum window function. All window functions require an *OVER* clause with a *PARTITION BY* and/or *ORDER BY* clause. Since the denominator should count all the records, I have added a *PARTITION BY* 1, which is a way to force the database to make it a window function but still read from the entire table. Finally, the result set is *ORDER*ed *BY* the magnitude:

```
SELECT mag
,count(id) as earthquakes
,round(count(id) * 100.0 / sum(count(id)) over (partition by 1),8)
 as pct_earthquakes
FROM earthquakes
WHERE mag is not null
GROUP BY 1
ORDER BY 1 desc
;

mag  earthquakes  pct_earthquakes
---  -----------  ---------------
9.1  1            0.00006719
8.8  1            0.00006719
8.6  1            0.00006719
8.3  2            0.00013439
```

```
...  ...        ...
6.9  53         0.00356124
6.8  45         0.00302370
6.7  60         0.00403160
...  ...        ...
```

There is only one each of the earthquakes that are over 8.5 in magnitude, but there are two that registered 8.3. By the value 6.9, there are double digits of earthquakes, but those still represent a very small percentage of the data. In our investigation, we should also check the other end of the sorting, the smallest values, by sorting ascending instead of descending:

```
SELECT mag
,count(id) as earthquakes
,round(count(id) * 100.0 / sum(count(id)) over (partition by 1),8)
 as pct_earthquakes
FROM earthquakes
WHERE mag is not null
GROUP BY 1
ORDER BY 1
;

mag    earthquakes  pct_earthquakes
---    -----------  ---------------
-9.99  258          0.01733587
-9     29           0.00194861
-5     1            0.00006719
-2.6   2            0.00013439
...    ...          ...
```

At the low end of values, –9.99 and –9 occur more frequently than we might expect. Although we can't take the logarithm of zero or a negative number, a logarithm can be negative when the argument is greater than zero and less than one. For example, log(0.5) is equal to approximately –0.301. The values –9.99 and –9 represent extremely small earthquake magnitudes, and we might question whether such small quakes could really be detected. Given the frequency of these values, I suspect they represent an unknown value rather than a truly tiny earthquake, and thus we may consider them anomalies.

In addition to sorting the overall data, it can be useful to *GROUP BY* one or more attribute fields to find anomalies within subsets of the data. For example, we might want to check the highest and lowest magnitudes recorded for specific geographies in the place field:

```
SELECT place, mag, count(*)
FROM earthquakes
WHERE mag is not null
 and place = 'Northern California'
GROUP BY 1,2
ORDER BY 1,2 desc
```

```
;

place                mag   count
------------------   ----  -----
Northern California  5.61
Northern California  4.73  1
Northern California  4.51  1
...                  ...   ...
Northern California  -1.1  7
Northern California  -1.2  2
Northern California  -1.6  1
```

"Northern California" is the most common `place` in the data set, and inspecting just the subset for it, we can see that the high and low values are not nearly as extreme as those for the data set as a whole. Earthquakes over 5.0 magnitude are not uncommon overall, but they are outliers for "Northern California."

Calculating Percentiles and Standard Deviations to Find Anomalies

Sorting and optionally grouping data and then reviewing the results visually is a useful approach for spotting anomalies, particularly when the data has values that are very extreme. Without domain knowledge, however, it might not be obvious that a 9.0 magnitude earthquake is such an anomaly. Quantifying the extremity of data points adds another layer of rigor to the analysis. There are two ways to do this: with percentiles or with standard deviations.

Percentiles represent the proportion of values in a distribution that are less than a particular value. The median of a distribution is the value at which half of the population has a lower value and half has a higher value. The median is so commonly used that it has its own SQL function, `median`, in many but not all databases. Other percentiles can be calculated as well. For example, we can find the 25th percentile, where 25% of the values are lower and 75% are higher, or the 89th percentile, where 89% of values are lower and 11% are higher. Percentiles are often found in academic contexts, such as standardized testing, but they can be applied to any domain.

SQL has a window function, `percent_rank`, that returns the percentile for each row within a partition. As with all window functions, the sorting direction is controlled with an *ORDER BY* statement. Similar to the `rank` function, `percent_rank` does not take any argument; it operates over all the rows returned by the query. The basic form is:

```
percent_rank() over (partition by ... order by ...)
```

Both the *PARTITION BY* and the *ORDER BY* are optional, but the function requires something in the *OVER* clause, and specifying the ordering is always a good idea. To find the percentile of the magnitudes of each earthquake for each place, we can first calculate the `percent_rank` for each row in the subquery and then count the occurrences of each magnitude in the outer query. Note that it's important to calculate the `percent_rank` first, before doing any aggregation, so that repeating values are taken into account in the calculation:

```
SELECT place, mag, percentile
,count(*)
FROM
(
    SELECT place, mag
    ,percent_rank() over (partition by place order by mag) as percentile
    FROM earthquakes
    WHERE mag is not null
    and place = 'Northern California'
) a
GROUP BY 1,2,3
ORDER BY 1,2 desc
;

place                 mag   percentile              count
-------------------   ----  ---------------------   -----
Northern California   5.6   1.0                     1
Northern California   4.73  0.9999870597065141      1
Northern California   4.51  0.9999741194130283      1
...                   ...   ...                     ...
Northern California   -1.1  3.8820880457568775E-5   7
Northern California   -1.2  1.2940293485856258E-5   2
Northern California   -1.6  0.0                     1
```

Within Northern California, the magnitude 5.6 earthquake has a percentile of 1, or 100%, indicating that all of the other values are less than this one. The magnitude −1.6 earthquake has a percentile of 0, indicating that no other data points are smaller.

In addition to finding the exact percentile of each row, SQL can carve the data set into a specified number of buckets and return the bucket each row belongs to with a function called `ntile`. For example, we might want to carve the data set up into 100 buckets:

```
SELECT place, mag
,ntile(100) over (partition by place order by mag) as ntile
FROM earthquakes
WHERE mag is not null
and place = 'Central Alaska'
ORDER BY 1,2 desc
;

place           mag   ntile
-------------   ----  -----
Central Alaska  5.4   100
Central Alaska  5.3   100
Central Alaska  5.2   100
...             ...   ...
Central Alaska  1.5   79
```

```
...              ...   ...
Central Alaska   -0.5  1
Central Alaska   -0.5  1
Central Alaska   -0.5  1
```

Looking at the results for "Central Alaska," we see that the three earthquakes greater than 5 are in the 100th percentile, 1.5 falls within the 79th percentile, and the smallest values of –0.5 fall in the first percentile. After calculating these values, we can then find the boundaries of each ntile, using max and min. For this example, we'll use four ntiles to keep the display simpler, but any positive integer is allowed in the ntile argument:

```
SELECT place, ntile
,max(mag) as maximum
,min(mag) as minimum
FROM
(
    SELECT place, mag
    ,ntile(4) over (partition by place order by mag) as ntile
    FROM earthquakes
    WHERE mag is not null
    and place = 'Central Alaska'
) a
GROUP BY 1,2
ORDER BY 1,2 desc
;

place           ntile  maximum  minimum
-------------   -----  -------  -------
Central Alaska  4      5.4      1.4
Central Alaska  3      1.4      1.1
Central Alaska  2      1.1      0.8
Central Alaska  1      0.8      -0.5
```

The highest ntile, 4, which represents the 75th to 100th percentiles, has the widest range, spanning from 1.4 to 5.4. On the other hand, the middle 50 percent of values, which include ntiles 2 and 3, range only from 0.8 to 1.4.

In addition to finding the percentile or ntile for each row, we can calculate specific percentiles across the entire result set of a query. To do this, we can use the percen tile_cont function or the percentile_disc function. Both are window functions, but with a slightly different syntax than other window functions discussed previously because they require a *WITHIN GROUP* clause. The form of the functions is:

```
percentile_cont(numeric) within group (order by field_name) over (partition by
    field_name)
```

The numeric is a value between 0 and 1 that represents the percentile to return. For example, 0.25 returns the 25th percentile. The *ORDER BY* clause specifies the field to return the percentile from, as well as the ordering. *ASC* or *DESC* can optionally be added, with *ASC* the default, as in all *ORDER BY* clauses in SQL. The *OVER (PARTI-TION BY...)* clause is optional (and confusingly, some databases don't support it, so check your documentation if you run into errors).

The `percentile_cont` function will return an interpolated (calculated) value that corresponds to the exact percentile but that may not exist in the data set. The `percentile_disc` (discontinuous percentile) function, on the other hand, returns the value in the data set that is closest to the requested percentile. For large data sets, or for ones with fairly continuous values, there is often little practical difference between the output of the two functions, but it's worth considering which is more appropriate for your analysis. Let's take a look at an example to see how this looks in practice. We'll calculate the 25th, 50th (or median), and 75th percentile magnitudes for all nonnull magnitudes in Central Alaska:

```
SELECT
percentile_cont(0.25) within group (order by mag) as pct_25
,percentile_cont(0.5) within group (order by mag) as pct_50
,percentile_cont(0.75) within group (order by mag) as pct_75
FROM earthquakes
WHERE mag is not null
and place = 'Central Alaska'
;

pct_25  pct_50  pct_75
------  ------  ------
0.8     1.1     1.4
```

The query returns the requested percentiles, summarized across the data set. Notice that the values correspond to the maximum values for ntiles 1, 2, and 3 calculated in the previous example. Percentiles for different fields can be calculated within the same query by changing the field in the *ORDER BY* clause:

```
SELECT
percentile_cont(0.25) within group (order by mag) as pct_25_mag
,percentile_cont(0.25) within group (order by depth) as pct_25_depth
FROM earthquakes
WHERE mag is not null
and place = 'Central Alaska'
;

pct_25_mag  pct_25_depth
----------  ------------
0.8         7.1
```

Unlike other window functions, `percentile_cont` and `percentile_disc` require a *GROUP BY* clause at the query level when other fields are present in the query. For example, if we want to consider two areas within Alaska, and so include the place field, the query must also include it in the *GROUP BY*, and the percentiles are calculated per place:

```
SELECT place
,percentile_cont(0.25) within group (order by mag) as pct_25_mag
,percentile_cont(0.25) within group (order by depth) as pct_25_depth
FROM earthquakes
WHERE mag is not null
and place in ('Central Alaska', 'Southern Alaska')
GROUP BY place
;
```

place	pct_25_mag	pct_25_depth
Central Alaska	0.8	7.1
Southern Alaska	1.2	10.1

With these functions, we can find any percentile required for analysis. Since the median value is so commonly calculated, a number of databases have implemented a median function that has only one argument, the field for which to calculate the median. This is a handy and certainly much simpler syntax, but note that the same can be accomplished with percentile_cont if a median function is not available.

 The percentile and median functions can be slow and computationally intensive on large data sets. This is because the database must sort and rank all the records, usually in memory. Some database vendors have implemented approximate versions of the functions, such as approximate_percentile, that are much faster and return results very close to the function that calculates the entire data set.

Finding the percentiles or ntiles of a data set allows us to add some quantification to anomalies. We'll see later in the chapter how these values also give us some tools for handling anomalies in data sets. Since percentiles are always scaled between 0 and 100, however, they don't give a sense of just how unusual certain values are. For that we can turn to additional statistical functions supported by SQL.

To measure how extreme values in a data set are, we can use the *standard deviation*. The standard deviation is a measure of the variation in a set of values. A lower value means less variation, while a higher number means more variation. When data is normally distributed around the mean, about 68% of the values lie within +/- one standard deviation from the mean, and about 95% lie within two standard deviations. The standard deviation is calculated as the square root of the sum of differences from the mean, divided by the number of observations:

$$\sqrt{\Sigma(x_i - \mu)^2 / N}$$

In this formula, x_i is an observation, μ is the average of all the observations, Σ indicates that all of the values should be summed, and N is the number of observations. Refer to any good statistics text or online resource[1] for more information about how the standard deviation is derived.

Most databases have three standard deviation functions. The `stddev_pop` function finds the standard deviation of a population. If the data set represents the entire population, as is often the case with a customer data set, use the `stddev_pop`. The `stddev_samp` finds the standard deviation of a sample and differs from the above formula by dividing by $N - 1$ instead of N. This has the effect of increasing the standard deviation, reflecting the loss of accuracy when only a sample of the entire population is used. The `stddev` function available in many databases is identical to the `stddev_samp` function and may be used simply because it is shorter. If you're working with data that is a sample, such as from a survey or study from a larger population, use the `stddev_samp` or `stddev`. In practice, when you are working with large data sets, there is usually little difference between the `stddev_pop` and `stddev_samp` results. For example, across the 1.5 million records in the `earthquakes` table, the values diverge only after five decimal places:

```
SELECT stddev_pop(mag) as stddev_pop_mag
,stddev_samp(mag) as stddev_samp_mag
FROM earthquakes
;

stddev_pop_mag         stddev_samp_mag
-------------------    -------------------
1.273605805569390395   1.273606233458381515
```

These differences are small enough that in most practical applications, it doesn't matter which standard deviation function you use.

With this function, we can now calculate the number of standard deviations from the mean for each value in the data set. This value is known as the *z-score* and is a way of standardizing data. Values that are above the average have a positive z-score, and those below the average have a negative z-score. Figure 6-2 shows how z-scores and standard deviations relate to the normal distribution.

---

1 *https://www.mathsisfun.com/data/standard-deviation-formulas.html* has a good explanation.

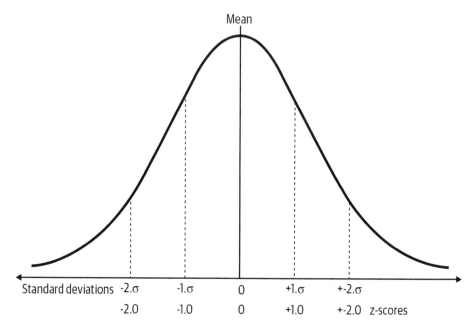

Figure 6-2. Standard deviations and z-scores for a normal distribution

To find the z-scores for the earthquakes, first calculate the average and standard deviation for the entire data set in a subquery. Then *JOIN* this back to the data set using a
Cartesian *JOIN*, so that the average and standard deviation values are *JOINed* to each
earthquake row. This is accomplished with the 1 = 1 syntax, since most databases
require that some *JOIN* condition be specified.

In the outer query, subtract the average magnitude from each individual magnitude
and then divide by the standard deviation:

```
SELECT a.place, a.mag
,b.avg_mag, b.std_dev
,(a.mag - b.avg_mag) / b.std_dev as z_score
FROM earthquakes a
JOIN
(
    SELECT avg(mag) as avg_mag
    ,stddev_pop(mag) as std_dev
    FROM earthquakes
    WHERE mag is not null
) b on 1 = 1
WHERE a.mag is not null
ORDER BY 2 desc
;
```

```
place                                      mag  avg_mag  std_dev  z_score
----------------------------------------   ---  -------  -------  -------
2011 Great Tohoku Earthquake, Japan        9.1   1.6251   1.2736   5.8691
offshore Bio-Bio, Chile                    8.8   1.6251   1.2736   5.6335
off the west coast of northern Sumatra     8.6   1.6251   1.2736   5.4765
...                                        ...   ...      ...      ...
Nevada                                    -2.5   1.6251   1.2736  -3.2389
Nevada                                    -2.6   1.6251   1.2736  -3.3174
Nevada                                    -2.6   1.6251   1.2736  -3.3174
```

The largest earthquakes have a z-score of almost 6, whereas the smallest (excluding the –9 and –9.99 earthquakes that appear to be data entry anomalies) have z-scores close to 3. We can conclude that the largest earthquakes are more extreme outliers than the ones at the low end.

Graphing to Find Anomalies Visually

In addition to sorting the data and calculating percentiles and standard deviations to find anomalies, visualizing the data in one of several graph formats can also help in finding anomalies. As we've seen in previous chapters, one strength of graphs is their ability to summarize and present many data points in a compact form. By inspecting graphs, we can often spot patterns and outliers that we might otherwise miss if only considering the raw output. Finally, graphs assist in the task of describing the data, and any potential problems with the data related to anomalies, to other people.

In this section, I'll present three types of graphs that are useful for anomaly detection: bar graphs, scatter plots, and box plots. The SQL needed to generate output for these graphs is straightforward, though you might need to enlist pivoting strategies discussed in previous chapters, depending on the capabilities and limitations of the software used to create the graphs. Any major BI tool or spreadsheet software, or languages such as Python or R, will be able to produce these graph types. The graphs in this section were created using Python with Matplotlib.

The *bar graph* is used to plot a histogram or distribution of the values in a field and is useful for both characterizing the data and spotting outliers. The full extent of values are plotted along one axis, and the number of occurrences of each value is plotted on the other axis. The extreme high and low values are interesting, as is the shape of the plot. We can quickly determine whether the distribution is approximately normal (symmetric around a peak or average value), has another type of distribution, or has peaks at particular values.

To graph a histogram for the earthquake magnitudes, first create a data set that groups the magnitudes and counts the earthquakes. Then plot the output, as in Figure 6-3.

```
SELECT mag
,count(*) as earthquakes
FROM earthquakes
GROUP BY 1
ORDER BY 1
;

mag     earthquakes
-----   -----------
-9.99   258
-9      29
-5      1
...     ...
```

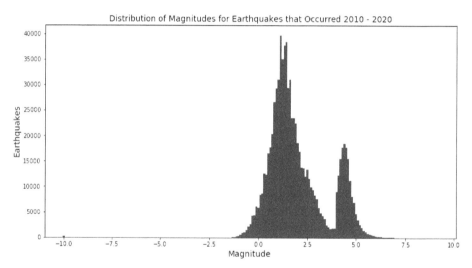

Figure 6-3. Distribution of earthquake magnitudes

The graph extends from –10.0 to +10.0, which makes sense given our previous exploration of the data. It peaks and is roughly symmetric around a value in the range of 1.1 to 1.4 with almost 40,000 earthquakes of each magnitude, but it has a second peak of almost 20,000 earthquakes around the value 4.4. We'll explore the reason for this second peak in the next section on forms of anomalies. The extreme values are hard to spot in this graph, however, so we might want to zoom in on a subsection of the graph, as in Figure 6-4.

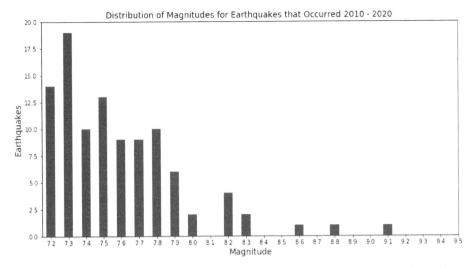

Figure 6-4. A zoomed-in view of the distribution of earthquake magnitudes, focused on the highest magnitudes

Here the frequencies of these very high-intensity earthquakes are easier to see, as is the decrease in frequency from more than 10 to only 1 as the value goes from the low 7s to over 8. Thankfully these temblors are extremely rare.

A second type of graph that can be used to characterize data and spot outliers is the *scatter plot*. A scatter plot is appropriate when the data set contains at least two numeric values of interest. The x-axis displays the range of values of the first data field, the y-axis displays the range of values of the second data field, and a dot is graphed for every pair of x and y values in the data set. For example, we can graph the magnitude against the depth of earthquakes in the data set. First, query the data to create a data set of each pair of values. Then graph the output, as in Figure 6-5:

```
SELECT mag, depth
,count(*) as earthquakes
FROM earthquakes
GROUP BY 1,2
ORDER BY 1,2
;

mag     depth  earthquakes
-----   -----  -----------
-9.99   -0.59  1
-9.99   -0.35  1
-9.99   -0.11  1
...     ...    ...
```

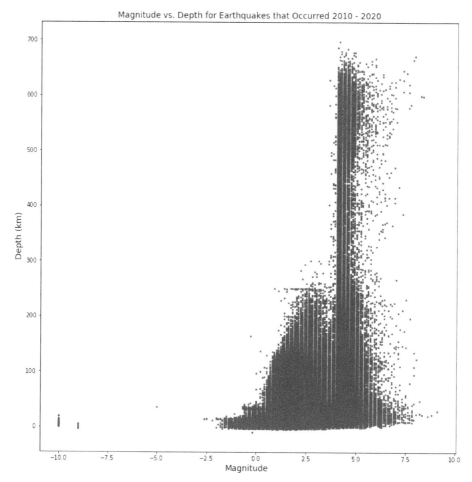

Figure 6-5. Scatter plot of the magnitude and depth of earthquakes

In this graph, we can see the same range of magnitudes, now plotted against the depths, which range from just below zero to around 700 kilometers. Interestingly, the high depth values, over 300, correspond to magnitudes that are roughly 4 and higher. Perhaps such deep earthquakes can be detected only after they reach a minimum magnitude. Note that, due to the volume of data, I have taken a shortcut and grouped the values by magnitude and depth combination, rather than plotting all 1.5 million data points. The count of earthquakes can be used to size each circle in the scatter, as in Figure 6-6, which is zoomed in to the range of magnitudes from 4.0 to 7.0, and depths from 0 to 50 km.

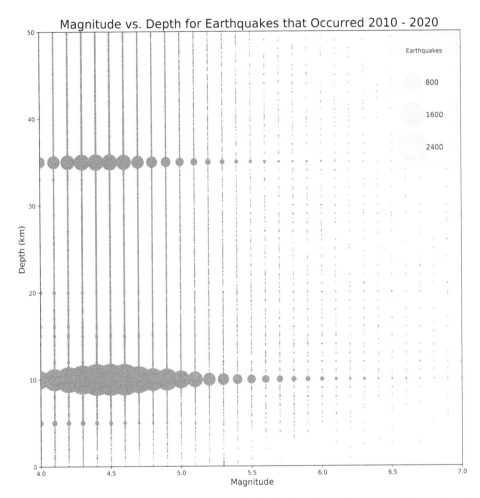

Figure 6-6. Scatter plot of the magnitude and depth of earthquakes, zoomed in and with circles sized by the number of earthquakes

A third type of graph useful in finding and analyzing outliers is the *box plot*, also known as the *box-and-whisker plot*. These graphs summarize data in the middle of the range of values while retaining the outliers. The graph type is named for the box, or rectangle, in the middle. The line that forms the bottom of the rectangle is located at the 25th percentile value, the line that forms the top is located at the 75th percentile, and the line through the middle is located at the 50th percentile, or median, value. Percentiles should be familiar from our discussion in the preceding section. The "whiskers" of the box plot are lines that extend out from the box, typically to 1.5 times the *interquartile range*. The interquartile range is simply the difference between the 75th percentile value and the 25th percentile value. Any values beyond the whiskers are plotted on the graph as outliers.

 Whichever software or programming language you use for graphing box plots will take care of the calculations of the percentiles and interquartile range. Many also offer options to plot the whiskers based on standard deviations from the mean, or on wider percentiles such as the 10th and 90th. The calculation will always be symmetric around the midpoint (such as one standard deviation above and below the mean), but the length of the upper and lower whiskers can differ based on the data.

Typically, all of the values are plotted in a box plot. Since the data set is so large, for this example we'll look at the subset of 16,036 earthquakes that include "Japan" in the place field. First, create the data set with SQL, which is a simple *SELECT* of all of the mag values that meet the filter criteria:

```
SELECT mag
FROM earthquakes
WHERE place like '%Japan%'
ORDER BY 1
;

mag
---
2.7
3.1
3.2
...
```

Then create a box plot in our graphing software of choice, as shown in Figure 6-7.

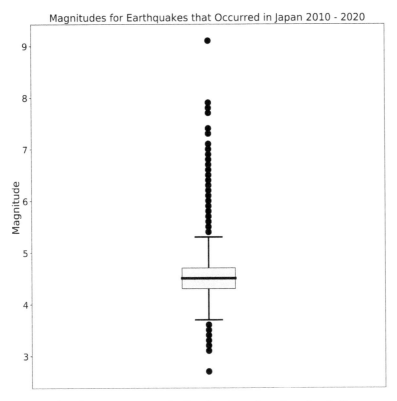

Figure 6-7. Box plot showing magnitude distribution of earthquakes in Japan

Although the graphing software will often provide this information, we can also find the key values for the box plot with SQL:

```
SELECT ntile_25, median, ntile_75
,(ntile_75 - ntile_25) * 1.5 as iqr
,ntile_25 - (ntile_75 - ntile_25) * 1.5 as lower_whisker
,ntile_75 + (ntile_75 - ntile_25) * 1.5 as upper_whisker
FROM
(
    SELECT
    percentile_cont(0.25) within group (order by mag) as ntile_25
    ,percentile_cont(0.5) within group (order by mag) as median
    ,percentile_cont(0.75) within group (order by mag) as ntile_75
    FROM earthquakes
    WHERE place like '%Japan%'
) a
;

ntile_25 median ntile_75 iqr  lower_whisker  upper_whisker
-------- ------ -------- ---- -------------  -------------
4.3      4.5    4.7      0.60 3.70           5.30
```

The median Japanese earthquake had a magnitude of 4.5, and the whiskers extend from 3.7 to 5.3. The plotted circles represent outlier earthquakes, both small and large. The Great Tohoku Earthquake of 2011, at 9.1, is an obvious outlier, even among the larger earthquakes Japan experienced.

 In my experience, box plots are one of the more difficult visualizations to explain to those who don't have a statistics background, or who don't spend all day making and looking at visualizations. The interquartile range is a particularly confusing concept, though the notion of outliers seems to make sense to most people. If you're not absolutely sure your audience knows how to interpret a box plot, take the time to explain it in clear but not overly technical terms. I keep a drawing like Figure 6-8 that explains the parts of a box plot and send it along with my work "just in case" my audience needs a refresher.

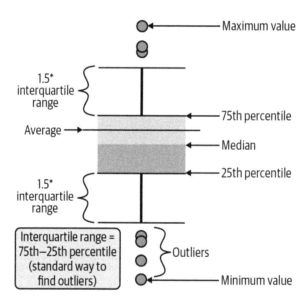

Figure 6-8. Diagram of parts of a box plot

Box plots can also be used to compare across groupings of the data to further identify and diagnose where outliers occur. For example, we can compare earthquakes in Japan in different years. First add the year of the time field into the SQL output and then graph, as in Figure 6-9:

```
SELECT date_part('year',time)::int as year
,mag
FROM earthquakes
WHERE place like '%Japan%'
ORDER BY 1,2
;

year  mag
----  ---
2010  3.6
2010  3.7
2010  3.7
...   ...
```

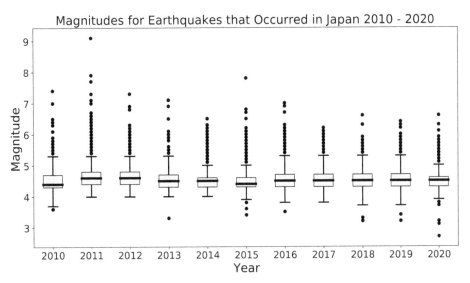

Figure 6-9. Box plot of magnitudes of earthquakes in Japan, by year

Although the median and the range of the boxes fluctuate a bit from year to year, they are consistently between 4 and 5. Japan experienced large outlier earthquakes every year, with at least one greater than 6.0, and in six of the years it experienced at least one earthquake at or larger than 7.0. Japan is undoubtedly a very seismically active region.

Bar graphs, scatter plots, and box plots are commonly used to detect and characterize outliers in data sets. They allow us to quickly absorb the complexity of large amounts of data and to start to tell the story behind it. Along with sorting, percentiles, and standard deviations, graphs are an important part of the anomaly detection toolkit. With these tools in hand, we're ready to discuss the various forms that anomalies can take in addition to those we've seen so far.

Forms of Anomalies

Anomalies can come in all shapes and sizes. In this section, I will discuss three general categories of anomalies: values, counts or frequencies, and presence or absence. These are starting points for investigating any data set, either as a profiling exercise or because anomalies are suspected. Outliers and other unusual values are often specific to a particular domain, so in general the more you know about how and why the data was generated, the better. However, these patterns and techniques for spotting anomalies are good starting places for investigation.

Anomalous Values

Perhaps the most common type of anomaly, and the first thing that comes to mind on this topic, is when single values are either extremely high or low outliers, or when values in the middle of the distribution are otherwise unusual.

In the last section, we looked at several ways to find outliers, through sorting, percentiles and standard deviations, and graphing. We discovered that the earthquakes data set has both unusually large values for the magnitude and some values that appear to be unusually small. The magnitudes also contain varying numbers of *significant digits*, or digits to the right of the decimal point. For example, we can look at a subset of values around 1 and find a pattern that repeats throughout the data set:

```
SELECT mag, count(*)
FROM earthquakes
WHERE mag > 1
GROUP BY 1
ORDER BY 1
limit 100
;

mag          count
----------   -----
...          ...
1.08         3863
1.08000004   1
1.09         3712
1.1          39728
1.11         3674
1.12         3995
....         ...
```

Every once in a while there is a value with 8 significant digits. Many values have two significant digits, but having only a single significant digit is more common. This is likely due to different levels of precision in the instruments collecting the magnitude data. Additionally, the database does not display a second significant digit when that digit is zero, so "1.10" appears simply as "1.1." However, the large number of records at "1.1" indicates that this is not just a display issue. Depending on the purpose of the analysis, we may or may not want to adjust the values to all have the same number of significant digits by rounding.

Often in addition to finding anomalous values, understanding why they happened or other attributes that are correlated with anomalies is useful. This is where creativity and data detective work come into play. For example, 1,215 records in the data set have very high depth values of more than 600 kilometers. We might want to know where these outliers occurred or how they were collected. Let's take a look at the source, which we can find in the net (for network) field:

```
SELECT net, count(*)
FROM earthquakes
WHERE depth > 600
GROUP BY 1
;


net  count
---  -----
us   1215
```

The USGS site indicates that this source is the USGS National Earthquake Information Center, PDE (*https://earthquake.usgs.gov/data/comcat/contributor/us*). This is not terribly informative, however, so let's check the place values, which contain the earthquake locations:

```
SELECT place, count(*)
FROM earthquakes
WHERE depth > 600
GROUP BY 1
;


place                             count
-------------------------------   -----
100km NW of Ndoi Island, Fiji     1
100km SSW of Ndoi Island, Fiji    1
100km SW of Ndoi Island, Fiji     1
...                               ...
```

Visual inspection suggests that many of these very deep earthquakes happen around Ndoi Island in Fiji. However, the place includes a distance and direction component, such as "100km NW of," that makes summarization more difficult. We can apply some text parsing to focus on the place itself for better insights. For places that contain some values and then " of " and some more values, split on the " of " string and take the second part:

```
SELECT
case when place like '% of %' then split_part(place,' of ',2)
     else place end as place_name
,count(*)
FROM earthquakes
```

```
WHERE depth > 600
GROUP BY 1
ORDER BY 2 desc
;

place_name          count
----------------    -----
Ndoi Island, Fiji   487
Fiji region         186
Lambasa, Fiji       140
...                 ...
```

We can now say with more confidence that the majority of the very deep values were recorded for earthquakes somewhere in Fiji, with a particular concentration around the small volcanic island of Ndoi. The analysis could continue to get more complex, for example, by parsing the text to group together all earthquakes recorded in the greater region, which would reveal that after Fiji, other very deep earthquakes have been recorded around Vanuatu and the Philippines.

Anomalies can come in the form of misspellings, variations in capitalization, or other text errors. The ease of finding these depends on the number of distinct values, or *cardinality*, of the field. Differences in capitalization can be detected by counting both the distinct values and the distinct values when a lower or upper function is applied:

```
SELECT count(distinct type) as distinct_types
,count(distinct lower(type)) as distinct_lower
FROM earthquakes
;

distinct_types  distinct_lower
--------------  --------------
25              24
```

There are 24 distinct values of the type field, but 25 different forms. To find the specific types, we can use a calculation to flag those values whose lowercase form doesn't match the actual value. Including the count of records for each form will help contextualize so that we can later decide how to handle the values:

```
SELECT type
,lower(type)
,type = lower(type) as flag
,count(*) as records
FROM earthquakes
GROUP BY 1,2,3
ORDER BY 2,4 desc
;

type       lower      flag   records
--------   --------   -----  -------
...        ...        ...    ...
explosion  explosion  true   9887
```

```
ice quake   ice quake   true    10136
Ice Quake   ice quake   false   1
...         ...         ...     ...
```

The anomalous value of "Ice quake" is easy to spot, since it is the only value for which the flag calculation returns `false`. Since there is only one record with this value, compared to 10,136 with the lowercase form, we can assume that it can be grouped together with the other records. Other text functions can be applied, such as `trim` if we suspect that the values contain extra leading or trailing spaces, or `replace` if we suspect that certain spellings have multiple forms, such as the number "2" and the word "two."

Misspellings can be more difficult to discover than other variations. If a known set of correct values and spellings exists, it can be used to validate the data either through an *OUTER JOIN* to a table containing the values or with a CASE statement combined with an IN list. In either case, the goal is to flag values that are unexpected or invalid. Without such a set of correct values, our options are often either to apply domain knowledge or to make educated guesses. In the `earthquakes` table, we can look at the `type` values with only a few records and then try to determine if there is another, more common value that can be substituted:

```
SELECT type, count(*) as records
FROM earthquakes
GROUP BY 1
ORDER BY 2 desc
;

type                        records
------------------------    -------
...                         ...
landslide                   15
mine collapse               12
experimental explosion      6
building collapse           5
...                         ...
meteorite                   1
accidental explosion        1
collapse                    1
induced or triggered event  1
Ice Quake                   1
rockslide                   1
```

We looked at "Ice Quake" previously and decided it was likely the same as "ice quake." There is only one record for "rockslide," though we might consider this close enough to another of the values, "landslide," which has 15 records. "Collapse" is more ambiguous, since the data set includes both "mine collapse" and "building collapse." What we do with these, or whether we do anything at all, depends on the goal of the analysis, as I'll discuss later in "Handling Anomalies" on page 260.

Anomalous Counts or Frequencies

Sometimes anomalies come not in the form of individual values but in the form of patterns or clusters of activity in the data. For example, a customer spending $100 on an ecommerce site may not be unusual, but that same customer spending $100 every hour over the course of 48 hours would almost certainly be an anomaly.

There are a number of dimensions on which clusters of activity can indicate anomalies, many of them dependent on the context of the data. Time and location are both common across many data sets and are features of the earthquakes data set, so I will use them to illustrate the techniques in this section. Keep in mind that these techniques can often be applied to other attributes as well.

Events that happen with unusual frequency over a short time span can indicate anomalous activity. This can be good, such as when a celebrity unexpectedly promotes a product, leading to a burst of sales of that product. They can also be bad, such as when unusual spikes indicate fraudulent credit card use or attempts to bring a website down with a flood of traffic. To understand these types of anomalies and whether there are deviations from the normal trend, we first apply appropriate aggregations and then use the techniques introduced earlier in this chapter, along with time series analysis techniques discussed in Chapter 3.

In the following examples, I'll go through a series of steps and queries that will help us understand the normal patterns and hunt for unusual ones. This is an iterative process that uses data profiling, domain knowledge, and insights from previous query results to guide each step. We'll start our journey by checking the counts of earthquakes by year, which we can do by truncating the time field to the year level, and counting the records. For databases that don't support date_trunc, consider extract or trunc instead:

```
SELECT date_trunc('year',time)::date as earthquake_year
,count(*) as earthquakes
FROM earthquakes
GROUP BY 1
;

earthquake_year  earthquakes
---------------  -----------
2010-01-01       122322
2011-01-01       107397
2012-01-01       105693
2013-01-01       114368
2014-01-01       135247
2015-01-01       122914
2016-01-01       122420
2017-01-01       130622
2018-01-01       179304
```

```
2019-01-01        171116
2020-01-01        184523
```

We can see that 2011 and 2012 had low numbers of earthquakes compared to other years. There was also a sharp increase in records in 2018 that was sustained through 2019 and 2020. This seems unusual, and we can hypothesize that the earth became more seismically active suddenly, that there is an error in the data such as duplication of records, or that something changed in the data collection process. Let's drill down to month level to see if this trend persists at a more granular level of time:

```
SELECT date_trunc('month',time)::date as earthquake_month
,count(*) as earthquakes
FROM earthquakes
GROUP BY 1
;

earthquake_month  earthquakes
----------------  -----------
2010-01-01        9651
2010-02-01        7697
2010-03-01        7750
...               ...
```

The output is displayed in Figure 6-10. We can see that although the number of earthquakes varies from month to month, there does appear to be an overall increase starting in 2017. We can also see that there are three outlier months, in April 2010, July 2018, and July 2019.

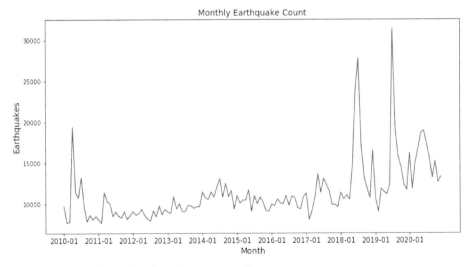

Figure 6-10. Number of earthquakes per month

From here we can continue checking the data at more granular time periods, perhaps optionally filtering the result set by a range of dates to focus in on these anomalous stretches of time. After narrowing in on the specific days or even times of day to pinpoint when the spikes occurred, we might want to break the data down further by other attributes in the data set. This can help explain the anomalies or at least narrow down the conditions in which they occurred. For example, it turns out that the increase in earthquakes starting in 2017 can be at least partially explained by the status field. The status indicates whether the event has been reviewed by a human ("reviewed") or was directly posted by a system without review ("automatic"):

```
SELECT date_trunc('month',time)::date as earthquake_month
,status
,count(*) as earthquakes
FROM earthquakes
GROUP BY 1,2
ORDER BY 1
;

earthquake_month   status      earthquakes
----------------   --------    -----------
2010-01-01         automatic   620
2010-01-01         reviewed    9031
2010-02-01         automatic   695
...                ...         ...
```

The trends of "automatic" and "reviewed" status are plotted in Figure 6-11.

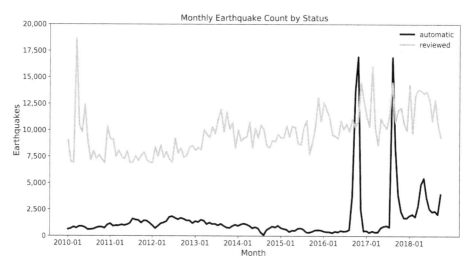

Figure 6-11. Number of earthquakes per month, split by status

In the graph, we can see that the outlier counts in July 2018 and July 2019 are due to large increases in the number of "automatic"-status earthquakes, whereas the spike in

April 2010 was in "reviewed"-status earthquakes. A new type of automatic recording equipment may have been added to the data set in 2017, or perhaps there hasn't been enough time to review all the recordings yet.

Analyzing location in data sets that have that information can be another powerful way to find and understand anomalies. The earthquakes table contains information about many thousands of very small earthquakes, potentially obscuring our view of the very large, very noteworthy earthquakes. Let's look at the locations of the biggest quakes, those of magnitude 6 or larger, and see where they cluster geographically:

```
SELECT place, count(*) as earthquakes
FROM earthquakes
WHERE mag >= 6
GROUP BY 1
ORDER BY 2 desc
;

place                                earthquakes
-----------------------------------  -----------
near the east coast of Honshu, Japan 52
off the east coast of Honshu, Japan  34
Vanuatu                              28
...                                  ...
```

In contrast to time, where we queried at progressively more granular levels, the place values are already so granular that it's a bit difficult to grasp the full picture, although the Honshu, Japan, region clearly stands out. We can apply some of the text analysis techniques from Chapter 5 to parse and then group the geographic information. In this case, we'll use split_part to remove the direction text (such as "near the coast of" or "100km N of") that often appears at the beginning of the place field:

```
SELECT
case when place like '% of %' then split_part(place,' of ',2)
     else place
     end as place
,count(*) as earthquakes
FROM earthquakes
WHERE mag >= 6
GROUP BY 1
ORDER BY 2 desc
;

place                   earthquakes
----------------------  -----------
Honshu, Japan           89
Vanuatu                 28
Lata, Solomon Islands   28
...                     ...
```

The region around Honshu, Japan, experienced 89 earthquakes, making it not only the location of the largest earthquake in the data set but also an outlier in the number of very large earthquakes recorded. We could continue to parse, clean, and group the place values to gain a more refined picture of where major earthquakes occur in the world.

Finding anomalous counts, sums, or frequencies in data is usually an exercise that involves a number of rounds of querying different levels of granularity in succession. It's common to start broad, then go more granular, zoom out again to compare to baseline trends, and zoom in again on specific splits or dimensions of the data. Fortunately, SQL is a great tool for this sort of rapid iteration. Combining techniques, especially from time series analysis, discussed in Chapter 3, and text analysis, discussed in Chapter 5, will bring even more richness to the analysis.

Anomalies from the Absence of Data

We've seen how unusually high frequencies of events can signal anomalies. Keep in mind that the absence of records can also signal anomalies. For example, the heartbeat of a patient undergoing surgery is monitored. The absence of a heartbeat at any time generates an alert, as do irregularities in the heartbeat. In many contexts, however, detecting the absence of data is difficult if you're not specifically looking for it. Customers don't always announce they are about to churn. They simply stop using the product or service and quietly drop out of the data set.

One way to ensure that absences in data are noticed is to use techniques from cohort analysis, discussed in Chapter 4. In particular, a *JOIN* to a date series or data dimension, to ensure that a record exists for every entity whether or not it was present in that time period, makes absences easier to detect.

Another way to detect absence is to query for gaps, or time since last seen. Some regions are more prone to large earthquakes due to the way tectonic plates are arranged around the globe. We've also detected some of this in the data in our previous examples. Earthquakes are notoriously hard to predict, even when we have a sense of where they are likely to occur. This doesn't stop some people from speculating about the next "big one" simply due to the amount of time that has passed since the last one. We can use SQL to find the gaps between large earthquakes and the time since the most recent one:

```
SELECT place
,extract('days' from '2020-12-31 23:59:59' - latest)
  as days_since_latest
,count(*) as earthquakes
,extract('days' from avg(gap)) as avg_gap
,extract('days' from max(gap)) as max_gap
FROM
(
```

```
SELECT place
,time
,lead(time) over (partition by place order by time) as next_time
,lead(time) over (partition by place order by time) - time as gap
,max(time) over (partition by place) as latest
FROM
(
    SELECT
    replace(
      initcap(
      case when place ~ ', [A-Z]' then split_part(place,', ',2)
           when place like '% of %' then split_part(place,' of ',2)
           else place end
    )
    ,'Region','')
    as place
    ,time
    FROM earthquakes
    WHERE mag > 5
  ) a
) a
GROUP BY 1,2
;

place               days_since_latest  earthquakes  avg_gap  max_gap
----------------    -----------------  -----------  -------  -------
Greece              62.0               109          36.0     256.0
Nevada              30.0               9            355.0    1234.0
Falkland Islands    2593.0             3            0.0      0.0
...                 ...                ...          ...      ...
```

In the innermost subquery, the place field is parsed and cleaned, returning larger regions or countries, along with the time of each earthquake, for all earthquakes of magnitude 5 or greater. The second subquery uses a lead function to find the time of the next earthquake, if any, for each place and time, and the gap between each earthquake and the next one. The max window function returns the most recent earthquake for each place. The outer query calculates the days since the latest 5+ earthquake in the data set, using the extract function to return just the days from the interval that is returned when two dates are subtracted. Since the data set includes records only through the end of 2020, the timestamp "2020-12-31 23:59:59" is used, though current_timestamp or an equivalent expression would be appropriate if the data were refreshed on an ongoing basis. Days are extracted in a similar fashion from the average and max of the gap value.

The time since the last major earthquake in a location may have little predictive power in practice, but in many domains, gaps and time since last seen metrics have practical applications. Understanding typical gaps between actions sets a baseline against which the current gap can be compared. When the current gap is within range of historical values, we might judge that a customer is retained, but when the current gap is much longer, the risk of churn increases. The result set from a query that returns historical gaps can itself become the subject of an anomaly detection analysis, answering questions such as the longest amount of time that a customer was gone before subsequently returning.

Handling Anomalies

Anomalies can appear in data sets for a number of reasons and can take a number of forms, as we've just seen. After detecting anomalies, the next step is to handle them in some fashion. How this is done depends on both the source of the anomaly—underlying process or data quality issue—and the end goal of the data set or analysis. The options include investigation without changes, removal, replacement, rescaling, and fixing upstream.

Investigation

Finding, or attempting to find, the cause of an anomaly is usually the first step in deciding what to do with it. This part of the process can be both fun and frustrating—fun in the sense that tracking down and solving a mystery engages our skills and creativity, but frustrating in the sense that we're often working under time pressure and tracking down anomalies can feel like going down an endless series of rabbit holes, leading us to wonder whether an entire analysis is flawed.

When I'm investigating anomalies, my process usually involves a series of queries that bounce back and forth between searching for patterns and looking at specific examples. A true outlier value is easy to spot. In such cases, I will usually query for the entire row that contains the outlier for clues as to the timing, source, and any other attributes that are available. Next, I'll check records that share those attributes to see if they have values that seem unusual. For example, I might check to see whether other records on the same day have normal or unusual values. Traffic from a particular website or purchases of a particular product might reveal other anomalies.

After investigating the source and attributes of anomalies when working on data produced internally in my organization, I get in touch with the stakeholders or product owners. Sometimes there is a known bug or flaw, but often enough there is a real issue in a process or system that needs to be addressed, and context information is useful. For external or public data sets, there may not be an opportunity to find the root cause. In these cases, my goal is to gather enough information to decide which of the options discussed next is appropriate.

Removal

One option for dealing with data anomalies is to simply remove them from the data set. If there is reason to suspect that there was an error in the data collection that might affect the entire record, removal is appropriate. Removal is also a good option when the data set is large enough that dropping a few records is unlikely to affect the conclusions. Another good reason to use removal is when the outliers are so extreme that they would skew the results enough that entirely inappropriate conclusions would be drawn.

We saw previously that the earthquakes data set contains a number of records with a magnitude of –9.99 and a few with –9. Since the earthquakes these values would correspond to are extremely small, we might suspect that they are erroneous values or were simply entered when the actual magnitude was unknown. Removing records with these values is straightforward in the *WHERE* clause:

```
SELECT time, mag, type
FROM earthquakes
WHERE mag not in (-9,-9.99)
limit 100
;
```

```
time                  mag   type
------------------    ----  ----------
2019-08-11 03:29:20   4.3   earthquake
2019-08-11 03:27:19   0.32  earthquake
2019-08-11 03:25:39   1.8   earthquake
```

Before removing the records, however, we might want to determine whether including the outliers actually makes a difference to the output. For example, we might want to know if removing the outliers affects the average magnitude, since averages can easily be skewed by outliers. We can do this by calculating the average across the entire data set, as well as the average excluding the extreme low values, using a CASE statement to exclude them:

```
SELECT avg(mag) as avg_mag
,avg(case when mag > -9 then mag end) as avg_mag_adjusted
FROM earthquakes
;
```

```
avg_mag               avg_mag_adjusted
-----------------     -----------------
1.6251015161530643    1.6273225642983641
```

The averages are different only at the third significant digit (1.625 versus 1.627), which is a fairly small difference. However, if we filter just to Yellowstone National Park, where many of the –9.99 values occur, the difference is more dramatic:

```
SELECT avg(mag) as avg_mag
,avg(case when mag > -9 then mag end) as avg_mag_adjusted
FROM earthquakes
WHERE place = 'Yellowstone National Park, Wyoming'
;
```

```
avg_mag                avg_mag_adjusted
---------------------  ---------------------
0.40639347873981053095 0.92332793709528214616
```

Although these are still small values, the difference between an average of 0.46 and 0.92 is big enough that we would likely choose to remove the outliers.

Notice that there are two options for doing so: either in the *WHERE* clause, which removes the outliers from all the results, or in a CASE statement, which removes them only from specific calculations. Which option you choose depends on the context of the analysis, as well as on whether it is important to preserve the rows in order to retain total counts, or useful values in other fields.

Replacement with Alternate Values

Anomalous values can often be handled by replacing them with other values rather than removing entire records. An alternate value can be a default, a substitute value, the nearest numerical value within a range, or a summary statistic such as the average or median.

We've seen previously that null values can be replaced with a default using the `coalesce` function. When values are not necessarily null but are problematic for some other reason, a CASE statement can be used to substitute a default value. For example, rather than report on all the various seismic events, we might want to group the types that are *not* earthquakes into a single "Other" value:

```
SELECT
case when type = 'earthquake' then type
     else 'Other'
     end as event_type
,count(*)
FROM earthquakes
GROUP BY 1
;
```

```
event_type count
---------- -------
earthquake 1461750
Other      34176
```

This reduces the amount of detail in the data, of course, but it can also be a way to summarize a data set that has a number of outlier values for `type`, as we saw previously. When you know that outlier values are incorrect, and you know the correct value, replacing them with a CASE statement is also a solution that preserves the row in the overall data set. For example, an extra 0 might have been added to the end of a record, or a value might have been recorded in inches instead of miles.

Another option for handling numeric outliers is to replace the extreme values with the nearest high or low value that is not extreme. This approach maintains much of the range of values but prevents misleading averages that can result from extreme outliers. *Winsorization* is a specific technique for this, where outliers are set to a specific percentile of the data. For example, values above the 95th percentile are set to the 95th percentile value, while values below the 5th percentile are set to the 5th percentile value. To calculate this in SQL, we first calculate the 5th and 95th percentile values:

```
SELECT percentile_cont(0.95) within group (order by mag)
 as percentile_95
,percentile_cont(0.05) within group (order by mag)
 as percentile_05
FROM earthquakes
;


percentile_95  percentile_05
-------------  -------------
4.5            0.12
```

We can put this calculation in a subquery and then use a CASE statement to handle setting values for outliers below the 5th percentile and above the 95th. Note the Cartesian *JOIN* that allows us to compare the percentile values with each individual magnitude:

```
SELECT a.time, a.place, a.mag
,case when a.mag > b.percentile_95 then b.percentile_95
      when a.mag < b.percentile_05 then b.percentile_05
      else a.mag
      end as mag_winsorized
FROM earthquakes a
JOIN
(
    SELECT percentile_cont(0.95) within group (order by mag)
     as percentile_95
    ,percentile_cont(0.05) within group (order by mag)
     as percentile_05
    FROM earthquakes
) b on 1 = 1
;


time                 place                       mag   mag_winsorize
-------------------  --------------------------  ----  -------------
2014-01-19 06:31:50  5 km SW of Volcano, Hawaii  -9    0.12
2012-06-11 01:59:01  Nevada                      -2.6  0.12
...                  ...                         ...   ...
2020-01-27 21:59:01  31km WNW of Alamo, Nevada   2     2.0
2013-07-07 08:38:59  54km S of Fredonia, Arizona 3.5   3.5
...                  ...                         ...   ...
2013-09-25 16:42:43  46km SSE of Acari, Peru     7.1   4.5
2015-04-25 06:11:25  36km E of Khudi, Nepal      7.8   4.5
...                  ...                         ...   ...
```

The 5th percentile value is 0.12, while the 95th percentile is 4.5. Values below and above these thresholds are changed to the threshold in the `mag_winsorize` field. Values between these thresholds remain the same. There is no set percentile threshold for winsorizing. The 1st and 99th percentiles or even the 0.01th and 99.9th percentiles can be used depending on the requirements for the analysis and how prevalent and extreme the outliers are.

Rescaling

Rather than filtering out records or changing the values of outliers, rescaling values provides a path that retains all the values but makes analysis and graphing easier.

We discussed the z-score previously, but it's worth pointing out that this can be used as a way to rescale values. The z-score is useful because it can be used with both positive and negative values.

Another common transformation is converting to logarithmic (log) scale. The benefit of transforming values into log scale is that they retain the same ordering, but small numbers get spread out more. Log transformations can also be transformed back into the original scale, easing interpretation. A downside is that the log transformation cannot be used on negative numbers. In the `earthquakes` data set, we learned that the magnitude is already expressed in log scale. The magnitude 9.1 Great Tohoku Earthquake is extreme, but the value would appear even more extreme were it not expressed in log scale!

The `depth` field is measured in kilometers. Here we'll query both the depth and the depth with the `log` function applied and then graph the output in Figures 6-12 and 6-13 in order to demonstrate the difference. The `log` function uses base 10 as a default. To reduce the result set for easier graphing, the depth is also rounded to one significant digit using the `round` function. The table is filtered to exclude values less than 0.05, as these would round to zero or less than zero:

```
SELECT round(depth,1) as depth
,log(round(depth,1)) as log_depth
,count(*) as earthquakes
FROM earthquakes
WHERE depth >= 0.05
GROUP BY 1,2
;

depth  log_depth            earthquakes
-----  -------------------  -----------
0.1    -1.0000000000000000  6994
0.2    -0.6989700043360188  6876
0.3    -0.5228787452803376  7269
...    ...                  ...
```

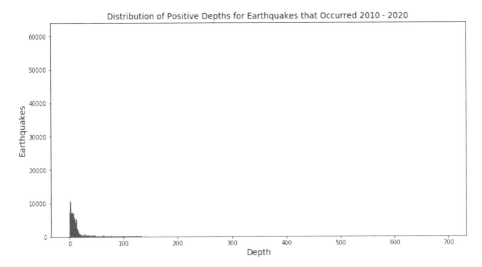

Figure 6-12. Distribution of earthquakes by depth, with unadjusted depths

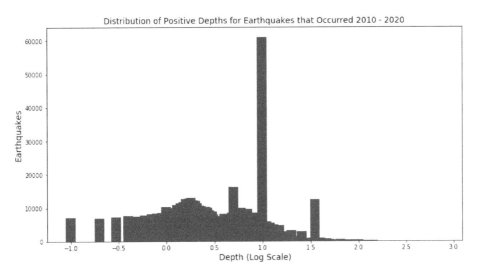

Figure 6-13. Distribution of earthquakes by depth on a log scale

In Figure 6-12, it's apparent that there are a large number of earthquakes between 0.05 and maybe 20, but beyond that it's difficult to see the distribution since the x-axis stretches all the way to 700 to capture the range of the data. When the depth is transformed to a log scale in Figure 6-13, however, the distribution of the smaller values is much easier to see. Notably, the spike at 1.0, which corresponds to a depth of 10 kilometers, is apparent.

Other types of scale transformations, while not necessarily appropriate for removing outliers, can be accomplished with SQL. Some common ones include:

- Square root: use the `sqrt` function
- Cube root: use the `cbrt` function
- Reciprocal transformation: 1 / `field_name`

Change the units, such as inches to feet or pounds to kilograms: multiply or divide by the appropriate conversion factor with * or /.

Rescaling can be done in SQL code, or often alternatively in the software or coding language used for graphing. The log transformation is particularly useful when there is a large spread of positive values and the patterns that are important to detect exist in the lower values.

As with all analysis, deciding how to handle anomalies depends on the purpose and the amount of context or domain knowledge you have about the data set. Removing outliers is the simplest method, but to retain all the records, techniques such as winsorizing and rescaling work well.

Conclusion

Anomaly detection is a common practice in analysis. The goal may be to detect the outliers, or it may be to manipulate them in order to prepare a data set for further analysis. In either case, the basic tools of sorting, calculating percentiles, and graphing the output of SQL queries can help you find them efficiently. Anomalies come in many varieties, with outlying values, unusual bursts of activity, and unusual absences being most common. Domain knowledge is almost always helpful as you go through the process of finding and gathering information about the causes of anomalies. Options for dealing with anomalies include investigation, removal, replacement with alternate values, and rescaling the data. The choice depends heavily on the goal, but any of these paths can be accomplished with SQL. In the next chapter, we'll turn our attention to experimentation, where the goal is to figure out whether a whole group of subjects differs from the norm of the control group.

CHAPTER 7

Experiment Analysis

Experimentation, also known as *A/B testing* or *split testing*, is considered the gold standard for establishing causality. Much data analysis work involves establishing correlations: one thing is more likely to happen when another thing also happens, whether that be an action, an attribute, or a seasonal pattern. You've probably heard the saying "correlation does not imply causation," however, and it is exactly this problem in data analysis that experimentation attempts to solve.

All experiments begin with a *hypothesis*: a guess about behavioral change that will result from some alteration to a product, process, or message. The change might be to a user interface, a new user onboarding flow, an algorithm that powers recommendations, marketing messaging or timing, or any number of other areas. If the organization built it or has control over it, it can be experimented on, at least in theory. Hypotheses are often driven by other data analysis work. For example, we might find that a high percentage of people drop out of the checkout flow, and we could hypothesize that more people might complete the checkout process if the number of steps were reduced.

The second element necessary for any experiment is a *success metric*. The behavioral change we hypothesize might be related to form completion, purchase conversion, click-through, retention, engagement, or any other behavior that is important to the organization's mission. The success metric should quantify this behavior, be reasonably easy to measure, and be sensitive enough to detect a change. Click-through, checkout completion, and time to complete a process are often good success metrics. Retention and customer satisfaction are often less suitable success metrics, despite being very important, because they are frequently influenced by many factors beyond what is being tested in any individual experiment and thus are less sensitive to the changes we'd like to test. Good success metrics are often ones that you already track as part of understanding company or organizational health.

You may wonder whether an experiment can have multiple success metrics. Certainly with SQL, it is usually possible to generate many different calculations and metrics. You should be aware of the multiple comparisons problem, however. I won't go into a full explanation here, but the gist is that the more places you look for a significant change, the more likely you are to find one. Check one metric, and you may or may not find a significant change in one of the experiment variants. Check 20 metrics, however, and there's a pretty good chance that at least one will show significance, whether or not the experiment had anything to do with that metric in the first place. As a rule of thumb, there should be one or maybe two primary success metrics. One to five additional metrics may be used for downside protection. These are sometimes called *guardrail metrics*. For example, you may want to ensure that an experiment doesn't hurt page-loading time, even though it's not the goal of the experiment to improve it.

The third element of experimentation is a system that randomly assigns entities to a control or experiment variant group and alters the experience accordingly. This type of system is also sometimes called a *cohorting system*. A number of software vendors offer experiment-cohorting tools, though some organizations choose to build them internally in order to achieve more flexibility. Either way, to perform experiment analysis with SQL, the entity-level assignment data must flow into a table in the database that also contains behavioral data.

The discussions of experiments in this chapter specifically refer to online experiments, in which variant assignment happens through a computer system and behavior is tracked digitally. There are certainly many types of experiments performed across science and social science disciplines. A key difference is that the success metrics and behaviors that are examined in online experiments are usually already tracked for other purposes, whereas in many scientific studies, the resulting behavior is tracked specifically for the experiment and only during the period of the experiment. With online experiments, we sometimes need to be creative about finding metrics that are good proxies for an impact when a direct measurement isn't possible.

With a hypothesis, a success metric, and a variant cohorting system in place, you can run experiments, collect the data, and analyze the outcomes using SQL.

Strengths and Limits of Experiment Analysis with SQL

SQL is useful for analyzing experiments. In many cases with experiment analysis, the experiment cohort data and behavioral data are already flowing into a database, making SQL a natural choice. Success metrics are often already part of an organization's reporting and analysis vocabulary, with SQL queries already developed. Joining variant assignment data to existing query logic is often relatively straightforward.

SQL is a good choice for automating experiment result reporting. The same query can be run for each experiment, substituting the name or identifier of the experiment in the *WHERE* clause. Many organizations with high volumes of experiments have created standardized reports to speed up readouts and simplify the interpretation process.

While SQL is useful for many of the steps involved with experiment analysis, it does have one major shortcoming: SQL is not able to calculate statistical significance. Many databases allow developers to extend SQL functionality with *user-defined functions* (UDFs). UDFs may be able to leverage statistical tests from languages such as Python, but they are beyond the scope of this book. A good option is to calculate summary statistics in SQL and then use an online calculator such as the one provided at Evanmiller.org (*https://oreil.ly/3uspA*) to determine whether the experiment result is statistically significant.

Why Correlation Is Not Causation: How Values Can Relate to Each Other

It's easier to prove that two values are correlated (they rise or fall together, or one exists primarily in the presence of the other) than it is to prove that one *causes* the other. Why is this the case? Although our brains are wired to detect causality, there are actually five ways in which two values, X and Y, can relate to each other:

1. *X causes Y:* This is of course what we're all trying to find. Through some mechanism, Y is the result of X.

2. *Y causes X:* The relationship is there, but the direction of causality is reversed. For example, umbrellas don't cause rain, but rather the presence of rain causes people to use umbrellas.

3. *X and Y have a common cause:* The values are related because there is some third variable that explains both of them. Sales of ice cream and use of air conditioners both rise in the summer, but neither causes the other. Higher temperatures cause both increases.

---

4. *A feedback loop exists between X and Y:* When Y increases, X increases to compensate, which leads to Y increasing in turn, and so on. This can happen when a customer is in the process of churning from a service. Fewer interactions lead to fewer items to suggest or remind, which leads to fewer interactions, and so on. Did the lack of recommendations cause less engagement, or is it the other way around?

5. *There is no relationship; it's just random:* Search long enough and you will find metrics that are correlated even though there is no actual relationship between them.

The Data Set

For this chapter, we will use a data set for a mobile game from the fictional Tanimura Studios. There are four tables. The game_users table contains records for people who downloaded the mobile game, along with the date and country. A sample of the data is shown in Figure 7-1.

*	user_id	created	country
1	1000	2020-01-01	Canada
2	1001	2020-01-01	United States
3	1002	2020-01-01	Canada
4	1003	2020-01-01	Australia
5	1004	2020-01-01	Germany
6	1005	2020-01-01	United States
7	1006	2020-01-01	United States
8	1007	2020-01-01	Canada
9	1008	2020-01-01	Australia
10	1009	2020-01-01	United States

Figure 7-1. Sample of the game_users table

The game_actions table contains records for things the users did in the game. A sample of the data is shown in Figure 7-2.

*	user_id	action	action_date
1	1000	email_optin	2020-01-01
2	1000	onboarding complete	2020-01-01
3	1001	email_optin	2020-01-01
4	1001	onboarding complete	2020-01-01
5	1002	onboarding complete	2020-01-01
6	1003	onboarding complete	2020-01-01
7	1003	email_optin	2020-01-01
8	1004	onboarding complete	2020-01-01
9	1005	onboarding complete	2020-01-01
10	1005	email_optin	2020-01-01

Figure 7-2. Sample of the game_actions table

The game_purchases table tracks purchases of in-game currency in US dollars. A sample of the data is shown in Figure 7-3.

*	user_id	purch_date	amount
1	1009	2020-01-10	50.00
2	1009	2020-01-02	2.99
3	1009	2020-01-02	10.00
4	1010	2020-01-16	25.00
5	1010	2020-01-22	25.00
6	1010	2020-01-09	50.00
7	1022	2020-01-07	25.00
8	1035	2020-01-07	10.00
9	1035	2020-01-02	2.99
10	1035	2020-01-01	2.99

Figure 7-3. Sample of the game_purchases table

Finally, the exp_assignment table contains records of which variant users were assigned to for a particular experiment. A sample of the data is shown in Figure 7-4.

*	exp_name	user_id	exp_date	variant
1	Onboarding	1000	2020-01-01	control
2	Onboarding	1001	2020-01-01	variant 1
3	Onboarding	1002	2020-01-01	control
4	Onboarding	1003	2020-01-01	variant 1
5	Onboarding	1004	2020-01-01	control
6	Onboarding	1005	2020-01-01	variant 1
7	Onboarding	1006	2020-01-01	control
8	Onboarding	1007	2020-01-01	variant 1
9	Onboarding	1008	2020-01-01	control
10	Onboarding	1009	2020-01-01	control

Figure 7-4. Sample of the exp_assignment table

All of the data in these tables is fictional, created with random number generators, though the structure is similar to what you might see in the database of a real digital gaming company.

Types of Experiments

There is a wide range of experiments. If you can change something that a user, customer, constituent, or other entity experiences, you can in theory test that change. From an analysis standpoint, there are two main types of experiments: those with binary outcomes and those with continuous outcomes.

Experiments with Binary Outcomes: The Chi-Squared Test

As you might expect, a binary outcome experiment has only two outcomes: either an action is taken or it isn't. Either a user completes a registration flow or they don't. A consumer clicks on a website ad or they don't. A student graduates or they don't. For these types of experiments, we calculate the proportion of each variant that completes the action. The numerator is the number of completers, while the denominator is all units that were exposed. This metric is also described as a rate: completion rate, click-through rate, graduation rate, and so on.

To determine whether the rates in the variants are statistically different, we can use the *chi-squared test*, which is a statistical test for categorical variables.[1] Data for a chi-squared test is often shown in the form of a *contingency table*, which shows the frequency of observations at the intersection of two attributes. This looks just like a pivot table to those who are familiar with that type of table.

Let's take a look at an example, using our mobile game data set. A product manager has introduced a new version of the onboarding flow, a series of screens that teach a new player how the game works. The product manager hopes that the new version will increase the number of players who complete the onboarding and start their first game session. The new version was introduced in an experiment called "Onboarding" that assigned users to either control or variant 1, as tracked in the exp_assignment table. An event called "onboarding complete" in the game_actions table indicates whether a user completed the onboarding flow.

The contingency table shows the frequency at the intersection of the variant assignment (control or variant 1) and whether or not onboarding was completed. We can use a query to find the values for the table. Here we count the number of users with and without an "onboarding complete" action and *GROUP BY* the variant:

---

1 See *https://www.mathsisfun.com/data/chi-square-test.html* for a good explanation of this test.

```
SELECT a.variant
,count(case when b.user_id is not null then a.user_id end) as completed
,count(case when b.user_id is null then a.user_id end) as not_completed
FROM exp_assignment a
LEFT JOIN game_actions b on a.user_id = b.user_id
 and b.action = 'onboarding complete'
WHERE a.exp_name = 'Onboarding'
GROUP BY 1
;

variant    completed  not_completed
---------  ---------  -------------
control    36268      13629
variant 1  38280      11995
```

Adding totals for each row and column turns this output into a contingency table, as in Figure 7-5.

Variant	Completed onboarding?		Total
	Yes	No	
Control	36,268	13,629	49,897
Variant 1	38,280	11,995	50,275
Total	74,548	25,624	100,172

Figure 7-5. Contingency table for onboarding completions

To make use of one of the online significance calculators, we will need the number of successes, or times when the action was taken, and the total number cohorted for each variant. The SQL to find the required data points is straightforward. The assigned variant and the count of users assigned to that variant are queried from the exp_assignment table. We then *LEFT JOIN* the game_actions table to find the count of users who completed onboarding. The *LEFT JOIN* is required since we expect that not all users completed the relevant action. Finally, we find the percent completed in each variant by dividing the number of users who completed by the total number cohorted:

```
SELECT a.variant
,count(a.user_id) as total_cohorted
,count(b.user_id) as completions
,count(b.user_id) / count(a.user_id) as pct_completed
FROM exp_assignment a
LEFT JOIN game_actions b on a.user_id = b.user_id
 and b.action = 'onboarding complete'
WHERE a.exp_name = 'Onboarding'
GROUP BY 1
;
```

variant	total_cohorted	completions	pct_completed
control	49897	36268	0.7269
variant 1	50275	38280	0.7614

We can see that variant 1 did indeed have more completions than the control experi-ence, with 76.14% completing compared to 72.69%. But is this difference statistically significant, allowing us to reject the hypothesis that there is no difference? For this, we plug our results into an online calculator and confirm that the completion rate for variant 1 was significantly higher at a 95% confidence level than the completion rate for the control. Variant 1 can be declared the winner.

 A 95% confidence level is commonly used, although this is not the only option. There are many online articles and discussions about the meaning of confidence levels, which level to use, and adjust-ments in scenarios in which you are comparing multiple variants to a control.

Binary outcome experiments follow this basic pattern. Calculate the successes or completions as well as the total members in each variant. The SQL used to derive the success events may be more complicated depending on the tables and how actions are stored in the database, but the output is consistent. Next, we'll turn to experiments with continuous outcomes.

Experiments with Continuous Outcomes: The t-Test

Many experiments seek to improve *continuous metrics*, rather than the binary out-comes discussed in the last section. Continuous metrics can take on a range of values. Examples include amount spent by customers, time spent on page, and days an app is used. Ecommerce sites often want to increase sales, and so they might experiment on product pages or checkout flows. Content sites may test layout, navigation, and head-lines to try to increase the number of stories read. A company running an app might run a remarketing campaign to remind users to come back to the app.

For these and other experiments with continuous success metrics, the goal is to figure out whether the average values in each variant differ from each other in a statistically significant way. The relevant statistical test is the *two-sample t-test*, which determines whether we can reject the null hypothesis that the averages are equal with a defined confidence interval, usually 95%. The statistical test has three inputs, all of which are straightforward to calculate with SQL: the mean, the standard deviation, and the count of observations.

Let's take a look at an example using our game data. In the last section, we looked at whether a new onboarding flow increased the completion rate. Now we will consider whether that new flow increased user spending on in-game currency. The success metric is the amount spent, so we need to calculate the mean and standard deviation of this value for each variant. First we need to calculate the amount per user, since users can make multiple purchases. Retrieve the cohort assignment from the exp_assignment table and count the users. Next, *LEFT JOIN* to the game_purchases table to gather the amount data. The *LEFT JOIN* is required since not all users make a purchase, but we still need to include them in the mean and standard deviation calculations. For users without purchases, the amount is set to a default of 0 with coalesce. Since the avg and stddev functions ignore nulls, the 0 default is required to ensure that these records are included. The outer query summarizes the output values by variant:

```
SELECT variant
,count(user_id) as total_cohorted
,avg(amount) as mean_amount
,stddev(amount) as stddev_amount
FROM
(
    SELECT a.variant
    ,a.user_id
    ,sum(coalesce(b.amount,0)) as amount
    FROM exp_assignment a
    LEFT JOIN game_purchases b on a.user_id = b.user_id
    WHERE a.exp_name = 'Onboarding'
    GROUP BY 1,2
) a
GROUP BY 1
;

variant     total_cohorted  mean_amount  stddev_amount
---------   --------------  -----------  -------------
control     49897           3.781        18.940
variant 1   50275           3.688        19.220
```

Next, we plug these values into an online calculator and find that there is no significant difference between the control and variant groups at a 95% confidence interval. The "variant 1" group appears to have increased onboarding completion rates but not the amount spent.

Another question we might consider is whether variant 1 affected spending among those users who completed the onboarding. Those who don't complete the onboarding never make it into the game and therefore don't even have the opportunity to make a purchase. To answer this question, we can use a query similar to the previous one, but we'll add an *INNER JOIN* to the game_actions table to restrict the users counted to only those who have an action of "onboarding complete":

```
SELECT variant
,count(user_id) as total_cohorted
,avg(amount) as mean_amount
,stddev(amount) as stddev_amount
```

```
FROM
(
    SELECT a.variant
    ,a.user_id
    ,sum(coalesce(b.amount,0)) as amount
    FROM exp_assignment a
    LEFT JOIN game_purchases b on a.user_id = b.user_id
    JOIN game_actions c on a.user_id = c.user_id
     and c.action = 'onboarding complete'
    WHERE a.exp_name = 'Onboarding'
    GROUP BY 1,2
) a
GROUP BY 1
;

variant     total_cohorted  mean_amount  stddev_amount
---------   --------------  -----------  -------------
control     36268           5.202        22.049
variant 1   38280           4.843        21.899
```

Plugging these values into the calculator reveals that the average for the control group is statistically significantly higher than that for variant 1 at a 95% confidence interval. This result may seem perplexing, but it illustrates why it is so important to agree on the success metric for an experiment up front. The experiment variant 1 had a positive effect on onboarding completion and so can be judged a success. It did not have an effect on the overall spending level. This could be due to a mix shift: the additional users who made it through onboarding in variant 1 were less likely to pay. If the underlying hypothesis was that increasing onboarding completion rates would increase revenue, then the experiment should not be judged a success, and the product managers should come up with some new ideas to test.

Challenges with Experiments and Options for Rescuing Flawed Experiments

Although experimentation is the gold standard for understanding causality, there are a number of ways experiments can go wrong. If the entire premise is flawed, there won't be much that SQL can do to save the day. If the flaw is more technical in nature, we may be able to query the data in such a way as to adjust or exclude problematic data points and still interpret some results. Running experiments has a cost in terms of the time spent by engineers, designers, or marketers who create variants. It also has *opportunity cost*, or the missed benefit that could have been gained by sending customers down an optimal conversion path or product experience. On a practical level, using SQL to help the organization at least learn something from an experiment is often time well spent.

Variant Assignment

Random assignment of experiment units (which can be users, sessions, or other entities) to control and variant groups is one of the key elements of experimentation. However, sometimes errors in the assignment process happen, whether because of a flaw in the experiment specification, a technical failure, or a limitation in the cohorting software. As a result, the control and variant groups may be of unequal sizes, fewer overall entities may have been cohorted than expected, or the assignment may not have actually been random.

SQL can sometimes help salvage an experiment in which too many units were cohorted. I have seen this happen when an experiment is meant to target only new users but all users are cohorted instead. Another way this can happen is when an experiment tests something that only a subset of users will see, either because it is a few clicks into the experience or because certain conditions must be met, such as previous purchase. Due to technical limitations, all users get cohorted, even though a chunk of them would never see the experiment treatment even if they are in that group. The solution is to add a *JOIN* into the SQL that restricts the users or entities considered to only those that were intended to be eligible. For example, in the case of a new user experiment, we can add an *INNER JOIN* to a table or subquery that contains user registration date and set a *WHERE* condition to exclude users who registered too far prior to the cohort event to be considered new. The same strategy can be used when a certain condition must be met to even see the experiment. Restrict the entities included by excluding those that shouldn't be eligible via *JOIN*s and *WHERE* conditions. After doing this, you should check to make sure that the resulting population is a large enough sample to produce significant results.

If too few users or entities are cohorted, it's important to check whether the sample is large enough to produce significant results. If not, run the experiment again. If the sample size is large enough, a second consideration is whether there is bias in who or what was cohorted. As an example, I have seen cases in which users on certain browsers or older app versions were not cohorted due to technical limitations. If populations that were excluded aren't random and represent differences in location, technical savvy, or socioeconomic status, it's important to consider both how large this population is relative to the rest and whether any adjustments should be made to include them in the final analysis.

Another possibility is that the variant assignment system is flawed and entities are not assigned randomly. This is fairly unusual with most modern experiment tools, but if it happens, it invalidates the whole experiment. Results that are "too good to be true" might signal a variant assignment problem. I have seen, for example, cases in which highly engaged users are accidentally assigned to both treatment and control due to a change in experiment configuration. Careful data profiling can check whether entities have been assigned to multiple variants or whether users with high or low engagement prior to the experiment are clustered in a particular variant.

 Running an A/A test can help uncover flaws in the variant assignment software. In this type of test, entities are cohorted and success metrics are compared, just like in any other experiment. However, no changes are made to the experience, and both cohorts receive the control experience. Since the groups receive the same experience, we should expect no significant differences in the success metric. If it turns out there is a difference, further investigation should be done to uncover and fix the problem.

Outliers

Statistical tests for analyzing continuous success metrics rely on averages. As a result, they are sensitive to unusually high or low outlier values. I have seen experiments in which the presence of one or two particularly high-spending customers in a variant gives that variant a statistically significant edge over others. Without those few high spenders, the result may be neutral or even the reverse. In most cases, we are more interested in whether a treatment has an effect across a range of individuals, and thus adjusting for these outliers can make an experiment result more meaningful.

We discussed anomaly detection in Chapter 6, and experiment analysis is another place in which those techniques can be applied. Outlier values can be determined either by analyzing the experiment results or by finding the base rate prior to the experiment. The outliers may be removed via a technique such as winsorizing (also discussed in Chapter 6), which removes values beyond a threshold, such as the 95th or 99th percentile. This can be done in SQL before moving on to the rest of the experiment analysis.

Another option for dealing with outliers in continuous success metrics is to turn the success metric into a binary outcome. For example, instead of comparing the average spend across the control and variant groups, which may be distorted due to a few very high spenders, compare the purchase rate between the two groups and then follow the procedure discussed in the section on experiments with binary outcomes. We could consider the conversion rate to purchaser among users who completed onboarding in the control and variant 1 groups from the "Onboarding" experiment:

```
SELECT a.variant
,count(distinct a.user_id) as total_cohorted
,count(distinct b.user_id) as purchasers
,count(distinct b.user_id) / count(distinct a.user_id)
 as pct_purchased
FROM exp_assignment a
LEFT JOIN game_purchases b on a.user_id = b.user_id
JOIN game_actions c on a.user_id = c.user_id
```

```
  and c.action = 'onboarding complete'
WHERE a.exp_name = 'Onboarding'
GROUP BY 1
;

variant    total_cohorted  purchasers  pct_purchased
--------   --------------  ----------  -------------
control    36268           4988        0.1000
variant 1  38280           4981        0.0991
```

We can look at the numbers and observe that even though there are more users in variant 1, there are fewer purchasers. The percentage of users who purchased in the control group is 10%, compared to 9.91% for variant 1. Next, we plug the data points into an online calculator. The conversion rate is statistically significantly higher for the control group. In this case, even though the rate of purchasing was higher for the control group, on a practical level we may be willing to accept this small decline if we believe that more users completing the onboarding process has other benefits. More players might boost rankings, for example, and players who enjoy the game may spread it to their friends via word of mouth, both of which can help growth and may then lead to attracting other new players who will become purchasers.

The success metric can also be set to a threshold, and the share of entities meeting that threshold compared. For example, the success metric could be reading at least three stories or using an app at least two times a week. An infinite number of metrics could be constructed in this way, so it's important to understand what is both important and meaningful to the organization.

Time Boxing

Experiments are often run over the course of several weeks. This means that individuals who enter the experiment earlier have a longer window in which to complete actions associated with the success metric. To control for this, we can apply *time boxing*—imposing a fixed length of time relative to the experiment entry date and considering actions only during that window. This concept was also covered in Chapter 4.

For experiments, the appropriate size of the time box depends on what you are measuring. The window could be as short as one hour when measuring an action that typically has an immediate response, such as clicking on an ad. For purchase conversion, experimenters often allow a window of 1 to 7 days. Shorter windows allow experiments to be analyzed sooner, since all cohorted entities need to be allowed the full time to complete actions. The best windows balance the need to obtain results with the actual dynamics of the organization. If customers typically convert in a few days, consider a 7-day window; if customers often take 20 or more days, consider a 30-day window.

As an example, we can revise our first example from experiments with continuous outcomes by only including purchases within 7 days of the cohorting event. Note that it is important to use the time the entity was assigned to a variant as the starting point of the time box. An additional *ON* clause is added, restricting the results to purchases that occurred within the interval "7 days":

```
SELECT variant
,count(user_id) as total_cohorted
,avg(amount) as mean_amount
,stddev(amount) as stddev_amount
FROM
(
    SELECT a.variant
    ,a.user_id
    ,sum(coalesce(b.amount,0)) as amount
    FROM exp_assignment a
    LEFT JOIN game_purchases b on a.user_id = b.user_id
     and b.purch_date <= a.exp_date + interval '7 days'
    WHERE a.exp_name = 'Onboarding'
    GROUP BY 1,2
) a
GROUP BY 1
;


variant    total_cohorted  mean_amount  stddev_amount
--------   --------------  -----------  -------------
control    49897           1.369        5.766
variant 1  50275           1.352        5.613
```

The means are similar, and in fact statistically they are not significantly different from each other. In this example, the time-boxed conclusion agrees with the conclusion when there was no time box.

In this case, purchase events are relatively rare. For metrics that measure common events and those that accumulate quickly, such as pageviews, clicks, likes, and articles read, using a time box can prevent the earliest cohorted users from looking substantially "better" than those cohorted later.

Repeated Exposure Experiments

In discussions of online experimentation, most examples are of what I like to call "one-and-done" experiences: the user encounters a treatment once, reacts to it, and does not pass that way again. User registration is a classic example: a consumer signs up for a particular service only once, and therefore any changes to the sign-up process affect only new users. Analyzing tests on these experiences is relatively straightforward.

There is another type of experience that I call "repeated exposure," in which an individual comes into contact with the change many times during the course of using a product or service. In any experiment involving these changes, we can expect individuals to encounter them more than once. Changes to an app's user interface, such as color, text, and placement of important information and links, are experienced by users throughout their app usage. Email marketing programs that send customers reminders or promotions on a regular basis also have this repeated exposure quality. Emails are experienced many times as subject lines in the inbox, and as content if opened.

Measuring repeated exposure experiments is trickier than measuring one-and-done experiments due to novelty effects and regression to the mean. A *novelty effect* is the tendency for behavior to change just because something is new, not because it is necessarily better. *Regression to the mean* is the tendency for phenomena to return to an average level over time. As an example, changing any part of a user interface tends to increase the number of people who interact with it, whether it is a new button color, logo, or placement of functionality. Initially the metrics look good, because the click-through rate or engagement goes up. This is the novelty effect. But over time, users get used to the change, and they tend to click or use the functionality at rates that return closer to the baseline. This is the regression to the mean. The important question to answer when running this kind of experiment is whether the new baseline is higher (or lower) than the previous one. One solution is to allow passage of a long enough time period, in which you might expect regression to happen, before evaluating the results. In some cases, this will be a few days; in others, it might be a few weeks or months.

When there are many changes, or the experiment comes in a series such as email or physical mail campaigns, figuring out whether the entire program makes a difference can be a challenge. It's easy to claim success when customers receiving a certain email variant purchase a product, but how do we know if they would have made that purchase anyway? One option is to set up a *long-term holdout*. This is a group that is set up to not receive any marketing messages or changes to the product experience. Note that this is different from simply comparing to users who have opted out of marketing messages, since there is usually some bias in who opts out and who doesn't. Setting up long-term holdouts can be complicated, but there are few better ways to truly measure the cumulative effects of campaigns and product changes.

Another option is to perform cohort analysis (discussed in Chapter 4) on the variants. The groups can be followed for a longer time period, from weeks to months. Retention or cumulative metrics can be calculated and tested to see whether effects differ between variants over the long term.

Even with the various challenges that can be encountered with experiments, they are still the best way to test and prove the causality around changes made to experiences ranging from marketing messaging and creative to in-product experience. We often encounter less than ideal situations in data analysis, however, so next we'll turn to some analysis options for when A/B testing isn't possible.

When Controlled Experiments Aren't Possible: Alternative Analyses

Randomized experiments are the gold standard for going beyond correlation to establish causality. However, there are a number of reasons why a randomized experiment may not be possible. It may be unethical to give different treatments to different groups, particularly in medical or educational settings. Regulatory requirements may prevent experiments in other settings, such as financial services. There may be practical reasons, such as the difficulty of restricting access to a variant treatment to only a randomized group. It's always worth considering whether there are pieces that are worth testing or are testable within ethical, regulatory, and practical boundaries. Wording, placement, and other design elements are some examples.

A second situation in which experimentation isn't possible is when a change happened in the past and the data has already been collected. Aside from reverting the change, going back and running an experiment isn't an option. Sometimes a data analyst or data scientist wasn't available to advise on experimentation. More than once, I have joined an organization and been asked to untangle the results of changes that would have been much more straightforward to understand had there been a holdout group. At other times, the change is unintended. Examples include site outages that affect some or all customers, errors in forms, and natural disasters such as storms, earthquakes, and wildfires.

Although causal conclusions aren't as strong in situations in which there was no experiment, there are a few quasi-experimental analysis methods that can be used to draw insights from the data. These rely on constructing groups from the available data that represent "control" and "treatment" conditions as closely as possible.

Pre-/Post-Analysis

A pre-/post-analysis compares either the same or similar populations before and after a change. The measurement of the population before the change is used as the control, while the measurement after the change is used as the variant or treatment.

Pre-/post-analysis works best when there is a clearly defined change that happened on a well-known date, so that the before and after groups can be cleanly divided. In this type of analysis, you will need to choose how long to measure before and after the change, but the periods should be equal or close to equal. For example, if two weeks have elapsed since a change, compare that period to the two weeks prior to the change. Consider comparing multiple periods, such as one week, two weeks, three weeks, and four weeks before and after the change. If the results agree across all these windows, you can have more confidence in the result than you would if the results differed.

Let's walk through an example. Imagine that the onboarding flow for our mobile game includes a step in which the user can check a box to indicate whether they want to receive emails with game news. This had always been checked by default, but a new regulation requires that it now be unchecked by default. On January 27, 2020, the change was released into the game, and we would like to find out if it had a negative effect on email opt-in rates. To do this, we will compare the two weeks before the change to the two weeks after the change and see whether the opt-in rate is statistically significantly different. We could use one-week or three-week periods, but two weeks is chosen because it is long enough to allow for some day-of-week variability and also short enough to restrict the number of other factors that could otherwise affect users' willingness to opt in.

The variants are assigned in the SQL query via a CASE statement: the users who were created in the time range prior to the change are labeled "pre," while those created after the change are labeled "post." Next, we count the number of users in each group from the game_users table. Then we count the number of users who opted in, which is accomplished with a *LEFT JOIN* to the game_actions table, restricting to the records with the "email_optin" action. Then we divide the values to find the percent who opted in. I like to include the count of days in each variant as a quality check, though it is not necessary to perform the rest of the analysis:

```
SELECT
case when a.created between '2020-01-13' and '2020-01-26' then 'pre'
     when a.created between '2020-01-27' and '2020-02-09' then 'post'
     end as variant
,count(distinct a.user_id) as cohorted
,count(distinct b.user_id) as opted_in
,count(distinct b.user_id) / count(distinct a.user_id) as pct_optin
,count(distinct a.created) as days
FROM game_users a
LEFT JOIN game_actions b on a.user_id = b.user_id
 and b.action = 'email_optin'
WHERE a.created between '2020-01-13' and '2020-02-09'
GROUP BY 1
;

variant  cohorted  opted_in  pct_optin  days
-------  --------  --------  ---------  ----
pre      24662     14489     0.5875     14
post     27617     11220     0.4063     14
```

Many databases will recognize dates entered as strings, as in `'2020-01-13'`. If your database does not, cast the string to a date using one of these options:

```
cast('2020-01-13' as date)

date('2020-01-13')

'2020-01-13'::date
```

In this case, we can see that the users who went through the onboarding flow before the change had a much higher email opt-in rate—58.75%, compared to 40.63% afterward. Plugging the values into an online calculator results in confirmation that the rate for the "pre" group is statistically significantly higher than the rate for the "post" group. In this example, there may not be much the game company can do, since the change is due to a regulation. Further tests could determine whether providing sample content or other information about the email program might encourage more new players to opt in, if this is a business goal.

When performing a pre-/post-analysis, keep in mind that other factors beyond the change that you're trying to learn about may cause an increase or a decrease in the metric. External events, seasonality, marketing promotions, and so on can drastically change the environment and customers' mindsets even within the span of a few weeks. As a result, this type of analysis is not as good as a true randomized experiment for proving causality. However, sometimes this is one of the few analysis options available, and it can generate working hypotheses that can be tested and refined in future controlled experiments.

Natural Experiment Analysis

A *natural experiment* occurs when entities end up with different experiences through some process that approximates randomness. One group receives the normal or control experience, and another receives some variation that may have a positive or negative effect. Usually these are unintentional, such as when a software bug is introduced, or when an event happens in one location but not in other locations. For this type of analysis to have validity, we must be able to clearly determine which entities were exposed. Additionally, a control group that is as similar as possible to the exposed group is needed.

SQL can be used to construct the variants and to calculate the size of cohorts and success events in the case of a binary outcome event (or the mean, standard deviation, and population sizes in the case of a continuous outcome event). The results can be plugged into an online calculator just like with any other experiment.

As an example in the video game data set, imagine that, during the time period of our data, users in Canada were accidentally given a different offer on the virtual currency purchase page the first time they looked at it: an extra zero was added to the number of virtual coins in each package. So, for example, instead of 10 coins the user would receive 100 game coins, or instead of 100 coins they would receive 1,000 game coins, and so on. The question we would like to answer is whether Canadians converted to buyers at a higher rate than other users. Rather than compare to the entire user base, we will compare only to users in the United States. The countries are close geographically, and most users in the two countries speak the same language—and for the sake of the example, we'll assume that we've done other analysis showing that their behavior is similar, while the behavior of users in other countries differs enough to exclude them.

To perform the analysis, we create the "variants" from whatever the distinguishing characteristic is—in this case, the country field from the game_users table—but note that sometimes more complex SQL will be required, depending on the data set. The counts of users cohorted, and those who purchased, are calculated in the same way we saw previously:

```
SELECT a.country
,count(distinct a.user_id) as total_cohorted
,count(distinct b.user_id) as purchasers
,count(distinct b.user_id) / count(distinct a.user_id)
 as pct_purchased
FROM game_users a
LEFT JOIN game_purchases b on a.user_id = b.user_id
WHERE a.country in ('United States','Canada')
GROUP BY 1
;


country        total_cohorted  purchasers  pct_purchased
-------------  --------------  ----------  -------------
Canada         20179           5011        0.2483
United States  45012           4958        0.1101
```

The share of users in Canada who purchased is in fact higher—24.83%, compared to 11.01% of those in the United States. Plugging these values into an online calculator confirms that the conversion rate in Canada is statistically significantly higher at a 95% confidence interval.

The hardest part of analyzing a natural experiment tends to be finding a comparable population and showing that the two populations are similar enough to support the conclusions from the statistical test. Although it is virtually impossible to prove that there are no confounding factors, careful comparison of population demographics and behaviors lends credibility to the results. Since a natural experiment is not a true random experiment, the evidence for causality is weaker, and this should be noted in the presentation of analysis of this type.

Analysis of Populations Around a Threshold

In some cases, there is a threshold value that results in some people or other subject units getting a treatment, while others do not. For example, a certain grade point average might qualify students for a scholarship, a certain income level might qualify households for subsidized health care, or a high churn risk score might trigger a sales rep to follow up with a customer. In such cases, we can leverage the idea that subjects on either side of the threshold value are likely quite similar to each other. So instead of comparing the entire populations that did and did not receive the reward or intervention, we can compare only those that were close to the threshold both on the positive and the negative side. The formal name for this is *regression discontinuity design* (RDD).

To perform this type of analysis, we can construct "variants" by splitting the data around the threshold value, similar to what we did in the pre-/post-analysis. Unfortunately, there is no hard-and-fast rule about how wide to make the bands of values on either side of the threshold. The "variants" should be similar in size, and they should be large enough to allow for significance in the results analysis. One option is to perform the analysis several times with a few different ranges. For example, you might analyze the differences between the "treated" group and the control when each group contains subjects that fall within 5%, 7.5%, and 10% of the threshold. If the conclusions from these analyses agree, there is more support for the conclusions. If they do not agree, however, the data may be considered inconclusive.

As with other types of nonexperimental analysis, results from RDD should be taken as proving causality less conclusively. Potential confounding factors should receive careful attention as well. For example, if customers with high churn risk receive interventions from multiple teams, or a special discount to encourage them to retain, in addition to a call from a sales rep, the data can potentially be tainted by those other changes.

Conclusion

Experiment analysis is a rich field that often incorporates different types of analysis seen in other parts of this book, from anomaly detection to cohort analysis. Data profiling can be useful in tracking down issues that occur. When randomized experiments are not possible, a variety of other techniques are available, and SQL can be used to create synthetic control and variant groups.

In the next chapter, we'll turn to constructing complex data sets for analysis, an area that brings together various topics that we've discussed in the book so far.

CHAPTER 8

Creating Complex Data Sets for Analysis

In Chapters 3 through 7, we looked at a number of ways in which SQL can be used to perform analysis on data in databases. In addition to these specific use cases, sometimes the goal of a query is to assemble a data set that is specific yet general-purpose enough that it can be used to perform a variety of further analyses. The destination might be a database table, a text file, or a business intelligence tool. The SQL that is needed might be simple, requiring only a few filters or aggregations. Often, however, the code or logic needed to achieve the desired data set can become very complex. Additionally, such code is likely to be updated over time, as stakeholders request additional data points or calculations. The organization, performance, and maintainability of your SQL code become critical in a way that isn't the case for one-time analyses.

In this chapter, I'll discuss principles for organizing code so that it's easier to share and update. Then I'll discuss when to keep query logic in the SQL and when to consider moving to permanent tables via ETL (extract-transform-load) code. Next, I'll explain the options for storing intermediate results—subqueries, temp tables, and common table expressions (CTEs)—and considerations for using them in your code. Finally, I'll wrap up with a look at techniques for reducing data set size and ideas for handling data privacy and removing personally identifiable information (PII).

When to Use SQL for Complex Data Sets

Almost all data sets prepared for further analysis contain some logic. The logic can range from the relatively simple—such as how tables are *JOIN*ed together and how filters are placed in the *WHERE* clause—to complex calculations that aggregate, categorize, parse, or perform window functions over partitions of the data. When creating data sets for further analysis, choosing whether to keep the logic within the SQL query or to push it upstream to an ETL job or downstream to another tool is often as much art as science. Convenience, performance, and availability of help from engineers all factor into the decision. There is often no single right answer, but you will develop intuition and confidence the longer you work with SQL.

Advantages of Using SQL

SQL is a very flexible language. Hopefully I convinced you in the earlier chapters that a wide variety of data preparation and analysis tasks can be accomplished using SQL. This flexibility is the main advantage of using SQL when developing complex data sets.

In the initial stages of working with a data set, you may execute many queries. Work often starts with several profiling queries to understand the data. This is followed by building up the query step-by-step, checking transformations and aggregations along the way to be sure that the results returned are correct. This may be interspersed with more profiling, when actual values turn out to differ from our expectations. Complex data sets may be built up by combining several subqueries that answer specific questions with *JOINs* or *UNIONs*. Running a query and examining the output is fast and allows for rapid iteration.

Aside from relying on the quality and timeliness of the data in the tables, SQL has few dependencies. Queries are run on demand and don't rely on a data engineer or a release process. Queries can often be embedded into business intelligence (BI) tools or into R or Python code by the analyst or data scientist, without requesting technical support. When a stakeholder needs another attribute or aggregation added to the output, changes can be made quickly.

Keeping logic in the SQL code itself is ideal when working on a new analysis and when you expect the logic and result set to undergo changes frequently. Additionally, when the query is fast and data is returned to stakeholders quickly, there may never be a need to move the logic anywhere else.

When to Build into ETL Instead

There are times when moving logic into an ETL process is a better choice than keeping all of it in a SQL query, especially when working in an organization that has a data warehouse or data lake. The two main reasons to use ETL are performance and visibility.

Performance of SQL queries depends on the complexity of the logic, the size of the tables queried, and the computational resources of the underlying database. Although many queries run fast, particularly on the newer databases and hardware, you will inevitably end up writing some queries that have complex calculations, involve *JOINs* of large tables or Cartesian *JOINs*, or otherwise cause query time to slow down to minutes or longer. An analyst or a data scientist may be willing to wait for a query to return. However, most consumers of data are used to websites' rapid response times and will get frustrated if they have to wait more than a few seconds for data.

ETL runs behind the scenes at scheduled times and writes the result to a table. Since it is behind the scenes, it can run for 30 seconds, five minutes, or an hour, and end users will not be affected. Schedules are often daily but can be set to shorter intervals. End users can query the resulting table directly, without need for *JOINs* or other logic, and thus experience fast query times.

A good example of when ETL is often a better choice than keeping all of the logic in a SQL query is the daily snapshot table. In many organizations, keeping a daily snapshot of customers, orders, or other entities is useful for answering analytical questions. For customers, we might want to calculate total orders or visits to date, current status in a sales pipeline, and other attributes that either change or accumulate. We've seen how to create daily series, including for days when an entity was not present, in the discussions of time series analysis in Chapter 3 and cohort analysis in Chapter 4. At the individual entity level, and over long time periods, such queries can become slow. Additionally, attributes such as current status may be overwritten in the source table, so capturing a daily snapshot may be the only way to preserve an accurate picture of history. Developing the ETL and storing daily snapshot results in a table are often worth the effort.

Visibility is a second reason to move logic into ETL. Often SQL queries exist on an individual's computer or are buried within report code. It can be difficult for others to even find the logic embedded in the query, let alone understand and check it for mistakes. Moving logic into ETL and storing the ETL code in a repository such as GitHub makes it easier for others in an organization to find, check, and iterate on it. Most repositories used by development teams also store change history, an additional benefit that allows you to see when a particular line in a query was added or changed.

There are good reasons to consider putting logic into ETL, but this approach also has its drawbacks. One is that fresh results are not available until the ETL job has run and refreshed the data, even if new data has arrived in the underlying table. This can be overcome by continuing to run SQL against the raw data for very new records but limiting it to a small time window so that the query runs quickly. This can optionally be combined with a query on the ETL table, using subqueries or *UNION*. Another drawback to placing logic in ETL is that it becomes harder to change. Updates or bug fixes often need to be handed to a data engineer and code tested, checked into the repository, and released into the production data warehouse. For this reason, I usually opt to wait until my SQL queries are past the period of rapid iteration, and the resulting data sets have been reviewed and are in use by the organization, before moving them into ETL. Of course, making code harder to change and enforcing code reviews are excellent ways to ensure consistency and data quality.

Views as an Alternative to ETL

When you want the reusability and code visibility of ETL but without actually storing the results and therefore taking up space permanently, a database *view* can be a good option. A view is essentially a saved query with a permanent alias that can be referenced just like any other table in the database. The query can be simple or complex and may involve table joins, filters, and any other elements of SQL.

Views can be used to ensure that everyone querying the data uses the same definitions, as defined in the underlying query—for example, by always filtering out test transactions. They can be used to shield users from the complexity of the underlying logic, helpful for more novice or occasional users of a database. Views can also be used to provide an extra layer of security by restricting access to certain rows or columns in a database. For example, a view might be created to exclude PII such as email addresses but allow query writers to view other acceptable customer attributes.

Views have a few drawbacks, however. They are objects in the database and thus require permissions to create and update their definitions. Views do not store the data, so each time a query is run with a view, the database must go back to the underlying table or tables to fetch the data. As a result, they are not a replacement for ETL that creates a precomputed table of data.

Most major databases also have *materialized views*, which are similar to views but do store the returned data in a table. Planning for the creation and refreshing of materialized views is usually best done in consultation with an experienced database administrator, as there are nuanced performance considerations beyond the scope of this book.

When to Put Logic in Other Tools

SQL code and the query results output in your query editor are frequently only part of an analysis. Results are often embedded in reports, visualized into tables and graphs, or further manipulated in a range of tools, from spreadsheets and BI software to environments in which statistical or machine learning code is applied. In addition to choosing when to move logic upstream into ETL, we also have choices about when to move logic downstream into other tools. Both performance and specific use cases are key factors in the decision.

Each type of tool has performance strengths and limitations. Spreadsheets are very flexible but are not known for being able to handle large numbers of rows or complex calculations across many rows. Databases definitely have a performance advantage, so it's often best to perform as much of the calculation as possible in the database and pass the smallest data set possible on to the spreadsheet.

BI tools have a range of capabilities, so it's important to understand both how the software handles calculations and how the data will be used. Some BI tools can *cache* data (keep a local copy) in an optimized format, speeding up calculations. Others issue a new query each time a field is added to or removed from a report and thus mainly leverage the computational power of the database. Certain calculations such as count distinct and median require detailed, entity-level data. If it's not possible to anticipate all the variations on these calculations in advance, it may be necessary to pass a larger, more detailed data set than otherwise might be ideal. Additionally, if the goal is to create a data set that allows exploration and slicing in many different ways, more detail is usually better. Figuring out the best combination of SQL, ETL, and BI tool computation can take some iteration.

When the goal is to perform statistical or machine learning analysis on the data set using a language such as R or Python, detailed data is usually better. Both of these languages can perform tasks that overlap with SQL, such as aggregation and text manipulation. It's often best to perform as much of the calculation as possible in SQL, to leverage the computational power of the database, but no more. Flexibility to iterate is usually an important part of the modeling process. The choice of whether to perform calculations in SQL or another language may also depend on your familiarity and comfort level with each. Those who are very comfortable in SQL may prefer to do more calculations in the database, while those who are more proficient in R or Python may prefer to do more calculations there.

 Although there are few rules to deciding where to put logic, I will encourage you to follow one rule in particular: avoid manual steps. It's easy enough to open a data set in a spreadsheet or text editor, make a small change, save, and move on. But when you need to iterate, or when new data arrives, it's easy to forget that manual step or to perform it inconsistently. In my experience, there's no such thing as a truly "one-off" request. Put logic into code somewhere, if at all possible.

SQL is a great tool and is incredibly flexible. It also sits within the analysis workflow and within an ecosystem of tools. Deciding where to put calculations can take some trial and error as you iterate through what is feasible among SQL, ETL, and downstream tools. The more familiarity and experience you have with all the available options, the better you will be able to estimate trade-offs and continue to improve the performance and flexibility of your work.

Code Organization

SQL has few formatting rules, which can lead to unruly queries. Query clauses must be in the correct order: *SELECT* is followed by *FROM*, and *GROUP BY* cannot precede *WHERE*, for example. A few keywords such as *SELECT* and *FROM* are *reserved* (i.e., they cannot be used as field names, table names, or aliases). However, unlike in some other languages, newlines, whitespace (other than the spaces that separate words), and capitalization are not important and are ignored by the database. Any of the example queries in this book could have been written on a single line, and with or without capital letters, except in quoted strings. As a result, the burden of code organization is on the person writing the query. Fortunately, we have some formal and informal tools for keeping code organized, from commenting to "cosmetic" formatting such as indentation and storage options for files of SQL code.

Commenting

Most coding languages have a way to indicate that a block of text should be treated as a comment and ignored during execution. SQL has two options. The first is to use two dash marks, which turns everything on the line that follows into a comment:

```
-- This is a comment
```

The second option is to use the slash (/) and star (*) characters to start a comment block, which can extend over multiple lines, followed by a star and slash to end the comment block:

```
/*
This is a comment block
with multiple lines
*/
```

Many SQL editors adjust the visual style of code inside comments, by graying them out or otherwise changing the color, to make them easier to spot.

Commenting code is a good practice, but admittedly it's one that many people struggle to do on a regular basis. SQL is often written quickly, and especially during exploration or profiling exercises, we don't expect to keep our code for the long term. Overly commented code can be just as difficult to read as code with no comments. And we all suffer from the idea that since we wrote the code, we will always be able to remember *why* we wrote the code. However, anyone who has inherited a long query written by a colleague or has stepped away from a query for a few months and then come back to update it will know that it can be frustrating and time consuming to decipher the code.

To balance the burden and the benefit of commenting, I try to follow a few rules of thumb. First, add a comment anywhere that a value has a nonobvious meaning. Many source systems will encode values as integers, and their meaning is easy to forget.

Leaving a note makes the meaning clear and makes the code easier to change if needed:

```
WHERE status in (1,2) -- 1 is Active, 2 is Pending
```

Second, comment on any other nonobvious calculations or transformations. These can be anything that someone who hasn't spent the time profiling the data set might not know, from data entry errors to the existence of outliers:

```
case when status = 'Live' then 'Active'
    else status end
    /* we used to call customers Live but in
    2020 we switched it to Active */
```

The third practice I try to follow around commenting is to leave notes when the query contains multiple subqueries. A quick line about what each subquery calculates makes it easy to skip to the relevant piece when coming back later to quality check or edit a longer query:

```
SELECT...
FROM
( -- find the first date for each customer
    SELECT ...
    FROM ...
) a
JOIN
( -- find all of the products for each customer
    SELECT ...
    FROM ...
) b on a.field = b.field
...
;
```

Commenting well takes practice and some discipline, but it's worth doing for most queries that are longer than a few lines. Commenting can also be used to add useful information to the overall query, such as purpose, author, date created, and so on. Be kind to your colleagues, and to your future self, by placing helpful comments in your code.

Capitalization, Indentation, Parentheses, and Other Formatting Tricks

Formatting, and consistent formatting especially, is a good way to keep SQL code organized and legible. Databases ignore capitalization and whitespace (spaces, tabs, and newlines) in SQL, so we can use these to our advantage to format code into more legible blocks. Parentheses can both control the order of execution, which we will discuss more later, and also visually group calculation elements.

Capitalized words stand out from the rest, as anyone who has received an email with an all-caps subject line can confirm. I like to use capitalization only for the main clauses: *SELECT, FROM, JOIN, WHERE*, and so on. Particularly in long or complex queries, being able to spot these quickly and thus to understand where the *SELECT* clause ends and the *FROM* clause begins saves me a lot of time.

Whitespace is another key way to organize and make parts of the query easier to find, and to understand which parts logically go together. Any SQL query could be written on a single line in the editor, but in most cases this would lead to a lot of scrolling left and right through code. I like to start each clause (*SELECT, FROM*, etc.) on a new line, which, along with capitalization, helps me keep track of where each one starts and ends. Additionally, I find that putting aggregations on their own lines, as well as functions that take up some space, helps with organization. For CASE statements with more than two WHEN conditions, separating them onto multiple lines is also a good way to easily see and keep track of what is happening in the code. As an example, we can query the `type` and `mag` (magnitude), parse `place`, and then count the records in the `earthquakes` table, with some filtering in the *WHERE* clause:

```
SELECT type, mag
,case when place like '%CA%' then 'California'
      when place like '%AK%' then 'Alaska'
      else trim(split_part(place,',',2))
      end as place
,count(*)
FROM earthquakes
WHERE date_part('year',time) >= 2019
and mag between 0 and 1
GROUP BY 1,2,3
;

type                mag place      count
-----------------   --- ---------- -----
chemical explosion  0   California 1
earthquake          0   Alaska     160
earthquake          0   Argentina  1
...                 ... ...        ...
```

Indentation is another trick for keeping code visually organized. Adding spaces or tabs to line up the WHEN items within a CASE statement is one example. You've also seen subqueries indented in examples throughout the book. This makes subqueries visually stand apart, and when a query has multiple levels of nested subqueries, it makes it easier to see and understand the order in which they will be evaluated and which subqueries are peers in terms of level:

```
SELECT...
FROM
(
    SELECT...
    FROM
    (
        SELECT...
```

```
        FROM...
    ) a
    JOIN
    (
        SELECT...
        FROM
    ) b on...
  ) a
  ...
  ;
```

Any number of other formatting choices can be made, and the query will return the same results. Long-term SQL writers tend to have their own formatting preferences. However, clear and consistent formatting makes creating, maintaining, and sharing SQL code much easier.

Many SQL query editors provide some form of query formatting and coloration. Usually keywords are colored, making them easier to spot within a query. These visual clues make both developing and reviewing SQL queries much easier. If you've been writing SQL in a query editor all along, try opening a *.sql* file in a plain text editor to see the difference coloration makes. Figure 8-1 shows an example of a SQL query editor, and the same code is shown in a plain text editor in Figure 8-2 (please note that these may appear in grayscale in some versions of this book).

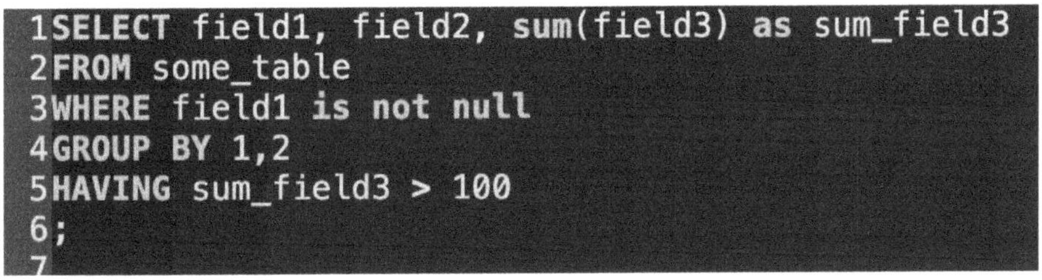

```
1 SELECT field1, field2, sum(field3) as sum_field3
2 FROM some_table
3 WHERE field1 is not null
4 GROUP BY 1,2
5 HAVING sum_field3 > 100
6 ;
7
```

Figure 8-1. Screenshot of keyword coloration in the SQL query editor DBVisualizer

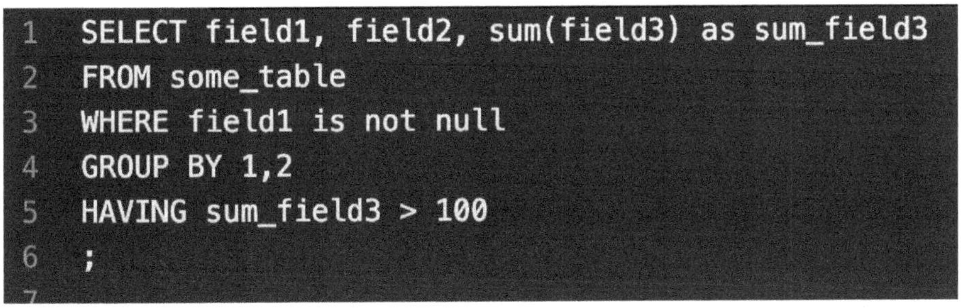

```
1   SELECT field1, field2, sum(field3) as sum_field3
2   FROM some_table
3   WHERE field1 is not null
4   GROUP BY 1,2
5   HAVING sum_field3 > 100
6   ;
7
```

Figure 8-2. The same code as plain text in the text editor Atom

Formatting is optional from the database perspective, but it's a good practice. Consistent use of spacing, capitalization, and other formatting options goes a long way toward keeping your code readable, therefore making it easier to share and maintain.

Storing Code

After going to the trouble of commenting and formatting code, it's a good idea to store it somewhere in case you need to use or reference it later.

Many data analysts and scientists work with a SQL editor, often a desktop piece of software. SQL editors are useful because they usually include tools for browsing the database schema alongside a code window. They save files with a *.sql* extension, and these text files can be opened and changed in any text editor. Files can be saved in local directories or in cloud-based file storage services.

Since they are text, SQL code files are easy to store in change control repositories such as GitHub. Using a repository provides a nice backup option and makes for easy sharing with others. Repositories also track the change history of files, which is useful when you need to figure out when a particular change was made, or when the change history is required for regulatory reasons. The main drawback of GitHub and other tools is that they are usually not a required step in the analysis workflow. You need to remember to update your code periodically, and as with any manual step, it's easy to forget to do it.

Organizing Computations

Two related problems we face when creating complex data sets are getting the logic right and getting good query performance. Logic must be correct, or the results will be meaningless. Query performance for analysis purposes, unlike for transactional systems, usually has a range of "good enough." Queries that don't return are problematic, but the difference between waiting 30 seconds and waiting a minute for results may not matter a great deal. With SQL, there is often more than one way to write a query that returns the correct results. We can use this to our advantage to both ensure correct logic and tune performance of long-running queries. There are three main ways to organize the calculation of intermediate results in SQL: the subquery, temp tables, and common table expressions (CTEs). Before we dive into them, we'll review the order of evaluation in SQL. To wrap up the section, I'll introduce `grouping sets`, which can replace the need to *UNION* queries together in certain cases.

Understanding Order of SQL Clause Evaluation

Databases translate SQL code into a set of operations that will be carried out in order to return the requested data. While understanding exactly how this happens isn't necessary to be good at writing SQL for analysis, understanding the order in which the database will perform its operations is incredibly useful (and is sometimes necessary to debug unexpected results).

 Many modern databases have sophisticated query optimizers that consider various parts of the query to come up with the most efficient plan for execution. Although they may consider parts of the query in a different order from that discussed here and therefore may need less query optimization from humans, they won't calculate intermediate results in a different order from that discussed here.

The general order of evaluation is shown in Table 8-1. SQL queries usually include only a subset of possible clauses, so actual evaluation includes only the steps relevant to the query.

Table 8-1. SQL query order of evaluation

1	FROM
	including *JOINs* and their *ON* clauses
2	WHERE
3	GROUP BY
	including aggregations
4	HAVING
5	Window functions
6	SELECT
7	DISTINCT
8	UNION
9	ORDER BY
10	LIMIT and OFFSET

First the tables in the *FROM* clause are evaluated, along with any *JOINs*. If the *FROM* clause includes any subqueries, these are evaluated before proceeding to the rest of the steps. In a *JOIN*, the *ON* clause specifies how the tables are to be *JOINed*, which may also filter the result set.

 FROM is always evaluated first, with one exception: when the query doesn't contain a *FROM* clause. In most databases, it's possible to query using only a *SELECT* clause, as seen in some of the examples in this book. A *SELECT*-only query can return system information such as the date and database version. It can also apply mathematical, date, text, and other functions to constants. While there is admittedly little use for such queries in final analyses, they are handy for testing out functions or iterating over tricky calculations rapidly.

Next, the *WHERE* clause is evaluated to determine which records should be included in further calculations. Note that *WHERE* falls early in the order of evaluation and so cannot include the results of calculations that happen in a later step.

GROUP BY is calculated next, including the related aggregations such as count, sum, and avg. As you might expect, *GROUP BY* will include only the values that exist in the *FROM* tables after any *JOIN*ing and filtering in the *WHERE* clause.

HAVING is evaluated next. Since it follows *GROUP BY*, *HAVING* can perform filtering on aggregated values returned by *GROUP BY*. The only other way to filter by aggregated values is to place the query in a subquery and apply the filters in the main query. For example, we might want to find all the states that have at least one thousand terms in the legislators_terms table, and we'll order by terms in descending order for good measure:

```
SELECT state
,count(*) as terms
FROM legislators_terms
GROUP BY 1
HAVING count(*) >= 1000
ORDER BY 2 desc
;

state   terms
-----   -----
NY      4159
PA      3252
OH      2239
...     ...
```

Window functions, if used, are evaluated next. Interestingly, since aggregates have already been calculated at this point, they can be used in the window function definition. For example, in the legislators data set from Chapter 4, we could calculate both the terms served per state and the average terms across all states in a single query:

```
SELECT state
,count(*) as terms
,avg(count(*)) over () as avg_terms
FROM legislators_terms
GROUP BY 1
;

state   terms   avg_terms
-----   -----   ---------
ND      170     746.830
NV      177     746.830
OH      2239    746.830
...     ...     ...
```

Aggregates can also be used in the *OVER* clause, as in the following query that ranks the states in descending order by the total number of terms:

```
SELECT state
,count(*) as terms
,rank() over (order by count(*) desc)
FROM legislators_terms
GROUP BY 1
;

state   terms   rank
-----   -----   ----
NY      4159    1
PA      3252    2
OH      2239    3
...     ...     ...
```

At this point, the *SELECT* clause is finally evaluated. This is a little counterintuitive since aggregations and window functions are typed in the *SELECT* section of the query. However, the database has already taken care of the calculations, and the results are then available for further manipulation or for display as is. For example, an aggregation can be placed within a CASE statement and have mathematical, date, or text functions applied if the result of the aggregation is one of those data types.

 The aggregators sum, count, and avg return numeric values. However, min and max functions return the same data type as the input and use the inherent ordering of that data type. For example, min and max dates return the earliest and latest calendar dates, while min and max on text fields use alphabetical order to determine the result.

Following *SELECT* is *DISTINCT*, if present in the query. This means that all the rows are calculated and then deduplication occurs.

UNION (or *UNION ALL*) is performed next. Up to this point, each query that makes up a *UNION* is evaluated independently. This stage is when the result sets are assembled together into one. This means that the queries can go about their calculations in very different ways or from different data sets. All *UNION* looks for is the same number of columns and for those columns to have compatible data types.

ORDER BY is almost the last step in evaluation. This means that it can access any of the prior calculations to sort the result set. The only caveat is that if *DISTINCT* is used, *ORDER BY* cannot include any fields that are not returned in the *SELECT* clause. Otherwise, it is entirely possible to order a result set by a field that doesn't otherwise appear in the query.

LIMIT and *OFFSET* are evaluated last in the query execution sequence. This ensures that the subset of results returned will have fully calculated results as specified by any of the other clauses that are in the query. This also means that *LIMIT* has somewhat limited use in controlling the amount of work the database does before the results are returned to you. This is perhaps most noticeable when a query contains a large *OFFSET* value. In order to *OFFSET* by, say, three million records, the database still needs to calculate the entire result set, figure out where the three millionth plus one record is, and then return the records specified by the *LIMIT*. This doesn't mean *LIMIT* isn't useful. Checking a few results can confirm calculations without overwhelming the network or your local machine with data. Also, using *LIMIT* as early in a query as possible, such as in a subquery, can still dramatically reduce the work required by the database as you develop a more complex query.

Now that we have a good understanding of the order in which databases evaluate queries and perform calculations, we'll turn to some options for controlling these operations in the context of a larger, complex query: subqueries, temporary tables, and CTEs.

Subqueries

Subqueries are usually the first way we learn how to control the order of evaluation in SQL, or to accomplish calculations that can't be achieved in a single main query. They are versatile and can help organize long queries into smaller chunks with discrete purposes.

A subquery is enclosed in parentheses, a notation that should be familiar from mathematics, where parentheses also force evaluation of some part of an equation prior to the rest. Within the parentheses is a standalone query that is evaluated before the main outer query. Assuming the subquery is in the *FROM* clause, the result set can then be queried by the main code, just like any other table. We've already seen many examples with subqueries in this book.

An exception to the standalone nature of a subquery is a special type called a *lateral subquery*, which can access results from previous items in the *FROM* clause. A comma and the keyword *LATERAL* are used instead of *JOIN*, and there is no *ON* clause. Instead, a prior query is used inside the subquery. As an example, imagine we wanted to analyze previous party membership for currently sitting legislators. We could find the first year they were a member of a different party, and check how common that is when grouped by their current party. In the first subquery, we find the currently sitting legislators. In the second, lateral subquery, we use the results from the first subquery to return the earliest `term_start` where the party is different from the current party:

```
SELECT date_part('year',c.first_term) as first_year
,a.party
,count(a.id_bioguide) as legislators
FROM
(
    SELECT distinct id_bioguide, party
    FROM legislators_terms
    WHERE term_end > '2020-06-01'
) a,
LATERAL
(
    SELECT b.id_bioguide
    ,min(term_start) as first_term
    FROM legislators_terms b
    WHERE b.id_bioguide = a.id_bioguide
    and b.party <> a.party
    GROUP BY 1
) c
GROUP BY 1,2
;

first_year    party         legislators
----------    ----------    -----------
1979.0        Republican    1
2011.0        Libertarian   1
2015.0        Democrat      1
```

This turns out to be fairly uncommon. Only three current legislators have switched parties, and no party has had more switchers than other parties. There are other ways to return the same result—for example, by changing the query to a *JOIN* and moving the criteria in the *WHERE* clause of the second subquery to the *ON* clause:

```
SELECT date_part('year',c.first_term) as first_year
,a.party
,count(a.id_bioguide) as legislators
FROM
(
    SELECT distinct id_bioguide, party
    FROM legislators_terms
    WHERE term_end > '2020-06-01'
) a
JOIN
(
    SELECT id_bioguide, party
    ,min(term_start) as first_term
    FROM legislators_terms
    GROUP BY 1,2
) c on c.id_bioguide = a.id_bioguide and c.party <> a.party
GROUP BY 1,2
;
```

If the second table is very large, filtering by a value returned in a previous subquery can speed up execution. In my experience, use of *LATERAL* is less common, and therefore less well understood, than other syntax, so it's good to reserve it for use cases that can't be solved efficiently another way.

Subqueries allow a lot of flexibility and control over the order of calculations. However, a complex series of calculations in the middle of a larger query can become difficult to understand and maintain. At other times, the performance of subqueries is too slow, or the query won't return results at all. Fortunately, SQL has some additional options that may help in these situations: temporary tables and common table expressions.

Temporary Tables

A *temporary (temp) table* is created in a similar way to any other table in the database, but with a key difference: it persists only for the duration of the current session. Temp tables are useful when you are working with only a small part of a very large table, as small tables are much faster to query. They are also useful when you want to use an intermediate result in multiple queries. Since the temp table is a standalone table, it can be queried many times within the same session. Yet another time they are useful is when you are working in certain databases, such as Redshift or Vertica, that partition data across nodes. *INSERT*ing data into a temp table can align the partitioning to other tables that will be *JOIN*ed together in a subsequent query. There are two main drawbacks to temp tables. First, they require database privileges to write data, which may not be allowed for security reasons. Second, some BI tools, such as Tableau and Metabase, allow only a single SQL statement to create a data set,[1] whereas a temp table requires at least two: the statement to *CREATE* and *INSERT* data into the temp table and the query using the temp table.

To create a temporary table, use the *CREATE* command, followed by the keyword TEMPORARY and the name you wish to give it. The table can then be defined and a second statement used to populate it, or you can use *CREATE as SELECT* to create and populate in one step. For example, you could create a temp table with the distinct states for which there have been legislators:

```
CREATE temporary table temp_states
(
state varchar primary key
)
;

INSERT into temp_states
SELECT distinct state
```

---

1 Though in the case of Tableau, you can get around this with the Initial SQL option.

```
FROM legislators_terms
;
```

The first statement creates the table, while the second statement populates the temp table with values from a query. Note that by defining the table first, I need to specify the data type for all the columns (in this case varchar for the state column) and can optionally use other elements of table definition, such as setting a primary key. I like to prefix temp table names with "temp_" or "tmp_" to remind myself of the fact that I'm using a temp table in the main query, but this isn't strictly necessary.

The faster and easier way to generate a temp table is the *CREATE as SELECT* method:

```
CREATE temporary table temp_states
as
SELECT distinct state
FROM legislators_terms
;
```

In this case, the database automatically decides the data type based on the data returned by the *SELECT* statement, and no primary key is set. Unless you need fine-grained control for performance reasons, this second method will serve you well.

Since temp tables are written to disk, if you need to repopulate them during a session, you will have to *DROP* and re-create the table or *TRUNCATE* the data. Disconnecting and reconnecting to the database also works.

Common Table Expressions

CTEs are a relative newcomer to the SQL language, having been introduced into many of the major databases only during the early 2000s. I wrote SQL for years without them, making do with subqueries and temp tables. I have to say that since I became aware of them a few years ago, they have steadily grown on me.

You can think of a *common table expression* as being like a subquery lifted out and placed at the beginning of the query execution. It creates a temporary result set that can then be used anywhere in the subsequent query. A query can have multiple CTEs, and CTEs can use results from previous CTEs to perform additional calculations.

CTEs are particularly useful when the result will be used multiple times in the rest of the query. The alternative, defining the same subquery multiple times, is both slow (since the database needs to execute the same query several times) and error-prone. Forgetting to update the logic in each identical subquery introduces error into the final result. Since CTEs are part of a single query, they don't require any special database permissions. They can also be a useful way to organize code into discrete chunks and avoid sprawling nested subqueries.

The main drawback of CTEs arises from the fact that they are defined at the beginning, separate from where they are used. This can make a query more difficult to decipher for others when the query is very long, as it's necessary to scroll to the beginning to check the definition and then back to where the CTE is used to understand what is happening. Good use of comments can help with this. A second challenge is that CTEs make execution of sections of long queries more difficult. To check intermediate results in a longer query, it's fairly easy to select and run just a subquery in a query development tool. If a CTE is involved, however, all of the surrounding code must be commented out first.

To create a CTE, we use the *WITH* keyword at the beginning of the overall query, followed by a name for the CTE and then the query that makes it up enclosed in parentheses. For example, we could create a CTE that calculates the first term for each legislator and then use this result in further calculation, such as the cohort calculation introduced in Chapter 4:

```
WITH first_term as
(
    SELECT id_bioguide
    ,min(term_start) as first_term
    FROM legislators_terms
    GROUP BY 1
)
SELECT date_part('year',age(b.term_start,a.first_term)) as periods
,count(distinct a.id_bioguide) as cohort_retained
FROM first_term a
JOIN legislators_terms b on a.id_bioguide = b.id_bioguide
GROUP BY 1
;

periods  cohort_retained
-------  ---------------
0.0      12518
1.0      3600
2.0      3619
...      ...
```

The query result is exactly the same as that returned by the alternate query using subqueries seen in Chapter 4. Multiple CTEs can be used in the same query, separated by commas:

```
WITH first_cte as
(
    SELECT...
),
second_cte as
(
    SELECT...
)
SELECT...
;
```

CTEs are a useful way to control the order of evaluation, improve performance in some instances, and organize your SQL code. They are easy to use once you are familiar with the syntax, and they are available in most major databases. There are often multiple ways to accomplish something in SQL, and although not required, CTEs add useful flexibility to your SQL skills toolbox.

grouping sets

Although this next topic isn't strictly about controlling the order of evaluation, it is a handy way to avoid *UNIONs* and get the database to do all the work in a single query statement. Within the *GROUP BY* clause, special syntax is available in many major databases that includes grouping sets, cube, and rollup (though Redshift is an exception, and MySQL only has rollup). They are useful when the data set needs to contain subtotals for various combinations of attributes.

For examples in this section, we'll use a data set of video game sales that is available on Kaggle (*https://oreil.ly/qIxRX*). It contains attributes for the name of each game as well as the platform, year, genre, and game publisher. Sales figures are provided for North America, the EU, Japan, Other (the rest of the world), and the global total. The table name is videogame_sales. Figure 8-3 shows a sample of the table.

rank	name	platform	year	genre	publisher	na_sales	eu_sales	jp_sales	other_sales	global_sales
1	1 Wii Sports	Wii	2006	Sports	Nintendo	41.49	29.02	3.77	8.46	82.74
2	2 Super Mario Bros.	NES	1985	Platform	Nintendo	29.08	3.58	6.81	0.77	40.24
3	3 Mario Kart Wii	Wii	2008	Racing	Nintendo	15.85	12.88	3.79	3.31	35.82
4	4 Wii Sports Resort	Wii	2009	Sports	Nintendo	15.75	11.01	3.28	2.96	33
5	5 Pokemon Red/Pokemon Blue	GB	1996	Role-Playing	Nintendo	11.27	8.89	10.22	1	31.37
6	6 Tetris	GB	1989	Puzzle	Nintendo	23.2	2.26	4.22	0.58	30.26
7	7 New Super Mario Bros.	DS	2006	Platform	Nintendo	11.38	9.23	6.5	2.9	30.01
8	8 Wii Play	Wii	2006	Misc	Nintendo	14.03	9.2	2.93	2.85	29.02
9	9 New Super Mario Bros. Wii	Wii	2009	Platform	Nintendo	14.59	7.06	4.7	2.26	28.62
10	10 Duck Hunt	NES	1984	Shooter	Nintendo	26.93	0.63	0.28	0.47	28.31
11	11 Nintendogs	DS	2005	Simulation	Nintendo	9.07	11	1.93	2.75	24.76
12	12 Mario Kart DS	DS	2005	Racing	Nintendo	9.81	7.57	4.13	1.92	23.42
13	13 Pokemon Gold/Pokemon Silver	GB	1999	Role-Playing	Nintendo	9	6.18	7.2	0.71	23.1
14	14 Wii Fit	Wii	2007	Sports	Nintendo	8.94	8.03	3.6	2.15	22.72
15	15 Wii Fit Plus	Wii	2009	Sports	Nintendo	9.09	8.59	2.53	1.79	22
16	16 Kinect Adventures!	X360	2010	Misc	Microsoft Game Studios	14.97	4.94	0.24	1.67	21.82
17	17 Grand Theft Auto V	PS3	2013	Action	Take-Two Interactive	7.01	9.27	0.97	4.14	21.4
18	18 Grand Theft Auto: San Andreas	PS2	2004	Action	Take-Two Interactive	9.43	0.4	0.41	10.57	20.81
19	19 Super Mario World	SNES	1990	Platform	Nintendo	12.78	3.75	3.54	0.55	20.61
20	20 Brain Age: Train Your Brain in Minutes a Day	DS	2005	Misc	Nintendo	4.75	9.26	4.16	2.05	20.22

Figure 8-3. Sample of the videogame_sales table

So in the video game data set, for example, we might want to aggregate global_sales by platform, genre, and publisher as standalone aggregations (rather than only the combinations of the three fields that exist in the data) but output the results in one query set. This can be accomplished by *UNIONing* together three queries. Note that each query must contain at least placeholders for all three of the grouping fields:

```
SELECT platform
,null as genre
,null as publisher
,sum(global_sales) as global_sales
FROM videogame_sales
GROUP BY 1,2,3
```

```
    UNION
SELECT null as platform
,genre
,null as publisher
,sum(global_sales) as global_sales
FROM videogame_sales
GROUP BY 1,2,3
    UNION
SELECT null as platform
,null as genre
,publisher
,sum(global_sales) as global_sales
FROM videogame_sales
GROUP BY 1,2,3
;

platform  genre     publisher         global_sales
--------  ------    ---------         ------------
2600      (null)    (null)            97.08
3DO       (null)    (null)            0.10
...       ...       ...               ...
(null)    Action    (null)            1751.18
(null)    Adventure (null)            239.04
...       ...       ...               ...
(null)    (null)    10TACLE Studios   0.11
(null)    (null)    1C Company        0.10
...       ...       ...               ...
```

This can be achieved in a more compact query using grouping sets. Within the *GROUP BY* clause, grouping sets is followed by the list of groupings to calculate. The previous query can be replaced by:

```
SELECT platform, genre, publisher
,sum(global_sales) as global_sales
FROM videogame_sales
GROUP BY grouping sets (platform, genre, publisher)
;

platform  genre     publisher         global_sales
--------  ------    ---------         ------------
2600      (null)    (null)            97.08
3DO       (null)    (null)            0.10
...       ...       ...               ...
(null)    Action    (null)            1751.18
(null)    Adventure (null)            239.04
...       ...       ...               ...
(null)    (null)    10TACLE Studios   0.11
(null)    (null)    1C Company        0.10
...       ...       ...               ...
```

The items inside the grouping sets parentheses can include blanks as well as comma-separated lists of columns. As an example, we can calculate the global sales without any grouping, in addition to the groupings by platform, genre, and publisher, by including a list item that is just a pair of parentheses. We'll also clean up the output by substituting "All" for the null items using coalesce:

```
SELECT coalesce(platform,'All') as platform
,coalesce(genre,'All') as genre
,coalesce(publisher,'All') as publisher
,sum(global_sales) as na_sales
FROM videogame_sales
GROUP BY grouping sets ((), platform, genre, publisher)
ORDER BY 1,2,3
;
```

platform	genre	publisher	global_sales
All	All	All	8920.44
2600	All	All	97.08
3DO	All	All	0.10
...	...	...	...
All	Action	All	1751.18
All	Adventure	All	239.04
...	...	...	...
All	All	10TACLE Studios	0.11
All	All	1C Company	0.10
...	...	...	...

If we want to calculate all possible combinations of platform, genre, and publisher, such as the individual subtotals just calculated, plus all combinations of platform and genre, platform and publisher, and genre and publisher, we could specify all of these combinations in the grouping sets. Or we can use the handy cube syntax, which handles all of this for us:

```
SELECT coalesce(platform,'All') as platform
,coalesce(genre,'All') as genre
,coalesce(publisher,'All') as publisher
,sum(global_sales) as global_sales
FROM videogame_sales
GROUP BY cube (platform, genre, publisher)
ORDER BY 1,2,3
;
```

platform	genre	publisher	global_sales
All	All	All	8920.44
PS3	All	All	957.84
PS3	Action	All	307.88
PS3	Action	Atari	0.2
All	Action	All	1751.18
All	Action	Atari	26.65
All	All	Atari	157.22
...	...	...	...

A third option is the function `rollup`, which returns a data set that has combinations determined by the ordering of fields in the parentheses, rather than all possible combinations. So the previous query with the following clause:

```
GROUP BY rollup (platform, genre, publisher)
```

returns aggregations for the combinations of:

```
platform, genre, publisher
platform, genre
platform
```

But the query does *not* return aggregations for the combinations of:

```
platform, publisher
genre,publisher
genre
publisher
```

Although it is possible to create the same output using *UNION*, the `grouping sets`, `cube`, and `rollup` options are big space and time savers when aggregations at multiple levels are needed, because they result in fewer lines of code and fewer scans of the underlying database tables. I once created a query hundreds of lines long using *UNION*s to generate output for a dynamic website graphic that needed to have all possible combinations of filters precalculated. Quality checking it was an enormous chore, and updating it was even worse. Leveraging `grouping sets`, and CTEs for that matter, could have gone a long way toward making the code more compact and easy to write and maintain.

Managing Data Set Size and Privacy Concerns

After taking care to properly work out the logic in our SQL, organize our code, and make it efficient, we're often faced with another challenge: the size of the result set. Data storage is ever cheaper, meaning that organizations are storing ever-larger data sets. Computational power is also always increasing, allowing us to crunch this data in the sophisticated ways we've seen in previous chapters. However, bottlenecks still occur, either in downstream systems such as BI tools or in the bandwidth available to pass large data sets between systems. Additionally, data privacy is a major concern that impacts how we handle sensitive data. For these reasons, in this section I'll discuss some ways to limit the size of data sets, as well as considerations for data privacy.

Sampling with %, mod

One way to reduce the size of a result set is to use a sample of the source data. *Sampling* means taking only a subset of the data points or observations. This is appropriate when the data set is large enough and a subset is representative of the entire population. You can often sample website traffic and still retain most of the useful insights, for example. There are two choices to make when sampling. The first is the size of the sample that achieves the right balance between reducing the size of the data set and not losing too much critical detail. The sample might include 10%, 1%, or 0.1% of the data points, depending on the starting volume. The second choice is the entity on which to perform the sampling. We might sample 1% of website *visits*, but if the goal of the analysis is to understand how users navigate the website, sampling 1% of website *visitors* would be a better choice in order to preserve all the data points for the users in the sample.

The most common way to sample is to filter query results in the *WHERE* clause by applying a function to an entity-level identifier. Many ID fields are stored as integers. If this is the case, taking a modulo is a quick way to achieve the right result. The modulo is the whole number remainder when one number is divided by another. For example, 10 divided by 3 is equal to 3 with a remainder (modulo) of 1. SQL has two equivalent ways to find the modulo—with the % sign and with the mod function:

```
SELECT 123456 % 100 as mod_100;

mod_100
-------
56

SELECT mod(123456,100) as mod_100;

mod_100
-------
56
```

Both return the same answer, 56, which is also the last two digits of the input value 123456. To generate a 1% sample of the data set, place either syntax in the *WHERE* clause and set it equal to an integer—in this case, 7:

```
SELECT user_id, ...
FROM table
WHERE user_id % 100 = 7
;
```

A mod of 100 creates a 1% sample, while a mod of 1,000 would create a 0.1% sample, and a mod of 10 would create a 10% sample. Although sampling in multiples of 10 is common, it's not required, and any integer will work.

Sampling from alphanumeric identifiers that include both letters and numbers isn't as straightforward as sampling purely numeric identifiers. String-parsing functions can be used to isolate just the first or last few characters, and filters can be applied to them. For example, we can sample only identifiers ending in the letter "b" by parsing the last character from a string using the right function:

```
SELECT user_id, ...
FROM table
WHERE right(user_id,1) = 'b'
;
```

Assuming that any upper- or lowercase letter or number is a possible value, this will result in a sample of approximately 1.6% (1/62). To return a larger sample, adjust the filter to allow multiple values:

```
SELECT user_id, ...
FROM table
WHERE right(user_id,1) in ('b','f','m')
;
```

To create a smaller sample, include multiple characters:

```
SELECT user_id, ...
FROM table
WHERE right(user_id,2) = 'c3'
;
```

 When sampling, it's worth validating that the function you use to generate a sample does create a random or close-to-random sampling of the data. In one of my previous roles, we discovered that certain types of users were more likely to have certain combinations of the last two digits in their user IDs. In this case, using the mod function to generate a 1% sample resulted in noticeable bias in the results. Alphanumeric identifiers in particular often have common patterns at the beginning or end of the string that data profiling can help identify.

Sampling is an easy way to reduce data set size by orders of magnitude. It can both speed up calculations within SQL statements and allow the final result to be more compact, making it faster and easier to transfer to another tool or system. Sometimes the loss of detail from sampling isn't acceptable, however, and other techniques are needed.

Reducing Dimensionality

The number of distinct combinations of attributes, or *dimensionality*, greatly impacts the number of records in a data set. To understand this, we can do a simple thought experiment. Imagine we have a field with 10 distinct values, and we count the number of records and *GROUP BY* that field. The query will return 10 results. Now add in a second field, also with 10 distinct values, count the number of records, and *GROUP BY* the two fields. The query will return 100 results. Add in a third field with 10 distinct values, and the query result grows to 1,000 results. Even if not all the combinations of the three fields actually exist in the table queried, it's clear that adding additional fields into a query can increase the size of the results dramatically.

When performing analysis, we can often control the number of fields and filter the values included in order to end up with a manageable output. However, when preparing data sets for further analysis in other tools, the goal is often to provide flexibility and therefore to include many different attributes and calculations. To retain as much detail as possible while managing the overall size of the data, we can use one or more grouping techniques.

Granularity of dates and times is often an obvious place to look to reduce the size of data. Talk to your stakeholders to determine whether daily data is needed, for example, or whether weekly or monthly aggregations would work just as well. Grouping data by month and day of week might be a solution to aggregating data while still providing visibility into patterns that differ on weekdays versus weekends. Restricting the length of time returned is always an option, but that can restrict exploration of longer-term trends. I have seen data teams provide one data set that aggregates to a monthly level and covers several years, while a companion data set includes the same attributes but with daily or even hourly data for a much shorter time window.

Text fields are another place to check for possible space savings. Differences in spelling or capitalization can result in many more distinct values than are useful. Applying text functions discussed in Chapter 5, such as lower, trim, or initcap, standardizes values and usually makes data more useful for stakeholders as well. REPLACE or CASE statements can be used to make more nuanced adjustments, such as adjusting spelling or changing a name that has been updated to a new value.

Sometimes only a few values out of a longer list are relevant for analysis, so retaining detail for those while grouping the rest together is effective. I have seen this frequently when working with geographic locations. There are close to two hundred countries in the world, but often only a handful have enough customers or other data points to make reporting on them individually worthwhile. The legislators data set used in Chapter 4 contains 59 values for state, which includes the 50 states plus US territories that have representatives. We might want to create a data set with detail for the five states with the largest populations (currently California, Texas, Florida, New York, and Pennsylvania), and then group the rest into an "other" category with a CASE statement:

```
SELECT case when state in ('CA','TX','FL','NY','PA') then state
            else 'Other' end as state_group
,count(*) as terms
FROM legislators_terms
GROUP BY 1
ORDER BY 2 desc
;
```

```
state_group    count
-----------    -----
Other          31980
NY             4159
PA             3252
CA             2121
TX             1692
FL             859
```

The query returns only 6 rows, down from 59, which represents a significant decrease. To make the list more dynamic, we can first rank the values in a subquery, in this case by the distinct id_bioguide (legislator ID) values, and then return the state value for the top 5 and "Other" for the rest:

```
SELECT case when b.rank <= 5 then a.state
            else 'Other' end as state_group
,count(distinct id_bioguide) as legislators
FROM legislators_terms a
JOIN
(
    SELECT state
    ,count(distinct id_bioguide)
    ,rank() over (order by count(distinct id_bioguide) desc)
    FROM legislators_terms
    GROUP BY 1
) b on a.state = b.state
GROUP BY 1
ORDER BY 2 desc
;

state_group    legislators
-----------    -----------
Other          8317
NY             1494
PA             1075
OH             694
IL             509
VA             451
```

Several of the states change in this second list. If we continue to update the data set with fresh data points, the dynamic query will ensure that the output always reflects the current top values.

Dimensionality can also be reduced by transforming the data into flag values. Flags are usually binary (i.e., they have only two values). BOOLEAN TRUE and FALSE can be used to encode flags, as can 1 and 0, "Yes" and "No," or any other pair of meaningful strings. Flags are useful when a threshold value is important, but detail beyond that is less interesting. For example, we might want to know whether or not a website visitor completed a purchase, but detail on the exact number of purchases is less important.

In the legislators data set, there are 28 distinct numbers of terms served by the legislators. Instead of the exact value, however, we might want to include in our output only whether a legislator has served at least two terms, which we can do by turning the detailed values into a flag:

```
SELECT case when terms >= 2 then true else false end as two_terms_flag
,count(*) as legislators
FROM
(
    SELECT id_bioguide
    ,count(term_id) as terms
    FROM legislators_terms
    GROUP BY 1
) a
GROUP BY 1
;


two_terms_flag  legislators
--------------  -----------
false           4139
true            8379
```

About twice as many legislators have served at least two terms as compared to those with only one term. When combined with other fields in a data set, this type of transformation can result in much smaller result sets.

Sometimes a simple true/false or presence/absence indicator is not quite enough to capture the needed nuance. In this case, numeric data can be transformed into several levels to maintain some additional detail. This is accomplished with a CASE statement, and the return value can be a number or string.

We might want to include not only whether a legislator served a second term but also another indicator for those who served 10 or more terms:

```
SELECT
case when terms >= 10 then '10+'
    when terms >= 2 then '2 - 9'
    else '1' end as terms_level
,count(*) as legislators
FROM
(
    SELECT id_bioguide
    ,count(term_id) as terms
    FROM legislators_terms
    GROUP BY 1
) a
GROUP BY 1
;
```

```
terms_level   legislators
-----------   -----------
1             4139
2 - 9         7496
10+           883
```

Here we have reduced 28 distinct values down to 3, while retaining the notion of single-term legislators, those who were reelected, and the ones who are exceptionally good at staying in office. Such groupings or distinctions occur in many domains. As with all the transformations discussed here, it may take some trial and error to find the exact thresholds that are most meaningful for stakeholders. Finding the right balance of detail and aggregation can greatly decrease data set size and therefore often speeds delivery time and performance of the downstream application.

PII and Data Privacy

Data privacy is one of the most important issues facing data professionals today. Large data sets with many attributes allow for more robust analysis with detailed insights and recommendations. However, when the data set is about individuals, we need to be mindful of both the ethical and the regulatory dimensions of the data collected and used. Regulations around the privacy of patients, students, and financial services customers have existed for many years. Laws regulating the data privacy rights of consumers have also come into force in recent years. The General Data Protection Regulation (GDPR) passed by the EU is probably the most widely known. Other regulations include the California Consumer Privacy Act (CCPA), the Australian Privacy Principles, and Brazil's General Data Protection Law (LGPD).

These and other regulations cover the handling, storage, and (in some cases) deletion of *personally identifiable information (PII)*. Some categories of PII are obvious: name, address, email, date of birth, and Social Security number. PII also includes health indicators such as heart rate, blood pressure, and medical diagnoses. Location information, such as GPS coordinates, is also considered PII, since a small number of GPS locations can uniquely identify an individual. For example, GPS readings at my house and at my children's school could uniquely identify someone in my household. A third GPS point at my office could uniquely identify me. As a data practitioner, it's worthwhile to become familiar with what these regulations cover and to discuss how they affect your work with the privacy lawyers at your organization, who will have the most up-to-date information.

A best practice when analyzing data that includes PII is to avoid including the PII itself in the outputs. This can be accomplished by aggregating data, substituting values, or hashing values.

For most analyses, the goal is to find trends and patterns. Counting customers and averaging their behavior, rather than including individual detail in the output, is often the purpose. Aggregations generally remove PII; however, be aware that a combination of attributes that have a user count of 1 could potentially be tied back to an individual. These can be treated as outliers and removed from the result in order to maintain a higher degree of privacy.

If individual data is needed for some reason—to be able to calculate distinct users in a downstream tool, for instance—we can replace problematic values with random alternate values that maintain uniqueness. The row_number window function can be used to assign a new value to each individual in a table:

```
SELECT email
,row_number() over (order by ...)
FROM users
;
```

The challenge in this case is to find a field to put in the *ORDER BY* that makes the ordering sufficiently random such that we can consider the resulting user identifier anonymized.

Hashing values is another option. Hashing takes an input value and uses an algorithm to create a new output value. A particular input value will always result in the same output, making this a good option for maintaining uniqueness while obscuring sensitive values. The md5 function can be used to generate a hashed value:

```
SELECT md5('my info');

md5
--------------------------------
0fb1d3f29f5dd1b7cabbad56cf043d1a
```

 The md5 function hashes input values but does not encrypt them, and therefore it can be reversed to obtain the original value. For highly sensitive data, you should work with a database administrator to truly encrypt the data.

Avoiding PII in the output of your SQL queries is always the best option if possible, since you avoid proliferating it into other systems or files. Replacing or masking the values is a second-best option. You can also explore secure methods to share data, such as developing a secured data pipeline directly between a database and an email system to avoid writing email addresses out to files, for example. With care and partnership with technical and legal colleagues, it is possible to achieve high-quality analysis while also preserving individuals' privacy.

Conclusion

Surrounding every analysis, there are a number of decisions to be made around organizing the code, managing complexity, optimizing query performance, and safeguarding privacy in the output. In this chapter, we've discussed a number of options and strategies and special SQL syntax that can help with these tasks. Try not to get overwhelmed by all of these options or to become concerned that, without mastery of these topics, you can't be an efficient data analyst or data scientist. Not all of the techniques are required in every analysis, and there are often other ways to get the job done. The longer you spend analyzing data with SQL, the more likely you are to come across situations in which one or more of these techniques come in handy.

CHAPTER 9

Conclusion

Throughout the book, we've seen how SQL is a flexible and powerful language for a range of data analysis tasks. From data profiling to time series, text analysis, and anomaly detection, SQL can tackle a number of common requirements. Techniques and functions can also be combined in any given SQL statement to perform experiment analysis and build complex data sets. While SQL can't accomplish all analysis goals, it fits well into the ecosystem of analysis tools.

In this final chapter, I'll discuss a few additional types of analysis and point out how various SQL techniques covered in the book can be combined to accomplish them. Then I'll wrap up with some resources that you can use to continue your journey of mastering data analysis or to dig deeper into specific topics.

Funnel Analysis

A funnel consists of a series of steps that must be completed to reach a defined goal. The goal might be registering for a service, completing a purchase, or obtaining a course completion certificate. Steps in a website purchase funnel, for example, might include clicking the "Add to Cart" button, filling out shipping information, entering a credit card, and finally clicking the "Place Order" button.

Funnel analysis combines elements of time series analysis, discussed in Chapter 3, and cohort analysis, discussed in Chapter 4. The data for funnel analysis comes from a time series of events, although in this case those events correspond to distinct real-world actions rather than being repetitions of the same event. Measuring retention from step to step is a key goal of funnel analysis, although in this context we often use the term *conversion*. Typically, entities drop out along the steps of the process, and a graph of their number at each stage ends up looking like a household funnel—hence the name.

This type of analysis is used to identify areas of friction, difficulty, or confusion. Steps at which large numbers of users drop out, or that many fail to complete, provide insight into opportunities for optimization. For example, a checkout process that asks for credit card information before showing the total amount including shipping might turn off some would-be purchasers. Showing the total before this step may encourage more purchase completions. Such changes are often subjects of experiments, discussed in Chapter 7. Funnels can also be monitored in order to detect unexpected external events. For example, changes in completion rates might correspond to good (or bad) PR or to a change in the pricing or tactics of a competitor.

The first step in a funnel analysis is to figure out the base population of all users, customers, or other entities that were eligible to enter the process. Next, assemble the data set of completion for each step of interest, including the final goal. Often this includes one or more *LEFT JOINs* in order to include all of the base population, along with those who completed each step. Then count the users in each step and divide these step-wise counts by the total count. There are two ways to set up the queries, depending on whether all steps are required.

When all steps in the funnel are required—or if you only want to include users who have completed all steps—*LEFT JOIN* each table to the previous table:

```
SELECT count(a.user_id) as all_users
,count(b.user_id) as step_one_users
,count(b.user_id) / count(a.user_id) as pct_step_one
,count(c.user_id) as step_two_users
,count(c.user_id) / count(b.user_id) as pct_one_to_two
FROM users a
LEFT JOIN step_one b on a.user_id = b.user_id
LEFT JOIN step_two c on b.user_id = c.user_id
;
```

When users can skip a step, or if you want to allow for this possibility, *LEFT JOIN* each table to the one containing the full population and calculate the share of that starting group:

```
SELECT count(a.user_id) as all_users
,count(b.user_id) as step_one_users
,count(b.user_id) / count(a.user_id) as pct_step_one
,count(c.user_id) as step_two_users
,count(c.user_id) / count(b.user_id) as pct_step_two
FROM users a
LEFT JOIN step_one b on a.user_id = b.user_id
LEFT JOIN step_two c on a.user_id = c.user_id
;
```

It's a subtle difference, but it's one worth paying attention to and tailoring to the specific context. Consider including time boxes, to only include users who complete an action within a specific time frame, if users can reenter the funnel after a lengthy absence. Funnel analyses can also include additional dimensions, such as cohort or other entity attributes, to facilitate comparisons and generate additional hypotheses about why a funnel is or is not performing well.

Churn, Lapse, and Other Definitions of Departure

The topic of churn came up in Chapter 4, since churn is essentially the opposite of retention. Often organizations want or need to come up with a specific definition of churn in order to measure it directly. In some cases, there is a contractually defined end date, such as with B2B software. But often churn is a fuzzier concept, and a time-based definition is more appropriate. Even when there is a contractual end date, measuring when a customer stops using a product can be an early warning sign of an imminent contract cancellation. Churn definitions can also be applied to certain products or features, even when the customer doesn't churn from the organization entirely.

A time-based churn metric counts customers as churned when they haven't purchased or interacted with a product for a period of time, usually ranging from 30 days to as much as a year. The exact length depends a lot on the type of business and on typical usage patterns. To arrive at a good churn definition, you can use gap analysis to find typical periods between purchases or usage. To do gap analysis, you will need a time series of actions or events, the lag window function, and some date math.

As an example, we can calculate the typical gaps between representatives' terms, using the legislators data set introduced in Chapter 4. We'll ignore the fact that politicians are often voted out of office rather than choosing to leave, since otherwise this data set has the right structure for this type of analysis. First we'll find the average gap. To do this, we create a subquery that calculates the gap between the start_date and the previous start_date for each legislator for each term, and then we find the average value in the outer query. The previous start_date can be found using the lag function, and the gap as a time interval is calculated with the age function:

```
SELECT avg(gap_interval) as avg_gap
FROM
(
    SELECT id_bioguide, term_start
    ,lag(term_start) over (partition by id_bioguide
                            order by term_start)
                            as prev
    ,age(term_start,
        lag(term_start) over (partition by id_bioguide
                                order by term_start)
        ) as gap_interval
    FROM legislators_terms
    WHERE term_type = 'rep'
) a
WHERE gap_interval is not null
;
```

```
avg_gap
-------------------------------------
2 years 2 mons 17 days 15:41:54.83805
```

As we might expect, the average is close to two years, which makes sense since the term length for this office is two years. We can also create a distribution of gaps in order to pick a realistic churn threshold. In this case, we'll transform the gap to months:

```
SELECT gap_months, count(*) as instances
FROM
(
    SELECT id_bioguide, term_start
    ,lag(term_start) over (partition by id_bioguide
                            order by term_start)
                            as prev
    ,age(term_start,
        lag(term_start) over (partition by id_bioguide
                                order by term_start)
        ) as gap_interval
    ,date_part('year',
            age(term_start,
                lag(term_start) over (partition by id_bioguide
                                        order by term_start)
                )
            ) * 12
    +
    date_part('month',
            age(term_start,
                lag(term_start) over (partition by id_bioguide
                                        order by term_start)
                )
            ) as gap_months
    FROM legislators_terms
    WHERE term_type = 'rep'
) a
GROUP BY 1
;

gap_months  instances
----------  ---------
1.0         25
2.0         4
3.0         2
...         ...
```

If date_part is not supported in your database, extract can be used as an alternative. (Refer to Chapter 3 for an explanation and examples.) The output can be plotted, as in Figure 9-1. Since there is a long tail of months, this plot is zoomed in to show the range in which most gaps fall. The most common gap is 24 months, but there are also several hundred instances per month out to 32 months. There is another small bump to over 100 at 47 and 48 months. With the average and distribution in hand, I would likely set a threshold of either 36 or 48 months and say that any representative who hasn't been reelected within this window has "churned."

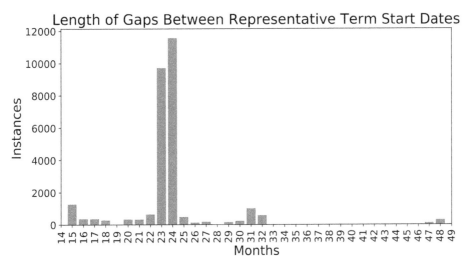

Figure 9-1. Distribution of length of gap between representative term start dates, showing range from 10 to 59 months

Once you have a defined threshold for churn, you can monitor the customer base with a "time since last" analysis. This can refer to last purchase, last payment, last time an app was opened, or whatever time-based metric is relevant for the organization. For this calculation, you need a data set that has the most recent date or timestamp for each customer. If starting with a time series, first find the most recent timestamp for each customer in a subquery. Then apply date math to find the time elapsed between that date and the current date, or the latest date in the data set if some time has elapsed since the data was assembled.

For example, we could find the distribution of years since the last election from the `legislators_terms` table. In the subquery, calculate the latest starting date using the `max` function and then find the time elapsed since then using the `age` function. In this case, the maximum data in the data set, May 5, 2019, is used. In a data set with up-to-date data, substitute `current_date` or an equivalent expression. The outer query finds the years from the interval using `date_part` and counts the number of legislators:

```
SELECT date_part('year',interval_since_last) as years_since_last
,count(*) as reps
FROM
(
    SELECT id_bioguide
```

```
          ,max(term_start) as max_date
          ,age('2020-05-19',max(term_start)) as interval_since_last
          FROM legislators_terms
          WHERE term_type = 'rep'
          GROUP BY 1
    ) a
    GROUP BY 1
    ;

    years_since_last  reps
    ----------------  -----
    0.0               6
    1.0               440
    2.0               1
    ...               ...
```

A related concept is "lapsed," which is often used as an intermediate stage between fully active customers and churned customers and might alternatively be called "dormant." A lapsed customer may be at higher risk of churning because we haven't seen them for a while but still have a decent likelihood of returning based on our past experience. In consumer services, I've seen "lapsed" cover periods from 7 to 30 days, with "churned" being defined as a customer not using the service for more than 30 days. Companies often experiment with reactivating lapsed users, using tactics ranging from email to support team outreach. Customers in each state can be defined by first finding their "time since last" as above and then tagging them with a CASE statement using the appropriate number of days or months. For example, we can group the representatives according to how long ago they were elected:

```
SELECT
case when months_since_last <= 23 then 'Current'
     when months_since_last <= 48 then 'Lapsed'
     else 'Churned'
     end as status
,sum(reps) as total_reps
FROM
(
    SELECT
    date_part('year',interval_since_last) * 12
      + date_part('month',interval_since_last)
      as months_since_last
    ,count(*) as reps
    FROM
    (
        SELECT id_bioguide
        ,max(term_start) as max_date
        ,age('2020-05-19',max(term_start)) as interval_since_last
        FROM legislators_terms
        WHERE term_type = 'rep'
        GROUP BY 1
    ) a
    GROUP BY 1
```

```
) a
GROUP BY 1
;

status     total_reps
-------    ----------
Churned    10685
Current    446
Lapsed     105
```

This data set contains more than two hundred years of legislator terms, so of course many of the people included have died, and some are still living but are retired. In the context of a business, we would hope that our churned customers didn't outnumber our current customers by such a wide margin, and we would want to know more about the lapsed customers.

Most organizations are very concerned about churn, since customers are generally more expensive to acquire than to retain. To learn more about the customers in any status or about the range of time since last seen, these analyses can be further sliced by any of the customer attributes available in the data set.

Basket Analysis

I have three kids, and when I go to the grocery store, my basket (or more often my shopping cart) fills up quickly with grocery items to feed them for the week. Milk, eggs, and bread are usually in there, but other items might change depending on what produce is in season, whether the kids are in school or on break, or if we're planning to cook a special meal. Basket analysis takes its name from the practice of analyzing the products consumers buy together to find patterns that can be used for marketing, store placement, or other strategic decisions. The goal of a basket analysis may be to find groups of items purchased together. It can also be framed around a particular product: when someone buys ice cream, what else do they buy?

Although basket analysis was originally framed around items purchased together in a single transaction, the concept can be extended in several ways. A retailer or an ecommerce store might be interested in the basket of items a customer purchases across their lifetime. Services and product feature usage can also be analyzed in this fashion. Services that are commonly purchased together might be bundled into a new offering, such as when travel sites offer deals if a flight, hotel, and rental car are booked together. Product features that are used together might be placed in the same navigation window or used to make suggestions for where to go next in an application. Basket analysis can also be used to identify stakeholder personas, or segments, which are then used in other types of analysis.

To find the most common baskets, using all items in a basket, we can use the `string_agg` function (or an analogous one, depending on the type of database—see

Chapter 5). For example, imagine we have a `purchases` table that has one row for each `product` bought by a `customer_id`. First, use the `string_agg` function to find the list of products purchased by each customer in a subquery. Then *GROUP BY* this list and `count` the number of customers:

```
SELECT products
,count(customer_id) as customers
FROM
(
    SELECT customer_id
    ,string_agg(product,', ') as products
    FROM purchases
    GROUP BY 1
) a
GROUP BY 1
ORDER BY 2 desc
;
```

This technique works well when there is a relatively small number of possible items. Another option is to find pairs of products purchased together. To do this, self-*JOIN* the `purchases` table to itself, *JOIN*ing on the `customer_id`. The second *JOIN* condition solves the problem of duplicate entries that differ only in their order. For example, imagine a customer who purchased apples and bananas—without this clause, the result set would include "apples, bananas" and "bananas, apples." The clause `b.prod uct > a.product` ensures only one of these variations is included and also filters out results in which a product is matched with itself:

```
SELECT product1, product2
,count(customer_id) as customers
FROM
(
    SELECT a.customer_id
    ,a.product as product1
    ,b.product as product2
    FROM purchases a
    JOIN purchases b on a.customer_id = b.customer_id
    and b.product > a.product
) a
GROUP BY 1,2
ORDER BY 3 desc
;
```

This can be extended to include three or more products by adding additional *JOIN*s. To include baskets that contain only one item, change the *JOIN* to a *LEFT JOIN*.

There are a few common challenges when running a basket analysis. The first is performance, particularly when there is a large catalog of products, services, or features. The resultant calculations can become slow on the database, particularly when the goal is to find groups of three or more items, and thus the SQL contains three or more self-*JOIN*s. Consider filtering the tables with *WHERE* clauses to remove infrequently purchased items before performing the *JOINs*. Another challenge occurs when a few items are so common that they swamp all other combinations. For example, milk is so frequently purchased that groups with it and any other item top the list of combinations. The query results, while accurate, may still be meaningless in a practical sense. In this case, consider removing the most common items entirely, again with a *WHERE* clause, before performing the *JOINs*. This should have the added benefit of improving query performance by making the data set smaller.

A final challenge with basket analysis is the self-fulfilling prophecy. Items that show up together in a basket analysis may then be marketed together, increasing the frequency with which they are purchased together. This may strengthen the case to market them together further, leading to more copurchasing, and so on. Products that are even better matches may never have a chance, simply because they didn't appear in the original analysis and become candidates for promotion. The famous beer and diapers correlation (*https://oreil.ly/4d5PF*) is only one example of this. Various machine learning techniques and large online companies have tried to tackle this problem, and there are plenty of interesting directions for analysis in this area still to be developed.

Resources

Data analysis as a profession (or even as a hobby!) requires a mix of technical proficiency, domain knowledge, curiosity, and communication skills. I thought I would share some of my favorite resources so that you might draw on them as you continue your journey, both to learn more and to practice your new skills on real data sets.

Books and Blogs

Although this book assumes a working knowledge of SQL, good resources for the basics or for a refresher are:

- Forta, Ben. Sams *Teach Yourself SQL in 10 Minutes a Day*. 5th ed. Hoboken, NJ: Sams, 2020.
- The software company Mode offers a SQL tutorial (*https://mode.com/sql-tutorial*) with an interactive query interface, useful for practicing your skills.

There is no single universally accepted SQL style, but you may find the SQL Style Guide (*https://www.sqlstyle.guide*) and the Modern SQL Style Guide (*https://oreil.ly/rsxBh*) useful. Note that their styles don't exactly match those used in this book, or each other. I believe that using a style that is both consistent with itself and readable is the most important consideration.

Your approach to analysis and to communicating the results can often matter just as much as the code you write. Two good books for sharpening both aspects are:

- Hubbard, Douglas W. *How to Measure Anything: Finding the Value of "Intangibles" in Business*. 2nd ed. Hoboken, NJ: Wiley, 2010.
- Kahneman, Daniel. *Thinking, Fast and Slow*. New York: Farrar, Straus and Giroux, 2011.

The Towards Data Science blog (*https://towardsdatascience.com*) is a great source for articles about many analysis topics. Although many of the posts there focus on Python as a programming language, approaches and techniques can often be adapted to SQL.

For an amusing take on correlation versus causation, see Tyler Vigen's Spurious Correlations (*http://tylervigen.com/spurious-correlations*).

Regular expressions can be tricky. If you're looking to increase your understanding or to solve complex cases not covered in this book, a good resource is:

- Forta, Ben. *Learning Regular Expressions*. Boston: Addison-Wesley, 2018.

Randomized testing has a long history and touches many fields across the natural and social sciences. Compared to statistics, however, analysis of online experiments is still relatively new. Many classic statistics texts give a good introduction but discuss problems in which the sample size is very small, so they fail to address many of the unique opportunities and challenges of online testing. A couple of good books that discuss online experiments are:

- Georgiev, Georgi Z. *Statistical Methods in Online A/B Testing*. Sofia, Bulgaria: self-published, 2019.
- Kohavi, Ron, Diane Tang, and Ya Xu. *Trustworthy Online Controlled Experiments: A Practical Guide to A/B Testing*. Cambridge, UK: Cambridge University Press, 2020.

Evan Miller's Awesome A/B Tools (*https://www.evanmiller.org/ab-testing*) has calculators for both binary and continuous outcome experiments, as well as several other tests that may be useful for experiment designs beyond the scope of this book.

Data Sets

The best way to learn and improve your SQL skills is to put them to use on real data. If you are employed and have access to a database within your organization, that's a good place to start since you probably already have context on how the data is produced and what it means. There are plenty of interesting public data sets that you can analyze instead, however, and these range across a wide variety of topics. Listed below are a few good places to start when looking for interesting data sets:

- Data Is Plural (*https://www.data-is-plural.com*) is a newsletter of new and interesting data sets, and the Data Is Plural archive (*https://dataset-finder.netlify.app*) is a searchable treasure trove of data sets.
- FiveThirtyEight (*https://fivethirtyeight.com*) is a journalism site that covers politics, sports, and science through a data lens. The data sets behind the stories are on the FiveThirtyEight GitHub site (*https://github.com/fivethirtyeight/data*).
- Gapminder (*https://www.gapminder.org/data*) is a Swedish foundation that publishes yearly data for many human and economic development indicators, including many sourced from the World Bank.
- The United Nations publishes a number of statistics. The UN's Department of Economic and Social Affairs produces data on population dynamics (*https://population.un.org/wpp/Download/Standard/Population*) in a relatively easy-to-use format.
- Kaggle hosts data analysis competitions and has a library of data sets (*https://www.kaggle.com/datasets*) that can be downloaded and analyzed even outside of the formal competitions.
- Many governments at all levels, from national to local, have adopted the open data movement and publish various statistics. Data.gov (*https://www.data.gov/open-gov*) maintains a list of sites both in the United States and around the world that is a good starting point.

Final Thoughts

I hope you've found the techniques and code in this book useful. I believe that it's important to have a good foundation in the tools you're using, and there are many useful SQL functions and expressions that can make your analyses faster and more accurate. Developing great analysis skills isn't just about learning the latest fancy techniques or language, however. Great analysis comes from asking good questions; taking the time to understand the data and the domain; applying appropriate analysis techniques to come up with high-quality, reliable answers; and finally, communicating the results to your audience in a way that is relevant and supports decision making. Even after almost 20 years of working with SQL, I still get excited about finding new ways to apply it, new data sets to apply it to, and all of the insights in the world patiently waiting to be discovered.

Index

Symbols

! (exclamation point) negation operator in regular expressions, 204

% (percent sign)
  modulo operator, 309
  wildcard matching with LIKE, 195

() (parentheses)
  enclosing expressions in regular expressions, 209
  in SQL code, 293
  using to control order of operations, 197

* (asterisk)
  matching multiple characters in regular expressions, 205
  matching zero or more times in regular expressions, 207

+ (plus sign)
  addition operator, 70
  concatenation operator, 68
  matching one or more times in regular expressions, 207

- (dash), indicating range of characters in regular expressions, 206

-- (double dash) single line comments in SQL, 292

. (period), matching any single character in regular expressions, 204

/* */ comment for multiple lines of code, 292

:: (double colon) operator, 190

? (question mark), matching zero or more times in regular expressions, 207

[] (brackets), enclosing character class in regular expressions, 205

\ (backslash)
  escape character in pattern matching, 195
  escape character in regular expressions, 208

\A, matching beginning of string in regular expressions, 211

\n line feed or newline, 209

\r carriage return, 209

\s space in regular expressions, 209

\y at beginning and end of patterns in regular expressions, 210

\Z, matching end of string in regular expressions, 211

_ (underscore), wildcard matching character, 195

{} (curly braces), matching a character set in regular expressions, 207

|| (concatenation) operator, 44, 219

~ (tilde)
  alternatives to, functions, 212
  comparator in regular expressions, 204
  ~* making comparator case insensitive, 204

∧ (caret), negating pattern matches in regular expressions, 208

– (minus sign) subtraction operator, 69

A

A/A tests, 278

A/B testing, 122, 267

absence of data, anomalies from, 258-260

active user calculations, 96

age function, 128, 321

aggregate functions
  aggregation returning one row per entity, 39
  in cohort analysis, 123
  followed by frequency count, 30

using temporary tables with, 302
views and materialized views, 290
DataFrames (Python), 8
date dimension, 102
date function, converting dates to/from strings, 44
DATE type
    casting to a TIMESTAMP, 44
datediff function, 69
    replacing age and date_part in retention analysis, 129
dates and times, 62-73
    casting fields into timestamps and dates, 190
    converting in/out of date or datetime formats with to_datatype functions, 44
    date and datetime type conversions, 43
    date dimension table, 50
    date, datetime, and time manipulations
        date and timestamp format conversions, 64-68
        date math, 68-71
        joining data from different sources, 72-73
        time math, 71-72
        time zone conversions, 62
    dates entered as strings, 284
    granularity of, adjusting to reduce data size, 311
    time-based churn metric, 319
datetime types, 20, 21
date_add or dateadd function, 71
date_format function, 65
date_from_parts or datefromparts function, 68
date_part function, 66, 70, 114, 320
    in PARTITION BY clause, 112, 118
    in retention analysis, 128
date_trunc function, 65, 254
DAU (daily active users), 96
day of week cyclicality, 107
day-time intervals, 69
dbplyr (R), 9
DBVisualizer editor, 295
DCL (Data Control Language), 6
DDL (Data Definition Language), 5
decimals
    DECIMAL type, 20
    rounding to various decimal places, 32
DELETE commands, 6
deletes, 6

in column-store databases, 15
delimiters, 223
denormalization, 14
dialects of SQL, 6
difference, ratio, and percent difference between time series in data set, 82
dimensionality, reducing, 310-314
DISTINCT keyword
    order of evaluation, 299
    using in removing duplicates, 38
    using to select dates needed, 104
distributions of data, 27-35
    binning, 31-33
    histograms and frequencies, 28
    n-tiles, 33-35
division by zero, 93
double colon (::) operator, 190
DOUBLE type, 20
DQL (Data Query Language), 5
DROP statements, 6
    deleting a table, 303
duplicates
    deduplication with GROUP BY and DISTINCT, 38
    detecting, 36-38

E

earthquakes data set (USGS), 229
EDA (exploratory data analysis), 28
editors (SQL), 296
ELSE statements, 31, 55
ELT (extract, load, transform), 11
empty strings, 46
    nulls versus, 191
escape character, backslash (\) in regular expressions, 208
ethical considerations with data, 3
ETL (extract, transform, load), 6, 11
    drawbacks to, 289
    using instead of SQL for complex data sets, 288
    views as alternative to, 290
experiment analysis, 267-286
    alternatives to controlled experiments, 282
        analysis of populations around a threshold, 286
        natural experiment analysis, 284
        pre-/post-analysis, 282

I

identifiers, 14, 30
    sampling on, 309-310
ILIKE operator, 196
imputation techniques, 48
IN operator, 40, 200-203
    CASE statement combined with, 253
    NOT IN, 200
indentation in code, 294
indexes
    for database tables, 14
    revealing percent of change over time, 90-94
initcap function, 187
INNER JOIN, 25, 275, 277
INSERT commands, 6
integers
    converting to strings, 43
    INT, SMALLINT, and BIGINT types, 20
interquartile range, 245
intervals
    addition with dates, 70
    in date math, 69
    finding number of months component, 70
    multiplying, 72
    requested date and time parts, 67
    subtracting from dates, 70
    subtracting from times, 72
    subtracting times to result in, 72
investigation into cause of anomalies, 260
IoT (Internet of Things), 12
ISO (International Organization for Standards), 4

J

JavaScript, 53
JOINs
    in basket analysis, 324
    Cartesian JOIN in standard deviation calculation, 240
    combining date and time data from different sources, 72-73
    date math in JOIN conditions, 71
    to date series or data dimension, 258
    duplicates created by hidden many-to-many JOIN, 36
    JOIN conditions and JOIN types, 25
    LEFT JOIN, 224
    LIKE operator in JOIN...ON clauses, 197
    ON clause, 297

restricting entities included for experiment, 277
    sales months table joined to date dimension, 102
    self-JOIN, 86, 88
        leveraging a Cartesian JOIN, 106
    unusual JOIN clause in indexing time series data, 93
    using on date dimensions, 51
    values derived through text transformations as criteria, 198
JSON
    databases' support of, 21
    using to deal with sparse data, 24

K

key-value stores, 17
keywords, 292
    coloration in SQL query editor, 295

L

lag function, 116, 319
    using in YoY and MoM comparisons, 109-111
    using to fill in missing data, 49
    using with partitioning to compare same month versus last year, 112-115
lapse, 322
lateral subqueries, 300
laws regulating data privacy, 314
lead function, 109, 259
    calculating term_end data, 136
    using to fill in missing data, 49
left function, 182-183
LEFT JOIN, 25, 273, 275
    in funnel analysis, 318
legislators data set, 125-126
    reducing dimensionality of, 311-314
length function, 179
LIKE operator, 195-200
    NOT LIKE, 196
    using in CASE statement, 197
    using in SELECT clause, 197
LIMIT clause, 26
    order of evaluation, 300
listagg function, 223
location information, 314
logarithms
    conversions to log scale, 264

SQL queries embedded in, 288

Q

qualitative analysis, 176
quantitative analysis, 176
quantitative versus qualitative data, 22
queries (SQL)
    limiting size of results with LIMIT and sampling, 26
    structure of, 25-27
query optimizers, 297

R

R language, 53, 229, 291
    SQL or Python versus, 8-9
    SQL queries embedded in, 288
range (frame type), 100
range, rows, and groups (frame type), 100
ranges in regular expressions, 206
ratios, 84
reciprocal transformation, 266
regexp_like function, 212
regexp_matches function, 213, 215
regexp_replace function, 215, 217-218
regexp_split_to_table function, 223
regexp_substr function, 213
regression discontinuity design (RDD), 286
regression to the mean, 281
regular expressions, 203-218
    finding and replacing with, 212-218
    matching character set multiple times, symbols for, 207
    matching whitespace characters, 209
    range patterns, 206
    using parentheses to enclose patterns, 209
relational databases, 4
removal of anomalies, 260
repeat purchase behavior, 158
    (see also returnship)
repeated exposure experiments, 280
replace function, 192, 253
    using with regexp_replace, 218
replacement of anomalous values, 262
replacing text in strings, 216
repository, storing ETL code in, 289
rescaling values, 264-266
reserved words, 292
reshaping text, 222-225
Retail Sales data set, 74

retention, 124, 127-153
    adjusting time series to increase accuracy of, 131
    analyzing, main question in, 127
    basic retention curve, SQL for, 128-131
    cohorts derived from time series itself, 137-142
    dealing with sparse cohorts, 146-150
    defining cohort from separate table, 142-146
    defining cohorts from dates other than first date, 151-153
    as success metric, 267
returnship, 124
    analysis of, 158-163
REVOKE commands, 6
right function, 27, 309
RIGHT JOIN, 25
rlike function, 212
rolling time windows, 95-107
    calculating, 97-102
    calculating cumulative values, 104-107
    important pieces in calculations, 95
    with sparse data, 102-104
rollup function, 305, 308
round function, 32, 264
rounding, 32
row-store databases, 13
rows (frame type), 100
row_number function, 315
rule-based systems, 177

S

SaaS (see software as a service)
sampling, 27, 308-310
scatter plots, 243
seasonality
    analyzing data with, 107-119
        comparing to multiple prior periods, 116-119
        period-over-period comparisons, same month versus last year, 112-115
        period-over-period comparisons, YoY and MoM, 109-111
        time scales, 107
second-party data, 23
segments versus cohorts, 123
SELECT clause, 5, 25
    date math in, 71
    LIKE operator in, 197

trim function, 253
    removing blank spaces at beginning and end of strings, 189
    removing characters from beginning or end of strings, 189
trunc function, 254
truncating dates and times, 65, 254
TTM (trailing twelve months), 95
two-sample t-test, 274
    (see also t-test)
type coercion, 44
type conversions, 43
    (see also data types)

U

UFO sightings data set, 178
UNBOUNDED FOLLOWING, 100
UNBOUNDED keyword, 100
UNBOUNDED PRECEDING, 100
UNION clauses
    combining three queries, 305
    creating same output as grouping sets, cube, and rollup, 308
    UNION and UNION ALL, order of evaluation, 299
UNION statements
    unpivoting with, 55-57
    UNION versus UNION ALL, 57
uniqueness, enforcing in tables with primary key, 14
Unix epochs, 67
unnest function (Postgres), 58
unpivot function, 58
unstructured data, 175
    structured data versus, 22
updates
    in column-store databases, 15
    UPDATE command, 6
upper function, 187
US Congress, legislators data set, 125
US Geological Survey (USGS), earthquakes data set, 229
US retail sales data set, 74
    (see also Retail Sales data set)
user-defined functions (UDFs), 269
UTC (Coordinated Universal Time), 63
    considerations when joining data from different sources, 73
    drawback to, 63
    offset for local time zones, 63

V

values, anomalous, 250
VARCHAR type, 20, 179
    converting integers to, 43
variant assignment, 268, 277-278
    in natural experiment analysis, 285
    in pre-/post-analysis, 283
variant cohorting system, 268
Vertica (database), 15
views as alternative to ETL, 290
visualizations, 12, 53
    (see also graphs)

W

WAU (weekly active users), 96
WHEN condition, 31
WHERE clause, 26
    date math in, 71
    filtering data to remove null values, 82
    filtering query results for sampling, 309
    filtering records with LIKE operator, 195
    nulls in, 47
    OR and AND operators in, 197
    order of evaluation, 298
    removing anomalous records, 261
    restricting users cohorted for experiment, 277
whitespace
    matching in regular expressions, 209
    splitting text on, 224
    in SQL, 292
    using in SQL code formatting, 294
wildcard matches using LIKE and ILIKE operators, 195-200
window functions, 34, 86, 88
    calculating moving average, 101
    calculating rolling time windows with advantages over JOINs, 107
    in indexing of time series data, 91
    n-tile functions, 34
    order of evaluation in SQL code, 298
    PARTITION BY statement, 96
    percentile_cont and percentile_disc, 236
    use for moving calculations self-JOINs versus, 101
windows, 95
    (see also rolling time windows)

About the Author

Cathy Tanimura has a passion for connecting people and organizations to the data they need to make an impact. She has been analyzing data for over 20 years across a wide range of industries, from finance to B2B software to consumer services. She has experience analyzing data with SQL across most of the major proprietary and open source databases. She has built and managed data teams and data infrastructure at a number of leading tech companies. Cathy is also a frequent speaker at top conferences, on topics including building data cultures, data-driven product development, and inclusive data analysis.

Colophon

The animal on the cover of *SQL for Data Analysis* is a green magpie (*Cissa chinensis*). Usually referred to as the common green magpie, this jewel-toned bird is a member of the crow family. Found throughout the lowland evergreen and bamboo forests of northeastern India, central Thailand, Malaysia, Sumatra, and northwestern Borneo, this species of bird is noisy and highly social. In the wild, they can be identified by their jade-colored plumage, which contrasts elegantly with their red beak and a black band running along the eyes. They also have a white-tipped tail and reddish wings.

Highly social and noisy, the green magpie can be identified by its piercing shrieks followed by a hollow and decisive-sounding "chup" note. They are also often difficult to spot because they glide from tree to tree in the middle-upper levels of the forest. They build their nests in trees, large shrubs, and tangles of various climbing vines. Sometimes referred to as the hunting cissas, they are primarily carnivorous—consuming a variety of invertebrates, as well as young birds and eggs, small reptiles, and mammals.

The green magpie is fascinating because of its ability to change colors. Although they are jade green in the wild, they have been observed to turn distinctly turquoise in captivity. They get their green coloration from a combination of two sources: a special feather structure that produces blue coloring due to the feather refracting light, and carotenoids—yellow, orange, and red pigments that come from the bird's diet. Prolonged exposure to harsh sunlight destroys the carotenoids, hence making the bird appear turquoise.

The green magpie species has an extremely large range and although the population trend seems to be decreasing, the decline is not rapid enough to push the species into the Vulnerable category. As such, their current conservation status is "Least Concern."

The cover illustration is by Karen Montgomery, based on a black-and-white engraving from *English Cyclopedia*. The cover fonts are Gilroy Semibold and Guardian Sans. The text font is Adobe Minion Pro; the heading font is Adobe Myriad Condensed; and the code font is Dalton Maag's Ubuntu Mono.

O'REILLY®

There's much more
where this came from.

Experience books, videos, live online training courses, and more from O'Reilly and our 200+ partners—all in one place.

Learn more at oreilly.com/online-learning